THE

HIGH

SCHOOL

REVOLUTIONARIES

THE HIGH SCHOOL REVOLUTIONARIES

Marc Libarle
and Tom Seligson
EDITORS

RANDOM HOUSE
New York
A Scanlan's Book

Library of Congress Catalog Card Number: 79–110620

Manufactured in the United States of America
by the Kingsport Press, Kingsport, Tennessee

First Edition

For
HIGH SCHOOL STUDENTS
EVERYWHERE

Preface

A methodological caveat is in order to explain how the editors obtained and selected the contributions presented in this book.

The project began in the late spring of 1969. At that time both editors were teachers in the New York City public school system. After reading of the high school protests occurring across the country, it was our opinion that a definitive, authoritative work on the subject was necessary.

We discovered that most of what was being written on high school students was interpretive and written by adults. As teachers, we felt that what was being written was misleading and insensitive. The "outside" adults had no real understanding of what students were doing. In articles such as "Revolutionaries Who Have to Be Home by 7:30" (which appeared in *The New York Times Magazine*), radical students were condescendingly dismissed as rebels without a cause. There was an obvious inability on the part of these adult critics to empathize with the students involved. High school radicals can speak for themselves. Knowing this to be the case, we concluded that a book written by a sampling of the nation's high school radicals was in order.

During the summer we made an extensive tour of the nation, spending hundreds of hours collecting information and interviewing students. Some students were asked to write on what they considered to be the formative elements of their radicalism, other students were exhaustively interviewed on tape. After an extensive cross section had been obtained, in terms of geographical distribution, urban and rural areas, public and private schools, ghetto, middle-class, and affluent neighborhoods, and the various other elements of the Movement, we selected those which we considered most representative of these areas.

To obtain a reportorial coverage of the High School Movement in its national setting, hundreds of newspapers were clipped. In reference to this task we would like to thank Wendy Kaplan, Dianne Dudzanoski, and Peter Michelson from the Center for Research and Education in American Liberties, at Columbia University.

About education itself, we recommend one book as the most stimulating, imaginative, and innovative study done on this subject in a long time. It is *Education and Ecstasy* by George Leonard.

We would like to thank Ramona Ripston, Dotson Rader, Gene Eisner, Ira Glasser, Maryann Hinckle, and Robert Clark; and at Random House—John Simon, Jane Clark Seitz, Laura Furman and Hilary Maddux. We would also like to thank Sidney Zion and Warren Hinckle for their inspirational guidance and never-ending praise during frustrating moments in the course of the work. We are especially grateful to Lacey Fosburgh, whose assistance was invaluable.

A note of thanks is due to Mrs. Virginia Markoe who laboriously transcribed the tapes.

Lastly, and most important, we would like to thank the hundreds of high school students who made this book possible. Among these we would especially like to thank the students in the book.

MARC LIBARLE
TOM SELIGSON

Contents

Introduction

It is Wellesley, Massachusetts, but it could be any one of the small towns and cities in which, during the last few years, students and adults have found themselves in violent opposition to each others' beliefs, styles, and values, and minor incidents have exploded into vicious confrontations.

The famous "Wellesley Incident" begins innocuously enough in Wellesley High School with a special program in the gym devoted to the problems of racism and poverty in America. It ends several days later with students in faded blue jeans and worn sweaters, and adults in neat shirts and pressed jackets, climbing on the auditorium chairs, yelling and screaming at each other, waving their arms and calling for each others' defeat. Outside it is a cool spring night, but inside there is tension, anger, and fear. One boy is arrested and countless numbers of students, numb and bewildered by this spectacle of chaos and reprisal, are radicalized.

For three periods on the morning it began, students and

teachers in the gymnasium saw documentary films and heard poetry by Langston Hughes. They listened to young men from the Boston ghettoes talk about slums and prejudice. Then, as they sat in hushed silence in chairs on the basketball court, they watched the Boston Theater Company perform a part of LeRoi Jones' play, *The Slave*.

Significantly, the school program on poverty and racism was punctuated with the anger of an author who used words like "shit" and "fuck" to communicate his opposition to a system and a society that has kept the black man oppressed.

The students were fascinated by the play, but—in an indication of what was to follow—teachers suddenly left the room or started to correct their tests and papers.

Later the word circulated ominously in Wellesley that the play was "revolting," and about a week later over thirteen hundred people showed up at the regular School Committee meeting to denounce the students for selecting such entertainment.

"Filth," "vulgar," the adults yelled across the crowded auditorium toward the lonely moderator trying to ascertain whether school funds had been improperly used. Speakers went to the platform, the pros and cons of the play were hurled about the room like lethal darts. Members of the John Birch Society, Veterans of Foreign Wars, and the American Legion contributed staunchly and loudly to the program; finally the editor of the school paper mounted the stage.

"I think one of the things that is affecting you the most," said this A-student and star athlete, "is the word 'fuck.' " He quoted a line from the play ending in "fuck you" and the audience was stunned.

"Well, the first time I heard the word 'fuck'," he went on, "was when I was five years old and that was right here in Wellesley. In fact, I know some people in Wellesley who cannot say a sentence without using the word 'fuck.' "

"Get him out," cried a man in the audience. "Arrest him," yelled others. "Stop him!" "What right does he have?" The adults stood up, climbed on the chairs, and cried, "Arrest him."

A uniformed policeman, summoned by the audience, jumped up on the stage, grabbed the boy, and arrested him. The vice principal started to scream at the high school students standing in the front of the auditorium. "We're trying to build a good school and you're wrecking it," he cried as the policeman went off stage with the young editor. "You're the ones who're wrecking it," he repeated.

"This whole wall of angry shouting people rose up around us," said one white student later, recalling the angry scene. "It was really terrifying, and for the first time we began to realize what we were up against in our fight for freedom. Up until then we had confronted only one man, the principal or the vice principal, but here were hundreds of people screaming and yelling."

"Here was America right before our eyes," he went on, echoing the words of countless hundreds of high school radicals, forced into their radicalism by similar discoveries and observations. "This is what America really is."

For the first time in history, high school students throughout the United States are protesting the situations in which they find themselves. The current generation in the high schools has discovered that the situation they confront as students is inhuman, and that the status they hold is one of subjugation. During the last few years these students have articulated both to themselves and to the world their need—in fact, their demand—for greater constitutional rights and freedoms. Simultaneously, the number of protests and demonstrations taking place either in high schools or involving high school students has increased enormously.

These students have become so vocal and active in expressing their dissatisfaction with the school system, and their protest activities have reached such dimensions, that a survey conducted in the spring of 1969 by the National Association of Secondary School Principals found that "Three out of five principals report some form of active protests in their schools." The report stated further that "many who note no protest as yet add they expect it in the near future." It also noted that 56 percent of the junior high schools participating in the survey had experienced protest activities.

This book is written by active, protesting students. It concerns their struggles for change and why they feel radical change in schools is necessary. The purpose of this introduction is not to explain the rationale of high school protests—that task is handled better by the students themselves—but to supply a brief survey of the scope, dimensions, and issues involved in the protests.

Significantly, these protests are limited neither to a geographical area nor to certain schools. Studies by newspapers, educators, and government officials reveal that they occur in all sections of the country, in all kinds of schools. Urban schools, rural schools, high and low caliber schools, have all experienced protest activity. Cities like New York (Pop. over 7 million) have been disrupted by demonstrations. So have Billings, Montana (Pop. 55,000) and Edcouch, Texas (Pop. 2,800).

The protests generally concern two grievous conditions in the schools—one is racial discrimination, the other is the discrimination levelled against all students, black and white equally. In both categories students are being denied the basic human rights and freedoms which the Constitution supposedly guarantees everyone, even those under twenty-one years of age.

The blacks face segregated conditions and unequal treatment in the North as well as in the South, in so-called good schools as well as in ghetto schools. In ghetto schools, however, the rooms are usually more crowded, the buildings more decayed, the facilities more inadequate. They are often without textbooks, teaching aids, or supplies, and frequently don't even have a minimum number of teachers and are forced to get along with incompetent substitutes. Learning under such conditions, the blacks protest, is virtually impossible.

Such conditions, however, reflect only part of the problem. The deeper problem lies with the racist practices which have become endemic to school systems everywhere. Such practices exist in the North as well as in the South where schools remain segregated despite the Supreme Court's reversal of the Nixon administration's refusal to speed desegregation.

In some areas, including large urban areas like New York, the question of segregation itself is not the prime target of protest. Here blacks want community control of their own schools and want their ghetto schools not only to be all black but also to have the same independence as suburban schools have elsewhere. Fed up with the artificial, token gesture of busing black children into white areas in order to achieve a semblance of integration, they want to be in control themselves, in order to pursue the desperately needed improvements which a racist, white-dominated society has often promised, but never delivered.

Today's black student has inverted the discrimination he has felt all his life into pride in being black. This has created problems in school systems where racism is institutionalized because black students want to honor black heroes with holidays and portraits on the wall, just as white students do for white heroes. Blacks want their schools to reflect a sense of pride in "blackness." They want a curriculum, teachers, and an administration that will be relevant to their needs. Their demands for a relevant curriculum are specific: black history and language courses, books by black authors in English literature courses and in the library, and educational assemblies to commemorate the birthdays of such men as Martin Luther King and Malcolm X. Outside the curriculum area they want more black administrators, black teachers, and counsellors. They demand that unfair and unequal disciplinary actions end, that discrimination against black teachers end, and that police be removed from school grounds.

The perceptive writings in this book of N. K. Jamal and Joe Harris, and the superb statements by James Brown and

Paul Gayton, address themselves to the following: what it's like to go to a ghetto school, racism in the classroom and on the football field, conditions in the school and the attitudes they foster, harassment by teachers and administrators.

What happened at Malverne High School on Long Island, New York, is a typical example of how school administrators handle student demands. The protests at Malverne concerned more black teachers, changes in the Black History Program, the hiring of a black guidance counsellor, and alleged discriminatory practices in the honor society. During February and March 1969, black students met with the Malverne School Board to discuss their grievances; yet for two months the board failed to make any decision about the students' demands and made no attempt to discuss with them the problems that might affect their adoption. The board told the students there was no substitute for orderly, step-by-step processes.

Finally the black students concluded that the officials had no intention of discussing the issues involved, and three hundred of them staged a sit-in in the high school lobby. Police were called to the school and 137 students were arrested for trespassing after they failed to leave the building. Eventually the school board agreed to eight of the fourteen demands, including two courses in Black Studies and a Student Advisory Committee to the School Board.

Malverne is an example of how attempts to make reforms and innovations through step-by-step bureaucratic procedures have failed and thoroughly disheartened the protesters. For two months the black students attempted to discuss the issues but the school board continued to be intransigent and neglectful. Only after the students were arrested and their protests became vocal did the Board agree to make certain concessions—but without ever setting a specific implementation date.

The school system in Edcouch, Texas, is comprised mostly of Mexican-American students. The Anglo-Saxon administration of the school exemplifies the authoritarian and obdurate nature of school administrations everywhere.

According to a school regulation, any pupil who fails to stand up during a pep rally or misses an appointment with a teacher is suspended for three days. Further, the students charge—and officials have not denied—that if they fail to dress for gym, even if their clothing has been stolen, they receive corporal punishment. In addition, any form of student government at Edcouch is meaningless because the student council is chosen by the schools' officials and therefore has an allegiance to the administration and not the student body.

Agitation started in Edcouch when the administration provocatively issued a statement saying that any "disruptive student" would be expelled for the rest of the semester, even though the school had been peaceful. As a result, the Mexican-American students created a major protest to challenge the arbitrary right of the administration to issue such a fiat. The administration responded by summoning the police and the National Guard, and ordered the students arrested. Although the actions of the administration and the school board were finally overturned in court, the authoritarian nature of the school, and the ill will and animosity between the administration and the students remain. Since then little has changed in the school system in Edcouch, Texas.

An incident which occurred in April 1969, at Seaford High School in Seaford, Delaware, shows the similarity between the responses of various administrators to student protests. At this time Seaford's black students organized a sit-in to emphasize their demands for Black History books and to show that despite repeated promises, no black had yet been selected to the varsity cheerleading squad. Although the athletic programs were integrated, no progress was being made in electing a black cheerleader. Ultimately the administration agreed to allow the student body to vote on the matter and it overwhelmingly supported the election of a black cheerleader.

The problem was easily resolved once the administration allowed the students to express their opinions in a school-wide vote; but significantly, the black students had to organize a sit-in before the administration recognized their grievance, even though the overwhelming majority of the student body supported them. Later, during spring vacation, the Board of Education held a special meeting in Seaford and, typically, decided that any future disruption of classes would be met with suspensions, expulsions, and police actions.

Although racial issues are a major factor behind school protests, there are other issues facing all students—black and white—which also lead to school protests. These concern the basic human rights and freedoms which the Constitution guarantees but which are virtually ignored. Our society clearly discriminates against those human beings who, under twenty-one or under eighteen, are considered minors.

Now, for the first time, a generation of people between the ages of ten and twenty are voicing concerns about their ineligibility for basic human rights and political freedoms. They want to know why they are punished if they don't go to school. They want to know why they must pledge allegiance to our flag. Why their hair must be kept a certain length, and why girls cannot wear the clothes they prefer. They want to know why they are punished for expressing certain political views and for actively supporting others. Why are they denied basic First Amendment freedoms concerning the press and the right to assemble?

Clearly students are an oppressed majority. Although schools purport to teach democracy and are supposed to serve as a tutelage for its traditions and procedures, they do not in fact do so. The typical high school is highly authoritarian in structure and attitude. Students are given the power to elect their government but that government has no power. Policies concerning student discipline, hiring teachers, budgets, and dress codes are determined by the school's administration or the Board of Education. Nor has the faculty any power. In some schools the faculty has a modicum of power over the curriculum, but in most, even this small deviation from an authoritarian system does not exist.

Any so-called democracy for students is a sham. There is no procedure in schools to examine student opinion on the curriculum or on teacher evaluation. Elected student representatives are denied the power to decide what organizations should be allowed in school. Student leaders are elected but have no power. The democracy students experience exists in a vacuum. Students are powerless and are controlled by the "school system."

A close examination by this writer of schools all over the country reveals that the American high school is an institution which functions according to traditions, customs, and bureaucratic procedures. Together these forces have produced a "system of education," e.g., organizational and procedural processes which determine the values of the school and regulate its functions. Arbitrary precedents which have been established over the years govern the codes and policies of schools, and have turned the "system of education" into a rigid bureaucratic organization. To be sure, the "system of education" varies, to some degree, from state to state and from urban to rural setting; but to the extent that high school protests have occurred in most states, in urban and rural areas, in ghetto and non-ghetto schools, all high schools obviously share the same conditions which generate the same feelings among students. It is in this sense that we can speak of a "system of education."

Basically, what has happened is that the present "system of education" no longer knows what it is educating for. Our educational system has not caught up with the scientific-technological revolution that has taken place over the past twenty years. The purpose of a high school education is no longer clear, in part, at least, because most of the jobs that a high school education once prepared students for no longer exist. Yet schools still continue to provide antiquated courses, training students senselessly and anachronistically for their future.

For most students, a high school education represents

one stage in the channeling process that continues throughout their lives. This channeling process is largely a function of the tracking system which is utilized in cities like New York, Chicago, and Los Angeles, to separate (track) children from the time they enter the second grade through the end of high school. Essentially, the tracking system—which is a target for high school radicals all across the country—consists of three categories: 1) academic, for college-bound students, 2) vocational or semi-professional training for students, or 3) general, for students who are expected to become common laborers or blue collar workers.

Benjamin Franklin High School in East Harlem, New York, illustrates how the tracking system affects the lives of students. There are three thousand students, 92 percent are black and Puerto Rican. In 1968, according to the New York City Board of Education, 2286 of them had been tracked since the second grade into the general program, 670 were in the academic program, and only 100 were enrolled in the vocational program. In 1967, twenty students graduated from the academic curriculum, fifty graduated from the vocational curriculum, and 130 graduated from the general curriculum. Of the original class scheduled to graduate that year, 60.2 percent were drop-outs, transfers, or unaccounted for. Of the original class that entered in September 1964, only 29.8 percent finally received diplomas, and only 1.8 percent of those were academic diplomas requisite for college entrance. For those students who do not obtain an academic diploma the alternatives are few: they can either spend their lives in menial work because they are technologically unemployable, or have careers in the army. Significantly, a recent study in Washington, D.C. showed that 80 percent of all public high school male graduates were in the army within two years after their graduation. This is what "the system of education" means to high school students. And in this book, Paul Gayton makes that point quite succinctly.

Students resent this control over their lives and consequently they challenge the school system's authority. Faced with such challenges to their authority, curriculum, purpose, and structure, school officials react not with imagination or innovation, but with repression. They resort to whatever means they have available to control students, and are bent more on silencing them than on discussing any issues of school reform. Administrators tighten their control by attacking spurious scapegoats. They enforce regulations that restrict the freedom of the student and give them an excuse to expell him if he protests. Invariably the issues students raise are merely ignored.

The need to articulate these issues had led to the birth of the underground high school newspaper. These organs provide vehicles for students to express disenchantment with the system. Indicating just how popular and important these underground papers are is the fact that from 1968 to 1969 over five hundred were established. Most of them are published by individual students for a particular school. There are, however, others, such as *The New York High School Free Press, The Bay Area F.P.,* and the Berkeley Student Union *Pack Rat,* which are printed on a broader scale for all high school students in the area. Such city-wide papers are usually accompanied by student coalitions and unions which solidify and coordinate all high school activities.

The official school policy toward these papers is generally to ban them as "unauthorized publications." Students are often suspended for distributing them or even possessing them. In two cases that have gone to court, in New York City and Hartford, Connecticut, judges have ruled against the students involved, on the ground that the papers could be "disruptive." In both cases, however, decisions were reached before the contents of the paper had been examined.

In general, these underground papers are a protest against official school papers which are controlled either by journalism departments or by administrators, who censor statements they consider critical of school policy or irrelevant to school, such as the war in Vietnam. For the students, therefore, the underground paper becomes the sole medium through which they can speak out on social or educational issues that are officially censored.

In these papers students demand the abolition of the present "tracking" system which systematically channels non-college preparatory students either into the army or into vocational fields which disappear as rapidly as technology progresses. They question the value of a school system that forces students to compete with one another for grades; they challenge the validity of grades and examinations as assessments of an individual's performance or capability. They call for an end to the draft and want ROTC and military recruiters removed from schools. Young editors ask administrators to stop giving students' names to draft boards, to end suspensions and expulsions, and to bar all police, plainclothesmen, and narcotic agents from school grounds. Students want to replace the school bureaucracy with a more democratic, relevant structure.

On a social level the underground papers provide a forum for young radicals to articulate the evils they see the government and the society perpetuating. Radical students denounce the Vietnam War, racism, economic imperialism, and, more fundamentally, the way the present "system of education" fosters and perpetuates these social injustices. Underground high school papers exist mainly because students are denied freedom of the press in official papers. In this book Toby Mamis, editor of the *New York Herald-Tribune* in New York, lucidly explains the birth, evolution, and role of the high school underground press.

Freedom of the press is not the only First Amendment freedom that is denied to high school students. Sometimes in subtle ways, sometimes in blatant ways, they are also denied freedom of speech.

A student at Mt. Greylock High School in Williamstown, Mass. for example, was not permitted to read a speech to a Veteran's Day assembly because the principal and the faculty faulted him for raising questions about national priorities for military and social spending.

In New Berlin, Wisconsin, to give another example, a boy was suspended because he told the student body during a pep rally, "It's not a question of whether you win or lose, and it's not the game either that's important." The principal explained that he suspended the boy because "he condemned the whole athletic program" (Waukesha *Freeman,* December 24, 1969).

In Minneapolis, Minnesota, fifty students participated in the Fourth National Resistance Day. Two were suspended: one, a seventeen-year-old girl, because she appeared in television coverage of the event; and the other, a girl also, because she had notified a school official that she had participated and should also be suspended. When the remaining forty-eight students challenged the principal for his selective punishment he told them that, "If particular students are suspended it should be no concern of yours." The students protested his statement and insisted that if students were suspended for something they had all done, then indeed it was very much their concern. Then the principal denounced them for "introducing a whole new idea" that was not relevant.

In Des Moines, Iowa, three students were suspended for wearing black armbands as a protest against the Vietnam War. The case became controversial and was finally resolved in the Supreme Court. The Court ruled that officials of public schools cannot interfere with the rights of students to express their political views during school hours, provided that the educational process is not disrupted. However, as most radical students point out, virtually all demonstrations (except perhaps for silent vigils) could be restricted on the ground that they could potentially disrupt the educational process. However, as attested to by Susan Snow in this book, most schools still do not observe this decision.

Another common issue involving political liberties has been the refusal of students to say the Pledge of Allegiance or sing the National Anthem. Two seventh-grade girls, for example, were suspended from their junior high school in

Queens, New York, in October 1969, for refusal to say the Pledge of Allegiance. The girls claimed they did not believe in God or in what the pledge says about "liberty and justice for all."

Elsewhere, in Darien, Connecticut, and at Jamaica High School in Queens, New York, school authorities created a major issue when individual students tried to exercise personal rights. In these cases both students explained their refusal to say the Pledge of Allegiance by saying they had seen too many injustices in America to still believe the country provided "liberty and justice for all."

Perhaps a less abstract but equally emotional issue which spurs high school students to protest, is dress code regulations. Dress codes vary throughout the country. Some schools are only concerned with the length of hair but others have strict rules regarding both hair and clothing.

In February 1961, approximately one hundred boys in blue jeans and girls in slacks were suspended from the Robbinsdale High School in Robbinsdale, Minnesota, for not conforming to the school's dress code. The previous day five students were suspended when they posted notices about the demonstration. For about a year before that the student council had been trying to reform the eight-year-old dress code which permitted boys to wear jeans in all colors except blue. Heretofore the policy had been to send students home to change if the code was broken.

The principal explained the ban on blue jeans in the *Minneapolis Tribune* (December 15, 1969). "Blue jeans used to have rivets that might have hurt the wooden furniture," he said. "Blue jeans are work clothes. You wouldn't wear work clothes to church or to a party either." The paper also reported that the school had changed several years earlier from wood to formica furniture, which cannot be harmed by blue jeans.

After the demonstration the school administration refused to admit that the demonstration had been caused by prevailing frustration among students over the fact that it was taking so long to change the code. "This is a well-organized resistance with information and help forthcoming from not only student union members but outside influences as well," the principal told the *Minneapolis Star*.

This tendency to blame "outside agitators" for trouble inside schools is a common practice among school administrators, and in this particular case such accusations prevented the administration from facing the possibility that it was in fact resistant to change and that the students had legitimate grievances.

Hair length is another issue related to the nationwide problem of old-fashioned dress codes. At Colfax High School in Colfax, Iowa, for example, hair must be kept one finger-width above the eyebrows, clear across the forehead. Susan Sims was sent home from Colfax High in December 1968 for wearing her hair too low. She trimmed her bangs, but when she returned to school, she learned they were still too long, and was sent home again.

The preamble to the Colfax School dress code states the administration's belief that students act the way they dress. During the four months in which Susan and her parents were fighting her case in court, no one explained why the behavior of students with hair less than one finger's width above the eyebrows was unacceptable. At a court hearing, however, the superintendent of schools did say, "There is a relationship between rules and the educational process. The school has an obligation to teach children discipline . . . Long hair is an impediment in playing such games as volleyball and basketball and also interferes with vision in the classroom" (*Des Moines Register,* January 14, 1969).

Shortly after Susan's suspension another girl was sent home for wearing a dress one-quarter of an inch too short, when a member of the administrative staff routinely measured—as was his custom with several "suspects" every day —the distance between her knee and the hem of her skirt.

During Michael Picler's Senior year at Garden Grove High School, California, his muttonchop sideburns became controversial. His school's regulations state that no beards, sideburns, or moustaches are permissible, with special emphasis on sideburns that extend below the ear or fan out perpendicular to it. In arguing his case with the school's administration, Michael pointed out that his counsellor was permitted to have a moustache and sideburns. Despite his pleadings and notwithstanding his A-minus average, Michael was suspended. He was allowed to attend another school for "problem students." Presumably the school authorities reasoned that "problem students" would not be bothered by Michael's sideburns, whereas regular students would be.

In all these cases and in others that students have taken to court, many different school administrators have responded in very similar ways. They are convinced that beards and miniskirts disrupt the classroom. They have adopted a hard line concerning the rules and have resorted to extreme measures to preserve their authority and ability to enforce the rules. In this book Joshua Mamis, age 12, describes the events that led to his filing suit in a federal court to protect his right to circulate a petition.

In order to challenge more effectively the school's authority, rules, and regulations, students have joined together and formed high school student unions. Because official student councils are powerless, extracurricular student associations, such as high school unions, are the natural and inevitable alternatives.

Significantly, during the last year such unions have been established in most metropolitan areas. They include: the New Jersey High School Liberation Movement; the Minnesota Student Union; the Montgomery County Student Alliance (MCSA) in Maryland; the Students' Rights Organization of Columbus, Ohio; the District of Columbia Student Coalition for Education; the Democratic Students' Coalition in Hewlitt, Long Island; the Newcastle County Student Union in Delaware; the famous New York High School Student Union (NYHSSU); the Bay Area Student Union and the Berkeley Student Union, both in California. Similarly, black student unions exist in virtually all schools where there are blacks; in New York City the city-wide Black High School Coalition coordinates most local Black Student Union activity.

Students belonging to these various unions and coalitions are probably more politically aware and sophisticated than their nonparticipating peers. Ironically, the most socially aware, perceptive, articulate, and brightest students are usually the most alienated from school and are considered by school officials to be the most dangerous of students. These officials view student activism and organization so ominously because they threaten the basic principles on which the authority and structure of the school system rest.

The goals, however, of these organizations and unions, coalitions and alliances, are the same: ameliorate conditions in the schools, end institutionalized racism, eliminate expulsions, suspensions, dress codes, censorship, and other regulations; recognize students' rights to assemble, to have a free press, and to exercise free speech.

Unfortunately, however, student union leaders are often intimidated, harassed, and expelled from their schools. In January 1969, members of the Montgomery County Student Alliance in Maryland announced their "program for change" at a press conference. Their program included student participation in curriculum and teacher evaluation; an end to censorship of school newspapers; freedom to publish and distribute independent publications in school; and the addition of germane courses. Less than a week after the press conference three members of the MCSA were suspended for leafletting. When other students released a pamphlet protesting their suspension, they too were suspended.

The New York High School Student Union (NYHSSU), composed of some of the most articulate and politically perceptive students in the city, has experienced similar forms of repression. Formed as a city-wide student coalition dedicated to struggle for students' rights and reforms in the schools, the NYHSSU takes the position that students' problems are shared by black and white and that all students must stand together. The New York Union has become extremely powerful as a leader of school reform not only in New York City but in the nation. Independent, autonomous, and free from the ideological influence of such college groups as SDS and Progressive Labor, the group has managed to preserve the integrity of its original ideals.

This powerful group organized in New York City what was probably the largest and most disruptive high school demonstration anywhere in the country. In the spring of 1969, the Union issued an eleven-point program concerning student rights and called for a "spring offensive." This offensive brought thousands of students out of the schools and into the streets. All over the city there were strikes and demonstrations as high school students walked out of schools in support of the Union's program.

The Union however, has not escaped repression. Members known to school officials have been suspended or transferred to other schools. Students who have distributed or had possession of the *New York High School Free Press,* the Union paper, have been suspended, or in some cases have had their graduation speeded up. In other cases, students with failing grades were suddenly given passing grades and graduated. In still other cases, school officials telephoned the parents of Union members and claimed hysterically that the children were insane.

The politics, birth, and growth of high school student unions are poignantly discussed in this volume by Steve Wasserman and Tom Lindsay.

The movement to form high school student unions has not been restricted to public schools. Students who attend boarding schools have formed the National Prep School Union. The contribution in this book from Andover, a top New England boarding school, explains how private prep schools deny students their rights, and regiment and condition them.

Parochial and private schools are hardly exempt from student activism: many have been wracked with demonstrations and student strikes. In the pages that follow, a high school student describes the issues that students are raising at one of New York City's finest private schools, and Paula Smith describes the incredible repression that she experienced at a Catholic girls' school and the events that led to her expulsion.

As already mentioned, high school protests cut across all class, racial, economic, and geographical backgrounds. The fact that no school is immune from protests is attested to by the brilliant and perceptive statements of Michael Marqusee and David Romano, both of whom attend so-called "liberal and progressive" schools. The former describes an upper-class suburb, Scarsdale, New York, as culturally stultifying, with a school system as repressive as any. In a similar vein, the latter describes the influences of suburban life that have turned him into a radical revolutionary advocating violent confrontation as a means for change.

Students become radicals for many reasons. Mary Ann Kennedy describes how Fundamentalism influenced her radical evolution. And Richard Cohen discusses perceptively the forces of oppression that he experienced as a Jew attending a North Carolina high school.

The cultural aspects of the High School Movement —drugs, sex, music, and art—are described by Jane Thompson. She writes about why their present forms are so attractive to youth. Much talk and comment about the current cultural revolution centers around the Woodstock Festival that occurred in New York State in the summer of 1969; its analysts frequently assume that the event marked the birth of a mass cultural revolution. Perhaps not. In a brilliant and witty analysis in the pages ahead, Fred Silber discusses "Woodstock Culture" as a counter-revolutionary culture.

A new and important aspect of the radical High School

Movement is the demand for women's liberation. Virtually all programs of radical students include a demand to end the oppression of women in high schools. As Maxine Orris points out in this book, women are subjugated and oppressed from the moment they enter the first grade. Women are taught to be pretty, gentle, docile, and submissive. They are taught that their place is in the home, being mothers and housewives. Consequently, their education is geared for secretarial or assembly-line work. Maxine describes the politics of women's liberation and the struggle to end the oppression of women in high schools.

Some students are radicalized at a very early age. Jim Gardiner is thirteen and has been a radical for some time. In his writing he explains the forces that have led him to a militant radical analysis of both the school system and national politics.

No book is complete without some comment on the future. Pat Gunkel is a high school drop-out, a radical hyper-intellectual, and a futurist. Presently Pat is completing a multi-volume study of alternate world futures based on over six hundred books that he has read relating to the future. His contribution reflects the creativity and imagination that can result from unstructured education. It is powerfully written and will send readers scurrying to the unabridged dictionary.

What does the radical High School Movement mean? To understand its meaning it must be placed in its context in time. Quite simply, a majority of young Americans are rejecting age-old American ideals and values; as they proceed through life they are forming new concepts about the meaning of being "American" and what the "American way of life" should be. America is changing because the minds of those people destined to inherit the nation have changed. The seriousness of this change is reflected in their integrity and convictions. They will not compromise their basic precepts: liberty, equality, and freedom in education. They understand that education is an organic part of life and the key to the liberation and unleashing of human potential.

The "system of education" controls their life through its control over their minds. They will not allow this antiquated "system of education" to corrupt their future and the country's future.

MARC LIBARLE

THE

HIGH

SCHOOL

REVOLUTIONARIES

I

SUBURBAN RADICALS

It appears strange to adults that many of the young high school protesters come from middle- and upper middle-class families. Why, they ask, are these kids rebelling against their country and their schools, when they've always been given the best of everything? Raised in affluent surroundings, provided with the cars and trips that blacks and lower-class whites only dream about, and educated in the "better" schools, they still appear in large numbers among the demonstrators.

Is it a paradox that affluent white students are in the front ranks of the high school radicals? Michael Marqusee from Scarsdale, New York, and David Romano from Westport, Connecticut, think not. They both talk about what it is that leads to rebellion among the privileged. Michael and David spoke into the tape recorder.

I Saw America in the Streets

by David Romano

> *David Romano is eighteen years old and comes from the Connecticut suburb of Westport. His father is an engineer, and his mother helps run a local bookstore. He is considered by most of his Staples High School classmates to be the most articulate member of his class.*

A high school radical is someone who is willing to become actively, personally involved in bringing about changes that have to be made; a high school liberal is someone who feels that there is a need to bring about change, but he is too concerned with his social life or studies to become really involved in attending meetings, talking to people, circulating petitions, and doing the other things that have to be done to bring about change. High school liberals are willing to be active within the framework of what the school considers legal, while high school radicals are willing to become active and instigate the changes whether or not they meet school approval. Radicals would not let the fact that what they were doing was unusual or had not been done before—or might not meet with the approval of the school or the community—stop them if they felt that they were justified and right. The high school liberal is concerned with not making waves and not causing any chaos which would disrupt the school; the radical would be willing to disrupt the school if he felt it necessary.

Students are waking up to realize their own capacity to govern themselves. We don't need the remote principals and assistant principals to tell us what to do. After all, who knows us better, they or ourselves? I think students should have a role equal to that of any other participating group in the school—the teachers and the administration. I think students should be given a voice in choosing the curriculum. Students should be able to influence the assignment of teachers to different courses. Students, I think, are in a much better position than anyone else to decide which teachers are suited for which courses. If assignments were done on that basis, they would probably result in determining which teachers were hired and fired because of student interest. Critics of "student power" claim that students are not responsible enough to make such critical decisions, and that such evaluations of teachers would deteriorate into popularity contests. While I don't believe this would be the case, it still would be better than what we have today. If a student at least had a teacher whom he liked, then he would go to class and most probably learn something.

No matter how good the teacher may be, no matter how many books he may have published (there are many accomplished teachers at Staples: teachers with Ph.D.'s, teachers who have published, teachers who attended Harvard and Columbia), he is not going to be able to teach anything if his students don't come to class. It's almost impossible to get the kids to come to class now, and once they're in class the situation is so bad that instead of learning anything or even being in a neutral situation they have an adverse reaction to anything that is being taught to them. This student boredom is reflected in the large numbers of Staples' students who cut school and classes regularly. (Out of a school of about nineteen hundred students, approximately three hundred skip the entire day, every day, and the number of students who cut individual classes often totals up to nine hundred, or half the school.) I think this shows that students are not just bored with individual classes, but with school generally. The only students who attend classes consistently are those who are intimidated by their teachers. Staples is probably no better or no worse than most schools in this country.

I think the educational system from top to bottom, from kindergarten to college, is in pretty bad shape. The experience of a Staples Experimental English class is indicative of this. The course, instituted this year and open only to Seniors, allowed the students the option to either come to class or stay away. In class they were allowed to study anything they wanted, anything that interested them. With this freedom, almost all the Senior students, instead of putting it to good use, decided to stay away. After eleven years of stifling classroom experience, these students were unable to take advantage of this freedom. They'd come to class, sign out, and then they'd leave. They'd go down to the school lounge, or they'd smoke cigarettes, or they'd just leave campus. While a few students did put this opportunity to good use, most of them were too brainwashed to do so.

I think this country definitely needs a redistribution of wealth. The American dream of the European immigrant coming over and making it rich through his own hard work has so blinded people that even if they are members of the lower middle-class, they are unable to gain any real awareness of their situation in the society. You keep hearing that America is the richest country in the world, that anyone can be President, and this ideological brainwashing has just blinded people to the fact that there are enormous disparities between the rich and the poor in this country. We have a much greater proportion of poverty-stricken people than should be at all tolerable in a country this wealthy. As far as the numerous programs and agencies recently instituted by the government to deal with the problem of poverty go, I think there is no question that they've been worse than ineffective. There's been much talk and little action. A number of programs that have been started failed, through corruption, neglect, and lack of funds, and there really aren't any worthwhile programs going. Anyway, the amount of money allotted these programs in proportion to the amount allotted the war in Vietnam and the Space Race is utterly ridiculous.

With these grave problems persisting despite the efforts of liberal legislators, I think it is quite clear that electoral politics will not be able to solve them for us. The Liberal Tradition, with its reform movement, and its emphasis on gradual reform rather than on violent change is never going to succeed, because its reforms become outdated almost as soon as they're instituted. I approve of violence, disruption, and interference with the normal functions of such institutions as schools and draft boards, when these methods serve a particular political objective and can be realistically used. The consideration of whether they're legal or illegal, moral or immoral is a consideration which is applied by the society to the actions of the radicals merely because they have violated some of the precepts of the society. Who's to say whether the actions in themselves are moral or immoral, legal or illegal? They're legal or illegal in terms of the norms of the particular society, and those norms may not be the right norms.

There have been several factors which led to my disenchantment with traditional liberal politics and my embracing of radicalism. First of all, I had the good fortune of being brought up in a liberal home. My parents are themselves critically conscious of the society, and had themselves struggled to bring about change when they were kids. My home is progressive, middle class, and fairly traditional. But I guess the real starting point for my involvement in radical politics, where I made the decision myself based on information and experience that I myself had gathered, was after my stay in Chicago during last year's Democratic Party convention.

Just before the convention I heard for the first time about the Yippies—this new group, different from the hippies, from the radicals, and from anybody else—cultural revolutionaries. The Yippies interested me. I was very curious to find out what these people were all about and whether they were an effective way to bring about change, whether their philosophy had any validity. Chicago was going to be the big unveiling of the Yippie scene. This was where they were going to make themselves known, and I was interested in being there to see them. I was also interested in gaining first-hand experience on the street where my life and safety might perhaps be at stake. I wanted to be there myself rather than hear about it on TV, read books, or hear people talk about it. I sat up a couple of nights hearing reports from Chicago on WBAI and getting very worried, taking Seconal to get to sleep, and wondering what was going on and whether I should go out. Finally I caught a train into New York, and got on a National Mobilization bus (they had chartered a whole fleet of buses to take people to Chicago). I was doing this by myself. I wasn't with any of my friends. I got on the bus and went out to Chicago.

For all my liberal-radical feelings before this, I had never had any concrete experience opposing the power structure on the street, which is where it counts. This was the first time in my life that I was the enemy, they were the good guys, and they were out to get me. I participated in the breaking of the curfew at Lincoln Park. The Yippies decided that they wanted to stay all night, the people decided that the park belonged to the people, and they were going to hold it and use it as their base. The city of Chicago disagreed and decided that the Park would be closed at 11:00 P.M. and everybody would have to be out. For the first time in my life I personally encountered the power structure incarnate in the form of a policeman with a tear-gas mask on and a billyclub in his hand. He was out to get me. He was out to get me because I was a threat to the status quo, because I was refusing to obey the laws of the society which I thought were unjust. He was out to get me because I was refusing in a manner that was unorthodox and to him unacceptable. The reason it was unacceptable was that it might be effective, and the only methods the power structure consider acceptable for registering opposition are those which will ultimately fail.

For the first time in my life I actually encountered

oppression of an outright fascist nature, where the right of
the people to free assembly and to make their views known
was being intentionally thwarted. It was being thwarted by
the power structure no matter what the costs in life and
limb to those people out on the street. If they could not be
made to go indoors peaceably, then they were going to be
clouted over the head with a club, dragged away, and put in
a cell. It was this experience that first got me started in
radicalism. I saw the power structure through the medium
of the police clubbing down people on the street, gassing
people, employing any method at its command to meet its
ends. I saw the response of the people on the street to this
fascism: they got together. I think it was a radicalizing
experience for anyone who was there. I think that the street
action was similar to the action of the French students: the
building of barricades, the lighting of bonfires, the use of
rocks, Molotov cocktails, and pop bottles as weapons by the
people against the police who were armed with guns. I saw
the police using all their weapons, shooting people, gassing
people, and beating people. I met up with a friend of mine
out there who was severely beaten by the police. He was the
one who lowered the flag in Grant Park during one of the
rallies. The police charged in, they grabbed him, they
clubbed him, they took him down to the station, and they
beat him. They beat him up, and it was only much later that
he was able to contact National Mobilization lawyers who
came down and bailed him out. This was a frightening
experience for me as well as him. It made me realize that I
was up against raw power, power that could crush me,
power that would crush me if I let it. It was power that
would take any steps at all to suppress the voice of the
people. I felt, and still do, that I was justified in being in
Chicago. I sincerely felt that the election convention was a
farce, and I believe I was proved right by the kind of
activity that went on. They cut the phone wires, they dead-
ened phones inside the convention hall so that delegates
could not register protest against Daley's choice. Daley
packed the gallery with the city employees of Chicago, and

they instituted the system of passes and checkpoints to get into the convention It was something that you'd expect to find in Franco's Spain.

I felt after my experiences in Chicago that there was no longer any hope for the American electoral system, and there was no longer any hope for the liberal façade. I felt that the power structure had become totally corrupt and was totally unresponsive to the people's needs and the people's wants. I felt it would do anything to remain in power and to circumvent democracy and justice. The American government no longer represented for me the ideals that it was supposed to stand for, and I felt that the stronghold of real democracy and real justice lay with the radical movement in this country. I consequently made it my business to become concerned and involved to the fullest extent possible, because I felt it was absolutely necessary for those of us who still had some integrity left and some belief in human dignity to act. The country is going down the drain, and we have to do something.

The federal government and the power structure of this country, the military-industrial complex, has become corrupt to the point where there is no longer any hope of a reform movement, or a government-sponsored movement, bringing about any kind of real change. I think that the only way that the racial situation will ever work itself out to social equality for all people in this country is going to have to be through violent revolution in the cause of socialism. There has to be a socialist economy; America has to become a social democracy. The system of free enterprise has become totally corrupt. The military and the industrial sectors have become so intertwined, so hand-in-glove with each other, that they've stifled free enterprise. The big corporations all work together. I'm not necessarily implying conspiracy here, only that because their interests lie in the same direction—preserving and increasing their power, and squelching all opposition—it takes on the appearance of a conspiracy. As this process goes on, the people, and their wants and needs, are going to be increasingly ignored.

I don't think that the people who run this country are inherently evil. But I do think that with the present trend toward what I'd have to call fascism (though we are not in a fascist state at this time), we could easily become a fascist state. Until most of the American people become awakened to the utter corruption of the government, the total disregard that the government holds them in, a revolution is unlikely. The now-blind Americans can be awakened to the intransigent ways of the government by being brought into direct opposition to the power structure. They will find out, as I found out in Chicago, that instead of the power structure adapting itself and changing itself to meet the needs of the people, it will display at best indifference and at worst oppression. People will have to begin realizing this, realizing that they have been allowed to live the lives that they're living and to exist the way they're existing merely because they do not trouble anybody, merely because they did not get out onto the street and make their voices heard. People are going to have to begin standing up for their rights regardless of the consequences to themselves or to the country. That's the only way they are going to be able to live with themselves. If it takes a revolution to win the rights we're all entitled to, then so be it.

Many of the so-called "experts" on radical movements have compared the high school and college radicalism of the 1960's with the social movement of the 1930's, in which my parents and a lot of my friends' parents were involved. Seeing that the radicals of the 1930's lost their fire and became absorbed into traditional, respectable positions in the economy, the "experts" predict the same future for the youthful activists of today. This may very well be the case for my generation, and perhaps, though I doubt it, even for the next generation. But I think more and more students and young people, after having become involved at this age and seen the degree of the country's corruption, will remain disenchanted throughout their lives. Our efforts to effect change notwithstanding, I think the system carries within itself the seeds for its own destruction. I believe the society has created a condition that human nature will just inherently revolt against. I think the modern industrial society, as we can see it working here in America, is a society that cannot help collapsing. I don't think human beings can survive in the set-up that the power structure of this country would like them to survive in. Even if the radicals of today go on to become the liberals and reactionaries of tomorrow, they will find that the acquisition of material wealth (the bribe of the power structure which placated the activists of my parents' day) will no longer suffice. The absolute spiritual barrenness of their lives is going to cause them eventually to become totally disenchanted with this system. Then we'll institute a new system. The question, however, is whether people will become disenchanted soon enough to prevent a fascist state.

People think it's strange that middle-class kids like myself become radicals. What, they often ask, do these products of affluent homes have to be angry about? They've never wanted for anything, they've always been provided with the best that money could buy, and still they complain and condemn the system that provided all the benefits they enjoyed. Well you see, it's because this life is basically unhealthy that we take to the streets as we do. This life is flawed. The emphasis on material comforts, the emphasis on complacency and normalcy, the lack of individuality, the emphasis on keeping people in boxes and slots and defining them one-dimensionally, the idea of a person having a role and being defined by that role, all this adds up to something that human nature in general and we in particular find intolerable. Before cultural conditioning causes people to tolerate and live with it, some change must be made.

I've heard it said that high school radicals are really doing nothing more than aping their college seniors, that high school radicalism is merely a product of an adolescent need to identify with older brother who's almost an adult. I disagree with any such analysis that denies the High School Movement the individuality and meaning that it deserves.

Admittedly there is a lot of similarity between college radicalism and high school radicalism, but it's because we as radicals recognize that we have many goals in common. That is not to say however that high school radicalism is just a lower off-shoot of the college movement. High school radicalism is indigenous to the high schools, and came about in the high schools because of the conditions there. We as high school students want to acquire a relevant education now; later, after finishing school, we want to lead happy fulfilling lives in a country that has true equality and justice. The achievement of these goals, both in school and in the nation, will require change, and the only way to bring about meaningful change is through radical action.

Turn Left
at Scarsdale

by Michael Marqusee

*Michael Marqusee is a sixteen year old Junior in
Scarsdale High School. Scarsdale is a wealthy New
York City suburb, and Michael lives in a large, two-
story house. His father is a real-estate executive and
art book publisher in N.Y. Considered to be the most
articulate, outspoken student in his school, Michael
is a leader of the radical students in Scarsdale.*

I have lived in Scarsdale for most of my life, and I write
from the viewpoint of the affluent student turned radical.
This contradiction between my political thinking and economic and social background may seem strange, but it is
one of which I am constantly aware; in fact, it is my upbringing in this culture which has directly influenced my
radicalization and is in some ways the cause of it.

The Scarsdale community can be described as an upper
middle-class community. With the average income over
$25,000 and a virtually all-white population, Scarsdale is
the ideally insulated town, excluding the poor and the black.
It is a community of family units in which the father usually
commutes to New York City while the mother stays home to
tend the children who attend, for the most part, one of the
highly-rated Scarsdale public schools. The jobs that the men
in Scarsdale commute to are almost all either in one of the

professions or in business. In this community, my friends and myself are all the children of desk-sitters. Our fathers work in a 9 to 5, tie-and-jacket world where the guiding principle is usually that of finding the easiest path to the most money.

Obviously, laborers of any kind and low-ranking desk-job holders find no place for themselves in Scarsdale. In fact, for most of us, the only working-class people we ever have contact with are the employees our parents hire to clean house, do the gardening, or repair the washing machines, heaters, cars, stoves, and swimming pools.

Scarsdale prides itself on its cultural and intellectual interests. There are many patrons of Lincoln Center, frequent theaters-goers, and supposedly avid book-readers. Most of us live in large, one-family houses, among which there is little variety. The town has a calm, serene mood, with its quiet, uncrowded streets, and absence of night activity. There is a generally restrained and almost unfriendly attitude toward one's neighbors. The mothers of the town engage in various "wifely" activities: watching the kids, directing her staff, chatting on the phone, shopping, playing tennis, or maybe some occasional stuffing letters at a local political office.

Finally, in this catalogue of Scarsdale family elements, there are the children, and we are in many ways the center of family and community attention. Virtually all parents see their child's function within school as the attainment of high grades, or in other words, academic success and a better chance for admission to a highly-rated college. This is the goal and primary function of our high schools.

This purpose is reflected in the atmosphere and routine of the school. In the corridors, each morning before classes, there are many students, sitting on the floor. They look at their books, waiting without enthusiasm or even involvement, for school to begin. They've spent the night before either sweating over generally meaningless homework assignments or procrastinating and neglecting these assignments. In this case they have spent a night of anxiety and depression over their teacher's probable reactions to their misconduct the following day. With the exception of four or five scattered classes, there is no class which most students, given the chance, will not try to cut, either through legal excuses or by just taking off.

Although the school administration has not acknowledged this, cutting has become a major problem in recent years. There are those who cut all their classes constantly— the outcasts, heavy drug-users, or academic failures—but there is a new group of cutters. This new group includes many types of people: from "greasers" and "jocks" to average, liberal-oriented kids who do mediocre work in school, to those like myself, who see classes and school as a usually worthless activity and feel nothing but bitterness toward the rules. This broad group has one thing in common—none of us see going to classes as a useful, fulfilling, or truly important matter. This is not new. Students have felt that way about school for years. However, recently, we no longer just accept mandatory attendance. We look at those rows of desks, the other bored pupils, our unfinished homework, and some of our culturally mechanized teachers and say, "Fuck it." Usually, our decision to cut is impulsive, and the relief that comes when we finally resolve not to go to class seems to amply reward the risks we take. As more kids cut more often, the risk diminishes. In my school, cutting is so frequent that it has become virtually uncontrollable, and many teachers have resigned themselves to this fact. Still, cutting is probably the student crime most abhorred by faculty and administration, for it is a complete negation of the school's authority over the student: it is a rejection of the cherished tradition of student-teacher relationships as master-slave relationships.

Most students when in class blankly occupy their assigned place, and occasionally take notes. They infrequently participate in discussion, usually doing some mental tripping to take their minds off the boredom of their day-to-day routine. Some of the students (not necessarily the more intelligent or creative ones) participate actively in class discussions, either to impress the teacher, or relieve the dullness. Rarely is it out of genuine interest in the subject. When the period bell rings to signal the end of the class, we all stand up immediately, in Pavlovian response, and go to our next class, whether the discussion in the previous class is over or not.

Both teachers and students object to this procedure, but the school feels that the maintenance of this regimented pattern is more important than whether we become involved in the substance of a particular class. Once the student becomes aware that adherence to the schedule is of primary importance, he loses the desire to actively participate in his education. I know of one teacher who will stop in the middle of a sentence when the bell rings and continue that sentence at the beginning of the period next day as if nothing had happened and he was just speaking into a tape recorder. This is an extreme example, but it applies in part to all teachers. This pattern continues all day, every day, and within weeks after the beginning of school in September, the student bodies are demoralized, disinterested, and finally programmed. I use "programmed" because the process which each student undergoes in attending high school is akin to the computer data-organizing process. (Note here that my principal is a former data processor). The distribution of courses and schedules is completely impersonal; we are to the administrators little more than cards in a file.

Indeed, judging by the quantity of the different forms and records we fill out, each student is the sum of his "record"—that omnipresent, omnipotent fact which deans, teachers, and parents continuously remind us of. These "records" are the compilation of all the forms and fact sheets that contain information on us. They include medical forms, grade records, test scores, and evaluations filled out by teachers with questions such as: Is the student self-motivated in class discussion? (needs no outside encouragement, occasionally needs prodding, seldom participates voluntarily, never participates voluntarily—choose one). Not only do these files influence our high school career, but they are the primary information used by colleges in determining our acceptability. Therefore, from our entry into ninth grade until we graduate, our job is to build a "good record" and the school's job is to guide us in this task and ultimately into college. To describe the educational process as one of guidance is an understatement. Indeed, it is neither guidance nor influence, it is determined manipulation.

This manipulation does not start in high school, nor in any of the lower grades. It is, in fact, the function of the entire Scarsdale culture and society—from birth certificate to draft card. From an early age we are almost invariably taught basic, "humanistic" values: tolerance for others, freedom and equality for all, and general "do unto others . . ."-type rules which are taken quite seriously by most of us, and are a basis for the enormous respect parents demand of us when we are very young. Many children receive some form or another of religious instruction. Even before first grade, I had been inculcated with the knowledge that I am Jewish. Following this I worked my way through ten years of Sunday School. Moving from enthusiasm in the first years, through boredom, carelessness, and disinterest in the middle years, I finally became bitter and disgusted and I reacted against the whole process of religious education in Scarsdale.

I said above that at an early age, we are taught the "serious" values of justice and equality. My bitterness toward the Jewish culture in Scarsdale and especially the Sunday Schools, stems partly from my detection of the falseness and superficiality behind those primary teachings. In school, in temple, and at home, we are taught not to lie, cheat, or be dishonest, hypocritical, or intolerant in any way. Yet one learns that these teachings are meaningless. Our religious teachers make a mockery of the Bible—for most kids it has neither meaning nor value. Concepts of love, faith, peace, commitment, and social justice, seem useless when they are sermonized or lectured in a superficial, unreasoned, and thoughtless manner, as they are in most religious classes. Nowhere do the students and teacher come together and try to grasp, through sincere analysis, what these ideas mean and how they apply to everything from Agnew to the family gathering at the dinner table. What does brotherhood mean to us when we hear the sickening, racist comments our oh-so-proud, oh-so-Jewish elders make about Arabs and those "ungrateful," "anti-Semitic" black militants? What can religious values mean when they include the unquestioning dogmatic support of the militaristic, racist state of Israel simply because its populace is primarily Jewish? I am fed up with Sunday School curricula which supposedly deal with "black problems," the war, anti-Semitism, and premarital sex, from a point of view which dictates that through reasoned and informed analysis the student will come not to *a* conclusion but to *the* Jewish conclusion.

Why should we study these foreign problems which our teachers are not equipped to discuss, when Scarsdale itself is a spiritual void. Because most of us, in our different ways, have perceived the meaninglessness of this religious prattle, and the hypocrisy that lies behind our parents' culture, life becomes purposeless—a web of patterns and beaten paths that many kids in Scarsdale follow blindly.

When I speak of hypocrisy in the Scarsdale culture, I hope that this idea is not confused with fashionable suburban critiques seen in "Goodbye Columbus," "The Graduate," *Look* magazine, and endless trivia on the "younger generation." No, these are precisely the entertainments most popular among the pseudosophisticates of Scarsdale. Nearly everyone in Scarsdale sees other people completely in terms of roles or types. They all have their different images—each trying to appear more confident or correct than the other. The tragedy of this situation is not only that it forces (or again manipulates) people into limiting positions, but also that eventually if you play your various roles (including liberal, mod businessman, loud joker, sophisticated literati, conservative and cautious executive) often enough, you lose track of your personality; the being underneath the mask vanishes. Whether he realizes it or not, the youth in Scarsdale is constantly subjected to this in his parents, his friends,

his teachers, and the characters he observes nightly on TV.
He is absorbed into this pattern and too often the period of
adolescence is the period in which we are supposed to determine our various roles and their uses. To this end the community institutes many forms of teenage diversions. Besides
the all-American activities such as sports and dances, there
are the more subtle forms such as Bar Mitzvahs, clothes-
fashions, and above all school.

I return to the subject of school because finally it is the
center of all our activity and is the primary tool with which
the young of Scarsdale are molded into finished products.
The word "process" has repeatedly cropped up here because
it is indicative of the nature of existence in my community.
Thus, Scarsdale High seeks to produce college graduates
who are in turn directed into a field within the professional
or business community. This "process" is not so far removed
from the pattern whereby black kids in a ghetto school are
trained for "niggerly" jobs (or no jobs) or where working-
class kids are sent to vocational schools. As has been said,
the student is universally a nigger. We are subservient to all
authority and our lives are controlled by that authority from
the selection of our careers to the development of our values. This is a system which should be abhorrent to all who
hold supposedly "human," "progressive" values, yet it is endorsed by almost all in the adult world, for they see it as a
necessary preface to that wondrous goal—a career.

Choose anything you want but have a career—a definite, disciplined job or skill that involves a routine of
work. In that routine is security, happiness, and normalcy.
This is a standard defense of the school system. They preach
that this process aids in our attainment of fulfillment. It
gives us opportunities. Bullshit. This process, as I and my
friends in affluent Scarsdale have discovered, is one of limitation and misdirection. Imagine spending your entire
thinking life attending classes which have been planned by
someone thirty years older than you who usually has little in
common with you; having your daily schedule worked out
by someone who probably has never seen you; sitting down

in assigned desks at the signal of a bell and standing up again fifty minutes later at the same signal, only to move to another preplanned class and follow the same routine, all day, every day, in pursuit of a goal someone else has set for you and which, whether you believe in it or not, seems to offer as little excitement as the dreary schedule you now go through. This is the high school student, and that existence is one directed toward limitation, demoralization, and I repeat, manipulation. One of the weapons which the school uses in directing our course is a steady, subtle humiliation which starts the moment we learn in kindergarten that we must raise our hand (an absurd ritual) in order to get permission to go to the bathroom. It is continued in the hundreds of orderly lines we all form to move around elementary school, the disgrace we suffer when we make a wrong answer to an easy question, and the paranoia and tension that accompany the distribution of grades on all levels of education.

For a student, grades can become an obsessive force in life. All our activities in school revolve around our grades. However, few students actually believe they are an accurate measure of someone's intelligence or capabilities. Teachers often say they indicate a student's "performance." They picked the right word. Attaining high grades in school is usually just a matter of performing or acting out the role of dutiful student with a straight face. Given a talent for bull-shitting, anybody can pull an A. The difference between one grade or another, even if it's between a B+ and an A, can absorb some students to the point of neurosis. The parents are almost all excessively concerned with their child's grades, and some will punish or reward their kids according to their quarterly standing. All of them encourage and even push their kids into working for a higher grade whether that means learning anything or not. Often, we find ourselves orienting everything toward creating a good impression the last few weeks of each marking period and then dropping it at the beginning of a new one until report-card time comes around again.

We are forced into competition with one another—for grades, honor classes, admittance to college, athletic teams, and social acceptance. Through this competition, our honesty, awareness, and intelligence are not improved, but rather a capacity to wear a mask, be devious, take the safe and beaten path, and stomp on our peers is developed. But even this is not done by the students consciously. It is simply their adaptation to the school environment, the normal way to achieve "success" in the dreary, pre-packaged world of high school. This competitiveness is a series of humiliations, for all, even the successful one, and its ultimate purpose is to produce beings who have resigned themselves to the authority of this system. The being which the Scarsdale culture seeks to produce, is what my friends and I refer to as Plastic Man. He is a complex, built of TV commercials, AM radio, frozen dinners, *Life* magazine, shiny sports cars, and memories of years of boring, useless classes. Plastic Man does not regard these as wasted hours; they are merely the basis and background of his existence. He is not real. His life is synthetic, and has only the appearance of quality—he is normal.

The school and the society seek to manipulate us into a given career and social post through submission to authority. Supposedly, the system functions best in Scarsdale and therefore why did it produce a group of youths as embittered and hateful of the Establishment as we are? I think it is clear that part of the reason stems from the system itself and part from the climate of the times. When one has been humiliated, demoralized, and manipulated by unseen powers for most of his life, the expected result would be a complete resignation, a lack of rebellion. But one must remember that one of the principles of the system is to keep up the appearance of "creativity" and "progressiveness." This is part of the liberal doctrine—the appearance of freedom in order to maintain the status quo.

Part of our school's reputation is based on the idea that it is an "openminded" institution which encourages "free inquiry" and the development of "awareness." Not only is this image reported to outsiders but it is presented to us constantly. We are told, essentially, "Isn't this school great! Aren't we learning a lot, kids!" Most students swallow this crap. Yet, if one examines the school closely, it reveals itself as regimented, closed, and in many ways anti-openminded. We all are forced to take courses we don't want, courses in predetermined, rigid curricula that are forced on us without regard to our personal concerns. Most teachers still believe that their goal in instructing a class is to lead us to discover what the teacher has previously decided is the Truth about a particular book, event, person, idea, or subject. The school believes that whatever it decides will be the concern of each of our personal educations will be that which is most fruitful to us. We are not allowed to explore different fields on our own. This is not freedom, openness, or awareness. I had a teacher who took great pride in demonstrating his "open-mindedness" to us by criticizing Rockefeller's Latin American tour, but when I wrote an article for the school newspaper describing student-teacher relationships as master-slave relationships, he blew up. He insisted I had no right to say such things and listed all his degrees to prove his own superiority. Their progressiveness is a cover-up, a way of convincing the students that their plight could not be bad.

The system has backfired. We in the upper middle-class suburbs have grown up in an unreal world, without the natural beauty of the country or the urgency of the city. Suburbia is a vast map of "normalcy"—more likely banality. The process of growing up in this society is unreal because it does not involve awareness of what one is doing and why.

Adults in Scarsdale neither know nor understand the vastness or depth of drug usage in the high school. They regard it as an outside, unusual pattern of behavior. Growing up in Scarsdale is a matter of unreality, of fitting patterns. When we enter high school we have often reached a point where we need something beyond these patterns. To many, this need is filled by drugs, sometimes because it is fashionable, sometimes because it allows escape form the dreariness of school life, sometimes because the actual experience itself lends something new to perception of reality. Usually drug usage is a combination of all three. By my own observations, more than half of the students in Scarsdale High smoke grass and hash, and some have tripped on acid, mescaline, or psilocybin. The number of heroin and cocaine users is small but growing. The types of drugs that individuals use vary according to their temperament and social group, but the use of grass and hash is now so common as to have been accepted by many adults as just another teenage diversion like rock music or long hair. In many cases, this is true: kids get into drugs simply because it's an accepted social activity. There are those who use drugs, however, in a different manner, an antisocial manner. I don't use this term perjoratively at all, because by antisocial I mean our use of drugs is a method of responding to or reacting against the society we live in. In both its dreariness, its occupation with image, status, and money the society is an unblinking oppressor. In response to this, students often react by getting involved in different kinds of drugs, for drugs are a respite from Scarsdale life and an infinitely more real and personal experience than attending school or trying to succeed in suburban culture.

No creativity, no individuality, no questioning. We seem to be merely manipulated by a system (not by other individuals), from point to point with no purpose. Many of us feel powerless. Our only avenue to true self-expression and development is through rebellion against the society that created that monstrosity: Plastic Man. By criticizing and ultimately destroying this form of life we hope to free man from all kinds of oppression: economic, racial, cultural. Thus, here I am, an affluent radical, the most bourgeois of contradictions.

I I

BLACK STUDENTS

Most of the recent high school student protests center around the issue of race. What is the reason for this? Why is it that so many black students appear discontented with their schools? Are black students really discriminated against, and if so, how? What does a white student think of the racial violence in the schools?

Five students interviewed answer these important questions. N. K. Jamal writes about what it's like to be a student in New York's black ghettoes. James Brown from Peoria, Illinois speaks about the racism in his school—in the classroom and on the athletic field. Joe Harris has written a strong political analysis of high schools. Paul Gayton talks about the problems of black students in Denver, Colorado, and a white girl talks about the black-white conflicts in her Erie, Pennsylvania high school. She disagrees with her parents, and to avoid reprisals from them asked if she could remain anonymous. She will be referred to as Susan Snow.

Right On

by N. K. Jamal

N. K. Jamal is the former Chairman of the New York City Black High School Coalition. Before that he was President of the Afro-American Society at Brooklyn Technical High School. He writes poetry and short stories.

New York City is well known for many things, by a lot of people: its tall buildings, Broadway at night, the Manhattan skyline, the cultural affairs, the television shows that are produced here. Behind this phony, plastic, propman's idea of what a city is like, there is the real New York City. There are the crowded subways, the slow buses, the hot smelly streets during the summer, the ugly rushing crowds, and finally, the slums and tenements of Harlem, Brownsville, Bed-Stuy, and Morrisania. This is the real world.

Not least among New York City's braggings is its educational system, said to house and educate more than 1,120,000 students—in over ninety-one high schools, three hundred junior high schools, and an uncountable number of intermediate and elementary schools. The boasts are that this is one of the nation's largest educational systems, and that it is capable of being quite functional for its size. Here, however, the boasting stops.

The truth is that New York City is grossly incapable of handling the educational system as it should properly be handled. In fact, the city government, and even the Board of Education—the purported "policy making" branch of the school system—has little or no say in the proper handling of the system. Who then, you ask, does? Is it the teachers? The parents? The students themselves? The correct answer to each of these questions is a short, curt, and very definite *no!*

Most of the youth now entering, or who have entered the school system within the last five years, realize by the time they become Freshmen in high school, that there is something very wrong with their education. The problem for them is to find out what is wrong, and then to try to analyze and finally to correct these wrongs. This however, is not exactly that easy, since the student is often stopped either by society, religion, or the status quo for making his own evaluation instead of accepting the already formulated ones.

High school students like me, who come to realize the situations under which we function, usually reach this "insight" into what is going on in steps. Much of my time as a student is spent in trying to organize. I travel around the city to see exactly what the conditions are in each school. I speak to students at various schools. A student at my school, Brooklyn Technical High School, once related and analyzed the process of his radicalization with me.

David L—— is a brother. He entered Brooklyn Tech under the provisions of a special entrance program. He took the test for the school with about three hundred other "minority group" students, and was one of the few who passed and was accepted. It should be noted that the so-called "standards" for this test had been "lowered," and the students taking the test were told this. I believe this made them aware of the fact that they were considered different— below normal, thus limiting their hope for an equal chance to compete.

David had been shuffled off to Tech from one of Harlem's predominantly black junior high schools. David's analysis of his education led to this: his education up until high school had been very subtle. He had moved through kindergarten, elementary, and even junior high school with a smile on his face. But upon reaching the point at which he had to travel out of his own neighborhood to go to school, he found that he was lost. He had suddenly been taken out of a never-never world of school in the abstract, to the sudden, harsh realities of hard, cold Brooklyn life.

Look at what this could mean. Most black slum children are facing hard life every day. They walk down hot smelly streets in the summer. They walk down cold, slushy, dirty, dangerous streets during winter. Any season the sidewalks are strewn with uncovered garbage cans, some lying horizontally on the ground, trash falling into the children's paths. They walk past tall, dingy tenements on the way to school. They look up at the little old women who stare at them from three stories up—little women who sit there at the rusty, maybe broken and crumbled window ledge, reminiscing.

Traffic on the corner frightens children as they go to school. They never grow accustomed to the death-dealing automobiles that virtually fly past them in hordes in the early morning. They cross the streets, wary of broken glass that could cut them, possibly causing permanent injury.

On the school block, pimps coax the little girls as they walk past. Prostitutes pucker their lips at the little boys, telling them to come and see them when they grow up. Dope addicts nod, not at the children, not at anyone in particular, just nodding, in their vertical sleeping positions. Dope pushers attempt to sell the children little pieces of candy that are not as innocent as they look.

Further up the block gangs of boys and girls are giving one boy the shakedown. Others are yelling and screaming in fright or glee as two boys fight. Still others yelp as someone throws a bowl of hot, scalding water out of the third floor window of the adjoining tenement.

This is life as the average black student lives it—every

day. This is the sharp, focused world of reality. The world of the slum child.

Yet, once the student enters the classroom, this world mysteriously changes. The harsh roughness of existence is erased. The everyday life of Harlem, Watts, Detroit, Newark, or Washington, D.C. fades into the past. Everything that should have been used to determine the nature and direction of the student's education is discarded.

As David himself said, his education and mine have indeed been subtle. Education was not about the subjects of English, Math, and History, which were "taught," but rather about the workings of the system. Hypocritical education under false pretenses. The education we all received was actually about the subtleness of the structure that was educating us, the why of this subtleness, and the useful purposes we might later serve to the system. This was our education. We were awakening. David was awakening. We began to see a set, noted formula. A *pattern*. Guidelines by which the system knew it could prepare the student for his predetermined place in society.

The method? Soothe the student. Pull the kid out of the hard-hitting realities of life and push him up the path that leads into the soothing world of Mother Goose.

Kill the pessimism of his real life with the optimism of Honest Abe, the self-educated farmboy grown President.

Don't let him become aware of his color. Make him see no color. Let Dick and Jane become his everyday, colorless friends. Avoid questions about why Dick and Jane don't have a darker friend on their whole block.

Talk to him about Spot, and ask him if he has a dog of his own (don't let him trap you with discussion about the stray, rabid dogs roaming ghetto streets).

This was the formula—and if followed correctly, it worked.

The formula was set by the general society. Public education is society's baby. It arises from the need for society to determine what the individual should do with his life, and how he will live it. It arises from society's need to be able to control the individual—he belongs here, and she belongs there. Therefore, educate him to become this, and her to become that.

The formula is still being instituted by the entire school system, with the individual teacher being the most immediate and vulnerable component, the administration, principals, district supervisors, and the Board of Education and its members being the extensions, and *total control* being in the hands of a select group.

The method of institution of the formula is up to the individual teacher. In a circle of thirty or so teachers, there can be thirty stories about how each teacher managed to pull her student from the facts of his existence, to the bourgeois world of *Our Friends and Neighbors*—from the rugged tenements of Harlem to the clean-swept, mowed-lawn atmosphere of suburbia in a matter of minutes.

Then she will discourse on the success she has had in this transformation with minimal balking from her students during or after the transition. In short, she is proud that she can hide the discrepancy between life and the classroom from the student.

An amazing feat in itself, this process brings to mind the sad realization that the entire education the student receives is merely an escapist barbiturate to soothe and hold the student until he is ready to take his acceptable, pre-set place in society.

The nature of the education of the student is an incredible story. It would appear from the outset that the student's education should be geared to his environment. But, as has already been pointed out several times in the foregoing pages, the education was only to prepare the child for his "slot" in life (as a data-processing card has its slot in the computer, so has the student his "slot" in society).

The student can be going to school in a Harlem area—in fact, in middle Harlem, on 114th Street, down the block from one of the busiest dope and prostitution traffic corners in the world, and up the street from one of the most crime-ridden apartment buildings in New York City—and yet once he crosses the threshold of his school building and enters the classroom, a fantastic psychedelic illusion of truth, warmth, and everlasting beauty (as interpreted by the system), looms before him, inviting him to come in and be "educated."

He sees young boys and girls moving around in an impossible world of dreams and middle-class aspirations. He watches them, as they float in white shirts and ties that they cannot afford, blue skirts and blouses, doldrum uniforms reflecting the gray attitudes of the school administration.

Their thoughts and dreams aspire beyond reality—they reach for the white middle-class star that shines high above them. They prepare to make the necessary change—to usurp their inherited blackness to become half-white members of the "Negro Middle Class."

This is not their fault. This is their teaching. It is a fact that society's recognized position for these students is in the Negro Middle Class, where they best serve society as prime examples of "those who made it." These are the students who would, in centuries past, have been recognized as the former slave who escaped, got rich, and then decided that he needed a few black slaves of his own, because if "Massa has it, why cain't I . . . ?"

Then there are the others. Our student watches a group of kids walk by who do not conform. They don't obey the rules. They don't wear ties. They don't care about society. They fight, they lie, they cheat, and they steal. These are the victims of society. These are the ones most affected by their environment, and yet these are the ones who receive the least benefit from the school system. It is said of these, "They are too hard-headed," "He is uneducable," "She will never learn," and "I tried, but he won't listen." These are the students who *must* resign themselves to Gym, Shop, and Hygiene classes as their education. These are the ones who have only society's worst to look forward to—jobs as unskilled laborers, welfare, and the Selective Service.

Denise W—— goes to a junior high school in Harlem.

It is an all-girls' school. It's in one of the worst neighborhoods of New York. Outside—rape, murder, robbery, and undermining. Inside the school, much of the same . . . only this time done to girls by girls.

Denise lives in a bleak, dangerous, slum neighborhood, and yet her education is geared to the type of student that lives in white middle-class Scarsdale, N.Y., with its bourgeois ideals and settings. The fact that she lives in the worst, sub-standard conditions of housing, mental and physical health, and emotional stability, is not taken into account at all. She is taught by a formula, not by her capacity to relate to the things she is taught. It would be much easier for Denise to learn if her teacher did talk about the stray Spots in the street, the problems that Denise is having at home, the attitudes of the girls in the school toward one another, and the situations that arise in the community; but it is easier for the teacher to just give the lesson as she is told. This way, she doesn't have to breach the socio-economic and racial gaps between her and Denise.

The average aware student usually has had much opportunity to develop his thoughts. I myself spent many hours reviewing seemingly unrelated events and incidents, in the hope of finding the one missing link that would complete the chain. I remember that when I had first entered Brooklyn Tech as a Freshman I was swiftly caught up in a whirlwind of act, act, act. There was no time to think in which direction the action would lead me, but as long as a teacher said act, I had to act. Even though my awareness of certain basic facts relevant to my understanding did not come to a head until a few years later, I still felt at the time that there was something frighteningly wrong with my education. I began to realize exactly how warped the system is when I asked a Social Studies teacher (who considered himself a liberal) to tell me when the school was going to allow us to be taught about Africa.

"Son," I was told, "Next year, you will be taught all about Egypt and Mesopotamia."

This, of course, was unsatisfactory. Not only had he not answered my question, for I was concerned about learning about *all* of Africa, but I had also heard from those who had taken the course—and later I confirmed for myself—that, as taught, the Egyptians were not what we thought they were. They lived in Africa (no fault of theirs, though), but they were not Africans! Why, Mr. Teacher? Because they were considered to be Arabs or Cretans or Grecians—people who were of white origin. Arabs were "near-white." The scale, as taught to us, runs from black to brown to yellow to near-white, and then at the top stood—Whiteness Supreme!

Many times a student may be confronted with totally different conditions. They may be far from what he expects. Larry D—— is a student at Manhattan Vocational and Technical High School on East 96th Street, a predominantly black and Puerto Rican school in a predominantly Puerto Rican neighborhood. Larry himself is a beautiful Puerto Rican brother. He too realized that the purpose of schooling was not really to educate him. It was not to prepare him for a full, complete and uncontrolled life. It was not to prepare him to live for Larry . . .

Larry is one of the few brothers who did not stand for a lot of what was being shoved down his throat. He had been transferred from two junior highs and one senior high school, before ending up at Manhattan.

There his education took on a completely new form. No longer was he being soothed and babied (as his teachers in the previous schools had tried to do, asking him, "Why can't you be a *good* boy"—Larry hated both of those words, and even more so when they were put together—a *good boy!*), but now he was being pushed into the hard cold world of careerism. He was told, as so many black and Puerto Rican youths are still being told, that if he worked hard, kept in his place, and saluted the flag every day, he could become a top engineer with NASA, and maybe one day go to the moon, or maybe even Mars, and so what if your skin is a little dark, you're not black, you just have to work a little harder and wear a white suit and tie and shoes to match to work every day, just start from the bottom, and then prove to everybody that you can be as white as you want to!

The male teachers at Manhattan acted like seasoned factory bosses, transformed from the McCarthy period to now. They came on with the attitude that they were the kings and the students were the workers. In fact, the entire school did resemble a factory, with pre-set gongs and everyone bringing boxed lunches, and guys running around in denim aprons. And over all of this, presided the teacher— the vision of supreme authority, his pointer very often resembling a whipping switch.

The classes at the school were all geared to one concept —Engineering. Even the art classes dealt with drawing nuts and bolts and screws. Every class you went into prepared you for a career. The Gym teacher wanted you to become a Phys-Ed major. The Art teacher wanted you to become a draftsman's assistant. The whole purpose of going to school seemed, to Larry, to be to put him in a predetermined slot in life. Only when he realized that this was true was he able to grasp the meaning of his individual rebellion. Then he was able to communicate this meaning to others, and establish a resistance.

It is now easy for me to see and understand the extent of the roles that others played in my receiving a "proper education." I can now see the complete and full hypocrisy of education in America.

Scanning, now, I can see beyond the teacher. I look way beyond the administration of the school . . . beyond the city system, the state system, and even national systems of education.

I widen my range of vision and suddenly I see the government, the politicians, the priests, the organizations that are all interested in the education of youth. Then I begin to adjust, to narrow my line of sight, to focus. And there before me, as big and bright and dominating as a Christmas star high up on a naked tree, stands none other than Big Business and the Industrial-Military Interests.

Earlier I asked who, if the city and state couldn't, who then was handling the education of our youth? The answer, now, is simple—Wall Street, Madison Avenue, and the Pentagon! When I realized this, I then knew all the hows, whys, and wherefores of my education.

I was not being educated for my own benefit, but rather for the benefit of society in general, and business, industry, and the military, in specific. I could definitely be sure that for the benefit of society, upon my graduation or dropping out of school, one of the Big Three would be waiting for me: Wall Street wanted me as a big-time black broker or advertising manager; Ford wanted me to work in a factory as an assemblyman or as a janitor; and the army wanted me as a soldier. There was no out! One or another knew they could and would have me. After all, had I not been programmed for them?

Almost every high school in New York has some sort of black student organization. Usually it is a recognized, chartered, or semi-chartered group, but sometimes it takes the form of a loose gathering of friends who have decided to try to give themselves some direction.

At Brooklyn Tech, our group was chartered by the school's G.O. and was known as SONAC (Society for Negro American Culture). At the time, SONAC was more of a party club than anything else. The thing about SONAC that repelled me more than it could ever attract me, was that I too fully realized that this group was structured to follow the formula—"soothe them." And by soothing, we were blinded to the plight we were in. We "danced away our troubles," as one brother later put it.

We watched the teachers piss and shit all over us all during the week, every week of every month. But when Friday came along, just give us some music and we'd shuffle our feet, nod our heads, scratch, and even jump around every now and then. (Same old routine, but this time to a funkier rhythm than a whip crack). We smiled our troubles away (kick my ass, cut my throat, but give me my Friday night dance and everything will be all right). And this was the way the administration wanted it. This was why the SONAC club had been set up and approved. It was all part of the formula.

So here is where I knew I could possibly work. This was something I could try to work on.

My first efforts were toward offering alternatives to these "Negro society" clubs. So I tried to organize a group of youths from the streets of Harlem. Our thoughts were that we could begin in a given community, and then spread to other communities.

Our organization became known as the Black Youth Alliance, and we soon developed interests in the Marxist-Leninist and Maoist lines of philosophy and political ideology. All phases of proletariat struggle were scrutinized and even updated to apply to black people.

In our efforts to become a standing organization, we began to make odd-couple alliances—with SDS, SWP (Socialist Workers Party), YSA (Young Socialist Alliance), and later, the Black Panther Party. (Even later, from the threat of co-optation by something we couldn't really understand, we dropped all forms of Marxism and started to work as a general community youth organization.)

The immediate success of the BYA had its effect on SONAC. Some SONAC members became BYA members also. I involved myself a little more deeply in SONAC (which by this time had been renamed the Afro-American Society).

Eventually, my thoughts of offering an alternative dwindled, and I felt that there should be a movement from within to wake up the majority of black students still in the club. When I became president, by election, of the AAS at Brooklyn Tech, it gave me the opportunity to steer the organization in the direction I thought was correct, and to evaluate more deeply the effect the system has on controlling the students.

The realization of exactly how ingrained the formula is in the education system was flashed at me in full beam now! As we twisted and turned to get the club to move as we thought it should move for the benefit of the members, the rules, laws, and regulations of the administration were impressed upon us. Never before heard of, absurd rules were put into immediate practice by the teachers. Rules that had no direct bearing on the AAS were brought to bear on individual students. Members who had tried to make meetings were harassed by rules of stairway, hall, dress, and speech procedure that even some teachers never knew existed. Officers of the club were admonished that they should concentrate more on their school work, or face failure at the whim of the teacher.

Under these conditions, another well-known formula was beginning to have its effect. This formula?—that under repression, the forces of the people would react to counteract the repression. In other words, the administration was forcing the students to rebellion!

The brothers began to realize that the incidents of harassment were not isolated cases. Rather, they were calculated, and the administration took advantage of situations as they arose. The brothers realized that these harassments were subtly designed to make every student unsure of himself, his goals, the AAS, its goals, and its officers.

However, the effort had an adverse effect. The brothers banded together. They began to take issue. Demands were made. Ultimatums were sent. One hundred and three students were suspended in one day. The nature of the graffiti on the walls changed from general outbursts to well-directed political statements. Essays, book reports, and answers to questions in *every* class, began to take on a political nature. Radical books were appearing all over the school. A new awareness was being reached. Everyone in the school was now *truly* being educated—teachers included.

If I thought I had seen the worst the administration could do before, I was really about to see how it would worm and squirm until it could juggle everybody back into place.

The administration's attack was simple. It was two-pronged—first, a simple directive to the liberal teachers to be super-liberal, and a little coaxing of the right-wing conservative students by certain other teachers. When I left Brooklyn Tech, this is the way the situation stood.

The tone of my paper may seem to have been set along racial lines. School, teachers, ideas, all might sound as though I approached them from a black and white attitude. I'm not going to say this is not true, and I'm not going to set up defenses. But analyze:

The average slum child's whole world takes on one color up until school—and that color is black! His neighbors are black. His friends on the streets are black. The street cleaner, the garbage man, the newspaper man, all are black. The only times he sees anything other than this one color are when he momentarily ventures out of the ghetto, or when he goes to the local merchant.

On TV, in the papers, in his comic books, the faces are all white, but the difference does not occur to him. They, as far as he is concerned, are colorless people. They also, to him, have no personalities—this, in the end, is the important factor that makes them so acceptable to him.

When the child enters kindergarten, he is confronted with much of the same, but also something extra. What extra? Let's see.

You sit a five-year-old ghetto child down in a classroom. Usually in a slum there are only black Puerto Rican children in a kindergarten class.

Place before this child a *Fun With Dick and Jane* type of book, and next to it place the *Tales of Bre'r Rabbit*. Then ask him to tell you the difference—he'll either say he doesn't know, or if he's "exceptionally bright," he'll tell you that one book has animals in it, and one has *human beings* —he will not say one has animals, and one has white people. He *knows* no color.

But then, there is a factor in this classroom that you have overlooked, which does account for the child's future racial trends. *You!* You the teacher. Your attitudes. Most teachers do not realize that a child does not at first consider him or her white. The teacher makes the child aware of the difference as though it were a crime, and then she constantly reminds the child of this difference.

Either the teacher becomes too liberal or too conservative, but either way, it is constantly put before the child that he or she is different from what the teacher is used to seeing when she goes back home. The extremely liberal teacher is used to seeing when she goes back home. The extremely liberal teacher tries extra hard "not to be white" to her students. She attempts to hide *her* color behind a mask of "goodness" and "understanding." She attempts to lose her identity. She is naturally unsuccessful.

The student wants to know why the liberal teacher treats him so nice, while the darker, kinky-haired math teacher always tells him what to do and what not to do, and doesn't try so hard to "understand" him. The teacher also attempts to keep up with the current racial trends, and so she readily and happily announces to her students that "you are all Africans," without explaining to them what Africanism is—she doesn't really know herself.

On the other side, the conservative teacher attempts to let the kids know right off the bat where he stands. "I hate niggers, and I hate teaching, and shit, you ain't never gonna learn nothin' no how, and I'm only in this for the damned money—and go home niggers . . ."

This is the way it happens in elementary, junior high, and high school. Liberal or conservative, left or right, the teacher makes the student know that he is white, and you're black, and don't you forget it, you sweet little nigger you.

．　．　．

The fact that education is a process that programs people into society is probably the most shocking revelation a student can have. This insight—and its horrible implications—make up what is probably the single most important factor causing so many of the youths in our schools to rebel. It is the prime catalyst to many uprisings in the schools. Other crucial factors are: the racism that we meet in school and society; the plight of students who were so easily "educated" in a transposed environment; and the general apathy of the vast, unawakened majority of our brothers.

Now, as never before, the student is becoming deeply involved with the activities of his school. Not only on the level of being a member of a club or organization, but to the point of trying to change the rules and regulations, and to transfer the power that is inherent in the school kaleidoscope—to give the rule of education to the people. That is our goal. For to us, the people are the only ones who know the true meaning of the phrase "relevant education." We the students realize that our struggle, and everyone's struggle has just begun—and we also realize that we have a long way to go. We're going to get there. We will be victorious.

The Black Athlete

by James Brown

> *James Brown is an eighteen-year-old black student*
> *from Peoria, Illinois. A student in Peoria's Central*
> *High School, he works part-time in the local*
> *YMCA to help support his large family. He has six*
> *brothers and sisters and lives in the black ghetto*
> *of Peoria.*

My name is James Brown. I am black, and my school,
Peoria Central High, is dominated by whites. The blacks
don't really have a chance there, as there are so few of us.
There are two hundred blacks and about eighteen hundred
whites in the school. There are somewhere near 130 teachers, and only one black teacher out of that. Two years ago,
the issue about Black History and our endowed equal rights
and opportunities in school wasn't brought up. We just
wasn't together. When it was brought up by the older brothers and sisters we just came to realize that it is what we want
so that we can have it for our own children. We have to
fight for them like our parents fought for us. The white man
got his education and we want ours too. They talk about
blacks not having any education, this and that. I know now
that it's the white man's fault.

I started to realize that something was wrong in the
school when I began hearing a lot of things and actually
seeing a lot of things that were really being done wrong to

the blacks—the blacks everywhere, not only in the school. Especially when we've been working about two hundred to three hundred years hard labor. I got it in my mind that we don't need this, we don't want this. The blacks can go out and get an education like the white man if we had the chance. This all came to me then. I seen that the blacks have been treated so bad. I came to realize that why should I go do this for him. Why should I take all this from him? I say that we have been treated bad for two to three hundred years, and it is time for us to cut all this nonsense out. We are human beings.

When I was going to school at Central High, the black students were not treated the same as the whites. You go to class and you're late, you have to have a pass to go in. If you don't get a pass, you just miss out for the whole day or maybe even three days for nothing. When a white kid would be late, he would just say I was down talking to Mr. So and So. He wouldn't have a pass and he would have smoke all over his breath. Nothing would be done to him even though he'd probably been smoking in the bathroom. And the teachers weren't teaching the same. A black kid would go in and ask for help. They tell him to come back at 7:30 in the morning to catch up. School starts at a quarter after eight. How is he going to catch up by going at 7:30 in the morning? Most teachers don't even come till after 8:00. If a white student asks for extra help, he would get it right quick. Right then and there. If he would go up to the desk and ask how to get such and such, the teacher would stop everything she was doing and say something like, "You didn't take this test, you have this assignment to make up, and I'll give you help right after class and give you a pass to the next class." The teacher would provide for this kid while he was teaching class. He would stop and actually show him what is to be done.

A lot of the teachers discriminate against the blacks in other ways. They discriminate against them by the way they act. You can see a teacher and say hi to him and he would turn his head like you weren't there. And a white person would be walking down the hall and he would say, "Oh, hi Bill, or Roger, or Steve," the big men around the school. He would actually grip him. But they ignore the black kids.

They also discriminate against the blacks by talking about them. There's a woodshop teacher named Mr. W—— who says, "I sure would like to have the hide off a soul brother's back; it sure would make a good-ass wallet." There's this kid we call Bobo, his real name is Clarence. Bobo is kind of a dark brother, and W—— says, "Hey Bobo, where you been when I took role, hiding in a coal mine or something?" Bobo would talk back to him—like radical talk. He would talk for his own rights. When you're black, you don't want to be discriminated against like a piece of coal. You black, that's soul power. You understand. He would talk back to him and he would get kicked out of class. Every teacher was backed up by the principal, the dean, the people in the office, and the white kids. If Clarence went to the dean of students and complained about W——, saying he had discriminated against him, nothing would be done. The dean of boys, Mr. S——, hates his guts. He would say "Clarence Travis is nothing but a troublemaker. Everytime he comes to school he comes to school late." Really, Bobo's got problems. First of all, he don't have a car like the whites. Most black kids don't have cars. And he had problems at home. You know, when your mother and father is fighting, you would have problems. These are everyday problems. There is a work shift in Peoria and both his parents work. Bobo has about three or four brothers and sisters. He has to watch them until one of his parents comes home. He has to watch his little brothers and sisters until they come from a shift at work. The deans at school know about this, but they do not care at all.

They never care about our problems or about what we want. During the last part of my senior year, we were going to organize a BSA (Black Student Alliance). Before we got started, we asked Dr. Norcross, Superintendent of all schools, could we have a black meeting held in school for all the black students. This was mainly to talk to the students who didn't act right, what I mean by that—the kind that act like they think they are white. The upper-class blacks, the semi-blacks, the Negroes. We were trying to have this meeting to tell these Negroes, these Uncle Toms, how they really are. It is all right to have your white friends, but you better think black. I mean you don't wear no high bottom pants, no Beatle haircuts, no processed hair, no white socks and orange and loud colors. When you're black, you've got to act black and think black. We asked to have this meeting and the superintendent said, "All right." We called the principal and he said "No." The principal called Dr. Norcross and persuaded him to change his mind. Dr. Norcross then said that he thought we were trying to overcome the school, take over the administration, and threaten all the white kids. All this when there's only a population of two hundred blacks in the whole school.

There's also discrimination like when we're being punished; when there would be fighting going on between a black student and a white student, the black student would be kicked out for one whole week, and the white student would sit home on vacation. He would not be kicked out. The white would go around boasting that "Mr. S—— said I could have a vacation and he is going to put 'Suspended' on the bulletin board so the black students won't know about it." Stan Middlehall, a white kid, had a fight in the hall with Larry Brown who's black. Stan Middlehall got a vacation for two days. He came in our English class and told everyone that the principal gave him a two-day vacation. Larry Brown, the black student, got kicked out for one whole week. When he came back again, he got kicked out another three days for some reason. They made up some kind of excuse I didn't hear about, but all I seen on that bulletin was that he was kicked out for another three days. They just wanted to get rid of him. That's the way the deans feel about all the blacks.

Many of the teachers in Central discriminate against the blacks inside the classroom. Except the ones who are kind of uptight, and either live or have been around blacks. But

most all the other teachers teach like the whites are superior, which they think, and the blacks are dumb-dumbs.
Like they say, "All right, dumb-dumb, will you cut it out."
They will say that. And nobody takes that jive anymore.
Things are changing. When you say something back to the
teachers, that's insubordination—you get three days' detention. You ask a question that she thinks is not a legitimate
question, and she says, "No, we just can't put up with that."
Yet a white person can talk and give stupid answers. They
can even laugh and giggle and the teacher doesn't do a
thing. A black person can say, "Hey, loan me a pencil," and
boom, that's it. You're getting it from her—five or six
detentions, that's staying after school for an hour or so. But
that depends on how good you act in detention, it could be
longer. Detention is sort of like a study hall. You go there
and sleep or rest, waste your time. The white teachers
expect you to be good. They think of you as a "Good
Negro." You're supposed to be just perfect. All they want
you to do is to play their sports and run their games, so that
they can clap-clap for you. If you are good in sports, they
think of you as dumb.

If you're an athlete and you're black, you got a lot of
other problems. You've got to fight the discrimination of the
coaches. I was on the football team and the track team, and
I know. If you're black, you don't play football, not unless
you are the best black player ever in history. Really, like
Ray Taylor, he made the All-American team, third string.
He had to be good to play. He was elected captain. The
first black captain Peoria High had, and Peoria High is the
oldest school in the State of Illinois. You have to be excep-
tional. You have got to get down and kiss the coaches' ass
and you have to get down on your knees and do other
things too. You can't play your best, for one thing. If you
play defensive back in football and one of the star players is
a white boy, you got to be extra careful in practice. Say you
actually mess him up, hit him hard, and knock him down.
Man, that's just like saying you are going to get cut. You're
doing your job. You want to play, and you want to show

him you want to play. I went out for football for my two Varsity years. I banged my head for two years straight for football season, and I only got to play in four games. Four games. They knew I could run a 10.3 hundred and everything else. They did not let me play. And I couldn't talk to them about this because there wasn't any reason to. They just looked at their white boys. They brought up Freshmen and Sophomores to take the place of Seniors to play because they did not like the blacks. Only one black was playing; that was Jamie Laird and he was a straight-A honor-roll student. Even he didn't get to play much. Jamie was quick. I mean he could run a 10.2 hundred. Yet he played only one game of offense in his two years. He ran a 10.2 hundred and all he played was defensive back.

I was on the Varsity two years and only played in four games. I know I was better than a lot of whites. Like Beatleburg, he ran twenty-two touchdowns, and Curley, he's the captain of the All-Star team in the state of Illinois. I actually knocked Curley down, and I stopped Beatleburg in his tracks. They were ready to cut me for it. For being too good they want to cut me. When I tackled this white player one time he wanted to cut me. He said to a white guy, "The next time he's out there, R——, I want you to get that . . . ," but he didn't say it. "Just stomp him in the ground." He wanted to say "nigger," that's what he wanted to say.

In track there was discrimination from all the white players. Charles Harper, he was eighteen. He was kind of on the side where he wasn't that smart, you know. The teachers knew he could run track. This one coach, Mr. Saltfield, liked blacks, and he helped Charles out. Charles could run a 21.9 220, and tell me that's not fast. The white players running on the team would say, "He's not very good." And he was running a 10.1 hundred at the beginning of the season and he was bound to get better. But he pulled a leg muscle and he just didn't run too much 'till the end of the season. The whites would talk about all the blacks. And Jewish kids too. They'd say things like "Oh look at Joe (he's a long jumper), he runs like a Jew going to the synagogue for his daily prayers." The Jews in Peoria are also discriminated against by the other whites. They are considered about middle-white. The Jews live in one part of town, and when they go into another section the whites would say, "Hey, Jew-man, where you think you going?" They're actually afraid of them, and they would talk about them. The Jews are friendly with the blacks. I went to speak with this one guy. He did the long jump with me. And we sat down and practiced—me, James Laird, a black who also long-jumps, and Butch Banks. Butch is a Freshman broad-jumper and he's black too. And Joe, he was a Jew. And we would sit down and practice and talk all about the blacks and Jews and how we were discriminated against by the white players on the team.

I mean they didn't like the blacks. We scared them. We were coming up so quick doing everything. Like this one white guy, Scott Russell. That's all you heard from him for three whole years in track. "Those damn blacks! Those damn blacks!" Scott could run a 10.5 hundred when he was a Freshman. He could long jump 22.5 when he was a Sophomore. But he got heavy lifting weights, and me and Gene, two blacks, got better than him. Gene was second, I was third in the broad jump out of thirty-six guys in our area. The whites didn't like it at all. They didn't like it at all. They showed this by not treating us the same. They'd say things like, "You better go get a big sun hat before you get all burned up out in the sun. Track's no place for you." They would all say this. I mean they didn't like it one bit. They wanted all the glory for themselves. Like when Charles Harper, a black, ran a relay that broke the record, even though Charles was good, they didn't want him on the team. They didn't want a black person. They didn't want it.

And the teachers are all involved trying to flunk the blacks, trying to get them ineligible. Like Butch Banks. Butch is about 5'2" and Butch can leap like he was six feet. For a little guy he's really good. But his teacher in Algebra didn't want Butch to play. He had him declared ineligible. Fortunately Butch was one of Mr. Smith's players. Mr. Smith is a good coach, and he loves blacks. Butch was one of Mr. Smith's star players so Mr. Smith got up there on the teacher's ass and got him eligible. There's a guy named Darris Petty whose math teacher also wanted to keep him from playing. So I would help Darris with his homework. He would come over my house at night and we would do our homework together that we had in class. Darris did better, and the teacher had to let him play. He didn't want to though, because Darris was black. Do you hear me? That's the way the teachers are.

If the football team wins the season and gets its picture in the newspaper, the teachers and the coaches don't want a picture of a black guy in there. That's why they don't want a black guy to play—so Coach J—— can show Beatleburg, and Curley, Demler, Snyder, Roger Williams, and all the white guys. Show them white faces and not ours. But S—— our track coach, couldn't do anything *but* to show us. All his best men were black. If James Laird and James Brown wasn't in the broad jump, there was no points. If Charles Harper wasn't in the hundred, there was no points. If Tony Cornelius wasn't high jumping, there was no points. Tony's black too. He's jumping six feet and only a Sophomore. The coach had to give in. There was no other choice. That was the only way. If it wasn't for that, he'd keep the blacks on the bench. My Junior year in track I did not broad jump once. Not once. I only ran in one track meet. The last meet of the season is relays and I got to run in two relays. And that was it for my Junior year. The rest of the season I was burning in the sun. And I really didn't need that burn in the sun because I got my tan and I like it too. You understand, I'm gonna keep it. I did not jump all year. What did I do this year? I came out and I jumped twenty-one feet my first try. And the coach was so surprised—he didn't think a black person could jump like that. I was better than the rest of the jumpers. And this time he let me jump because there wasn't any alternative. I was beating his star, Scott Russell, who jumped 22.5 in his Junior year, Sophomore year too. I was beating him.

In the actual courses in Central High, there is discrimination against black people in general. Especially when the teachers talk about the history of this country. When you study America they say, America—land of the free, home of the brave. I know that brave, brave is the white man; free, free is the white man. I see blacks asking for freedom, but they don't get it. The black man is not free to do anything. You look at him trying to get into labor unions. They're not opening up their doors for him. These are lies, man. They just say these things. They want the other countries to get a good impression of America. Immigrants can come from any place across the seas and get ahead more than the black man can. They talk about things are changing. They aren't. And the teachers refuse to admit this. For example, if a teacher said that America is "land of the free," and I raised my hand and said, "It's not the home of the free. My father can't get into a labor union in Peoria because he's black," she would say something like maybe he doesn't have the qualifications. "Have you thought of that, Jim?" She wouldn't say James. Most of the white teachers say Jim. "Really, your father don't have the education. There are equal opportunities for him to get in, but maybe he just doesn't have the ability to do the work that the white man would have." And you can get any old white man with a ninth-grade education; he can go over there and scratch his little old name in, and boom, he's got the job, right then and there. The black man could have his diploma even, and still he's not qualified. That's the way she would really put it. He doesn't have the ability or he's not qualified. She won't admit the truth.

There's no black courses at Central High. There's hardly any around Peoria that I know of. Like they say, Uncle Tom was a good nigger and this is the way you should be. Who wants to read about that? We want to learn the truth about ourselves. I really didn't know about who discovered the North Pole till this year. You just don't know about any of this lost or strayed or stolen black history. I mean this was not lost or strayed; this was put away. They didn't want us to learn about ourselves, but about the white man. If it wasn't put away by a white man, it would be in the books. That's the way I feel. They say Columbus discovered America. Columbus was supposed to be white, but he could have been Jew, Gentile, any other thing. Nobody really knows. So they say Columbus discovered it: Columbus was white, and they want this to be a white America. White history all the way down. They don't give us any credit. You know, we fought the wars here, there; we built this, we built that. The white man wasn't doing much building. They had every one of them brothers and sisters on their hands and knees building bricks with their hands. That's the way it was. We was on our hands and knees. You didn't see too many of them on theirs. They had the whips standing over us, and you're not going to get up with no chain on your back and your feet tied and think you're going to fight somebody. Why, they just gonna stand there and kill you. The white man did a lot of that too.

When we request black courses they give us some dumb excuse. They talk about how a white teacher or a black teacher would have to study for so many years just to get this information across to you and explain it the way it was. "And by the time you get the information, it will be no good to you. It would only be good for the younger kids coming up, and even then it would be a waste of time to learn. White history is here and this is all that needs to be here because it's been here so long. Why not continue it?" Brain-wash the black—that's what they want. Make the black feel like he wants to be white, to be accepted as a white American so everything can be the way the white man wants it. They just want everything to be mellow; but they go about it in a different way. Things like, "Black history isn't really needed once you got white history, and what's there to learn about black history if you got white history? This is white America and why should we bother? Why should we go all out to give you blacks a little handful of knowledge you want about your relatives and all that when it's not really necessary?"

It was during my Junior year that the issue of black courses was brought up. It had been brought up before, a long time ago, but nobody really took any definite actions toward it. I just felt like I really wanted to know about my brothers and sisters; like the white man didn't build this all alone. He didn't pick the cotton that we grew. I wanted to find out about this myself. The issue of bringing up black history was there because it would be a different thing, something interesting. Instead of, "We brought you across from Africa to give you a home here away from home, a better place to live, equal opportunities, this and that." Nobody wants to hear that bullshit anymore. You read about slaves everywhere you go. That's the main thing about black courses, why we bring it up. We want the young black kids to know about more than that the blacks were just slaves. We were people in this world. There was some smart black people. They actually had offices, they held their own committees, and the white man didn't want them to get ahead like that, so they broke it all down. The white man didn't want all this to be published. They didn't want them to find out that one time or another the black man was successful—he had built his own empire. The black man got brains, and the white man didn't want us to know that we established something like our own country a long time ago. The whites all tried to keep it away.

But this isn't the case no more. There is going to be a change. The world is changing every time you look around. The white man is going to have to adjust. We blacks coming up are getting bigger, smarter, and better-off than before. This change is going to have to come, it's gonna move, it can't go slow like a snail. This is gonna have to come rapid. That's the way the changes in the world come about. The black man knows what he wants, the white man knows what he wants, but the white man don't want to give the black man what he wants. If we are going to just talk, we are going to get nothing. We're gonna have to make our

move to get what we want. Students and the way we refuse
to be treated and discriminated against—this is all part of
the change. You talk, talk, talk, but it doesn't change anything. War is progress. When you take a radical movement
against something, something gotta give. And that's what's
gonna happen when the black students make this effort to
move. We'll make this effort to move in one blow. When
you hit something, something gotta give. It's either you or
the idea you are hitting against. And that idea or object
gonna give. Because you are here and you are gonna be
here until the world ends. And that object gonna have to be
moved out of the way, like a barrier.

At Central High this past year we were trying to form
our BSA at school, our Black Student Alliance. We were
trying to make it easier for the younger brothers and sisters
because we were the black people there. We wanted all
power to the black people at the school—we wanted to
change the school. We were trying to make this change so it
would be easier on the younger brothers and sisters coming
up because we knew they were not as strong in mind as we
were then. We wanted to change the ideas, the way things
were about the school, how the blacks were being treated.
We wanted that change to come our year so that when our
brothers and sisters come up next year, the year after that,
and the year after that, it would be easier. And they all
would tell the people in their Junior year coming up to their
Senior year to keep this momentum going, keep that barrier
broken open, do not let anybody stop or seal it whatsoever.
Keep the momentum going. So it would be easier for the
other brothers and sisters.

In addition to establishing the Black Student Alliance,
we had a petition set up to get rid of the teachers who
actually discriminated against the blacks. The teachers like
Mr. W.——, and J——, the football coach, and some of the
others. I mean they really didn't dig blacks at all—not
unless we were outstanding. Blacks had to be Good Negroes
and Uncle Toms before they could like them. We didn't
need this. We couldn't be ourselves and be liked. We just

wasn't accepted in the school. About half of the blacks, all that weren't "Negroes," signed the petition, and we took it to Dr. Norcross, the Superintendent of Schools. We had a board meeting down at City Hall. No whites were in this. They didn't know anything about it. We wanted to keep the thing to ourselves, but we knew our Good Negroes would come to our meetings and tell the principal and the deans and everybody else in the school what was going on. They didn't like what we were doing. Gene Webster, president of the BSA at Bradley College here in Peoria, took over the meeting. He discussed the issues because if one of us would have brought it up, people would have said, "The hell with you." We needed somebody strong like Gene Webster to present what we wanted. People respected him, at least that's what we were thinking. We had to be thinking then. If I go, they'd think "put him down. He's just one person. They won't follow him." We needed a strong leader and that's why we picked Gene Webster.

We went there. We discussed the matters and everything. All they did was just discuss, discuss, discuss. It was close to graduation time, so they let it ride, ride, ride until graduation and then they threw it out the door. Everything out. And then they blamed everything on Gene Webster, and said the BSA created an uprising in the school. What happened wasn't really an uprising but a walk-out in the foyer, to demand what we wanted from these teachers who are really racist, and this school that doesn't care about us. The meeting just didn't accomplish anything really. It was like talking to a hole in the wall. We felt a good reason to leave school after that, so we left. The black students got up and went out, and the sisters and brothers of the college BSA distributed some letters supporting the twenty-five brothers and sisters who took their stand against the superintendent. The letter was to the rest of the black student body—to get them together. We gonna have to get them together. When the younger brothers and sisters come up, we gonna have to make it easier for them. When we left, the principal didn't do a thing. And when we came back he didn't say anything, probably 'cause he knew we were right. The school just went on like it was. However, the teachers hated the black kids more after this. They wouldn't let us make up our work for that day.

There was some other conflict before the end of the year, but nothing really organized. John Sturtevant got into a fight, him and John Miller, with some white boys. The principals said it was radical stuff but John said it was personal. The white man wanted to get it on John that it was a radical fight so me and the other blacks would be blamed. John wouldn't take it, so John fought again. Then there was a big fight, a racial fight in school, and everybody was fighting. They didn't know what they was fighting for, a lot of football players and basketball players jumped in for nothing. The principals didn't know it was a personal problem (it had to do with his sister), and they blamed everything on John. They kicked him out until graduation came —and then they gave him and John Miller their diplomas without any credits. That means they have legal diplomas but no credits. Just a piece of paper. Then the school year ended.

Looking toward the future at Peoria High, I know the movement is gonna be slow. The leader that's there now is Floyd Pickett. Floyd's a pretty good leader for a Sophomore. He was with all of the Seniors all of the way down to the real nitty-gritty. The rest of the people up there now are those dudes who are so-called Negroes. That's what they are. They call themselves lovers. I mean they grip everybody, every girl, black, white, as long as she's got a dress on, they don't care about anything at all. The only people who care are the Freshman. They are the only ones who went down with us to City Hall. The other people did not go. The movement is gonna be slow and I'm sure glad I'm out. In a way I'm glad I'm out because there will be nobody following. Back to normal.

If we were still in high school, if the older Senior class was still there, the movement would have kept going. We would have did some of everything. We would have did everything we could to get what we wanted. We went so far, and when the black student body left the school we were determined to put down some of the bullshit they were giving us. I mean, we were actually making our move, and we were actually breaking that barrier down. They were actually scared. When you go there and talk, talk, talk, they just sit back and laugh, laugh, laugh. When you go there and move, move, move, they get up and look, look, look. One day they gonna realize what's happening.

I don't know what we would've done next, but I know we'd have busted our brains. We couldn't just go in there and blow up the school. That wouldn't help. No, we had to out-think the white man; we had to sit down after school until one or two o'clock in the morning to see what our plans were going to be. We actually sat down together and talked about these things. That's how all this came about so slowly. And that's the thing we would have done again. But now I feel sorry for everybody at the school, because every-thing is going down the drain. I could tell when we was graduating, everything was going down the drain. The prin-cipal was saying about every black student, shaking their hands as they were leaving, "Oh, he was a fine boy at this school, they liked this boy, I hope he goes far. If there's any kind of help you want me to do, just look me up and I'll help you out." Oh, sure. He'll see if he can get him in ICC, some junior college nobody even knows about. He's just breathing easy 'cause he got rid of us.

Generally, we now know that the teachers and adminis-trators aren't going to change things. It's going to take our own efforts to do anything nowadays. We just can't go up to the desk and ask the teachers, can we go get a pencil out of our locker? and then go down to the principal and get a written excuse. We can't do that anymore. What you want in life, you are gonna have to work for. It's not going to be handed out anyway. What you want, you are gonna do what you have to do and take it in life. The Black Move-ment is gonna have to change; it's gonna have to move more and more. People just aren't gonna go for this anymore.

The high school students are going to have to come together. They gonna have to come together in order to do anything. If you're not together, you not anything. That's what the good brothers and sisters are doing now. They're getting themselves together. All this radical movement and all this progressive work in the last ten or twenty years is a lot compared to the two hundred or three hundred years before. The brothers and sisters are together; they know what's happening.

"All Power to the People!"

Firebomb

by Joe Harris

Joe Harris is fifteen and formerly attended Theodore Roosevelt High School in New York City. He works as an organizer when not in school.

The outside of the building is unattractive and without warmth. The inside is dark, depressing, and ugly. The whole interior is painted dull drab colors, the way prison halls and cells are painted. Guards walk the halls not unlike in prison, haranguing people with their mere presence. The stairways are in little closets, and fenced in like cages. A feeling of utter confinement would fall upon me whenever I was forced to use them. People are stopped in the halls and harassed and threatened while struggling to produce a paper to prove they belong there. Yet they do belong there. They belong there more than the pigs who they are trying to prove it to. This is supposed to be a school, not a prison or a jail. A school for the people, it is the people's school. To serve the people is the function of every school, and it is the people (community and students) alone who should decide how it can best work in their interests. And since the present "controllers"—pig administrators, corrupt politicians, fascist mayors, swine principals, and the mercenary UFT, have failed so completely in making the schools work for the people, control of the school should be taken from them immediately and given directly to the people by any means necessary.

Schools are nothing but the capitalist system's classification and processing centers. In the schools we are taught how to best become cogs to go into the capitalistic machine. Students that seem not to be able to do well in capitalist academic subjects are put either into commercial courses or general courses. General courses fuck the students. They are usually given to those who rarely come to school. They are given to students who think school is boring already. So classes get even more boring, making attendance almost nil. Out of all the hard-core absenters I used to know around school, very very few had academic or even commercial courses. Most students who get a general diploma can be nothing more than a janitor. For all the good a general course can do for you, you might as well throw it away. You might as well have dropped out of school. What they give you on graduation day is not a diploma but practically an induction notice because that's exactly where you're going to go. You're going to continue your education at Fort Jackson University or Fort Dix College, and join one of the biggest oppressive agencies the world has ever known. General courses must be stopped, and one diploma must be given for all. The school will not be used as a cannon fodder supplier. Students will not be taught ultra-bullshit. The time has come for school liberation and the end of meaningless education. The people will have meaningful education by any means necessary. General tracking isn't just poor education; general tracking is no education at all!

Academic education in the schools is just out and out warped bullshit. For example, we are taught that the American Indian was exterminated because he was a bloodthirsty savage always attacking and killing the "good" white settlers. That is bullshit. They were killed off because the white capitalist wanted their land. We are taught Chiang Kai-Shek was a great democratic general trying to rid China of the dirty commies, when it was proved in government reports that he had one of the most corrupt armies and administrations that ever existed. We are actually taught that slaves didn't have it so bad; they had a place to eat and sleep, etc. However, if they had been left in Africa they would have eaten and slept as well, and would have been spared fourteen hours a day of hard labor. It was this kind of labor that built the capitalist economy. The basic goal that all these studies have is to make us believe that Uncle Sam never did any wrong and always did things the American way. We are taught to keep on singing, "Three cheers for the red white and blue and kill the dirty commies too."

Many teachers in school are pathetic. Teachers in school don't usually care about anything but their monthly pay checks. They care little about how well or poorly students are doing. They teach in very boring ways that seem to make you forget before you've learned anything. Often teachers give preferential treatment to students who are doing well, and scorn and make it hard for students who are doing poorly. Often teachers give students bad marks and bad times just because they don't like them personally or politically. One student I know was told by his teacher in front of the whole class that "I'm so glad you fucked-up this marking period so I can fail you. I wanted to fail you last time but you did too well." Then she went on to say, "Sometimes you get a student you just can't stand and you want to fail him so bad, and boy you are one of those students." Yet this very same teacher was very human with other students she happened to like, like me and others, joking with us in class and shit like that.

Other teachers will argue and yell at you if they don't like your political beliefs. Once when I just started my new school (after being suspended from the last one I attended) I wore an "Eldridge Cleaver for President" button to school, and I was given an extra hard time by my teacher (who gave me hard times anyway for *no reason*). Then in class the point was brought up that a white man designed and built the city of Washington D.C. When I told her a black man also worked on it I was told I was wrong when she knew I was right. To add to this she told me I had a "problem" and that she knew what it was; meaning I was a racist cultural nationalist. I felt that the race of the man who designed Washington was irrelevant, but I brought it up to spite the teacher—it did. Also, this same teacher, when I came in the class for the first time, said I was showing her disrespect when to one of her questions I responded, "Huh, excuse me, what did you say?" She went on to say, "I have a group of good boys here, and anyone that comes in here and tries to change them will not be allowed in this class."

Teachers sometimes blackball a student. When teachers don't like a student they will tell all his teachers about him, often lying and telling stories about the student which play upon suspicions and prejudices. How can a student do well when all his teachers are against him for no reason?

Schools are depressing and ugly to begin with; if teachers are going to come in with fucked-up attitudes and irrelevant teaching methods, they just increase the malfunctioning of the school. Subjects must be taught in the context of the particular life in a particular community. Teachers who don't try to see the problems of the students, who do nothing more than give homework and read something out of a book, who play on prejudices for any reason and give students a hard time—these teachers should be dropped from teaching for being detrimental to the education of the people.

Many students are transferred for political reasons, and that is one of the most destructive things that can happen to a student. To be suspended illegally for three weeks and then put in a strange school with a trouble-maker brand makes passing and doing well almost impossible. (I was expelled for suggesting a sit-in in the principal's office—a sit-in that never took place.) When I went to my new school I brought with me a letter from the superintendent saying, "Although Joseph was engaging in activity contrary to school rules, he expresses a desire to continue his education." If a letter like that is carried by me to the school, I wonder what must have been said over the phone. Although I brought the letter to the dean expecting to start school that day, I was told a parent would have to accompany me before I could be enrolled. My father came with me the next day—for no good reason because he didn't sign a thing. I was told by the dean that the school didn't have to accept me, which was bullshit, and that I was not to enter into any discussions with teachers during class time. A lot of bullshit went down on how I've got to be a good boy and not disturb the running of the school whatsoever.

Although I had a 92 average at my old school, I found that in my new school it would be almost impossible to catch up the three weeks of school work that I missed. This inability to do well in a strange school with strange teachers depressed and angered me. For although I wanted to do well, the shit that was pulled was too heavy for me to overcome, and I failed for the term. But then, that gave me a whole term longer to try and liberate the schools from the oppressors.

Drug traffic in school is very heavy. Drugs like coke (cocaine) and scag (heroin) are sold frequently in the halls. The reason for the heavy sale of these drugs and the use of them in place of school is due to the pathetic conditions that the average student finds in school. With schools so motherfucking depressing, who could help but sample a joint or two before going into class? With teachers being the way they are and subjects being so boring, many can't help but go home after a period or two and snort some coke. People don't realize this and I feel they are very stupid, because the reasons for it are right in front of their eyes.

Most teachers' attitudes toward people who turn on— even to grass—are warped. The people who use drugs are called "stupid, asses, and dummies," when all the teachers know about taking them is what they have heard or read in some book. My feelings toward drugs in schools are that if the schools were brightened up, if teachers would change

their attitudes toward students, and if more relevant subjects were taught with more relevant methods, attendance in
schools would soar, cutting would be greatly reduced, and
drug-taking during school or in place of school would be
greatly reduced. I'm not saying it would disappear, because
there's always going to be someone who feels like getting
high. Everyone likes to get high once in a while. But with
some basic changes nobody will want to get high every day,
at least not because of what he feels about school. Drugs
have their place outside of school; a school where a person
has to get high to face—and then sometimes not face—
class, has to be very bad.

Principals are among the main reasons for the inadequate functioning of schools. They seem to be nothing but
mercenary opportunists. They sit in their comfortable,
wall-to-wall carpeted, air-conditioned offices, ruling the
schools in much the same way that a king would rule his
empire. Meanwhile the schools deteriorate and decay. Yet
administrators attribute the poor functioning of schools to
inadequate funds. Money, the people's money, can be put to
much better use than to pamper these overweight, incompetent tyrants. Principals are like invisible men whom the
average student rarely or never sees. They sit back and
control their schools through their various flunkies and
lackeys such as assistant principals, secretaries, and so-
called student leaders. The whole running of the school is
nothing more than a bureaucratic dictatorship. Principals
rarely if ever see what's going on in the school themselves.
And they never take an active position to try and see why
the students are angry. This is another fault of the schools
—mercenary, indifferent principals who must be replaced
by community control of the schools.

My first encounter with my principal showed me a man
who, with his antagonistic attitudes towards students,
shouldn't have even been made janitor. I was giving out
"unauthorized literature" one day in front of the school
before my first class. When I went into the building,

I was pushed into the dean's office and then taken to the principal. The conversation went as follows: "Are you a Black Panther?" he said.

"No, but I attend political education with them," I said.

"Why do you go to political education with them when you are failing all your subjects here?" This very arrogant statement by the principal showed his attitude toward students who are doing political things. He automatically brands them as stupid and failing without stopping to look, for I had a 92 average, my lowest mark was 85, and beside that he didn't even know me. He told me it was illegal to pass out leaflets on the school block. That was a motherfucking lie, for my lawyer said it was perfectly legal. Then he told me I could do more for my race if I stayed in school and excelled and became a leader. In other words, he out and out told me to become a bootlicking NAACP type leader. Now here was a white man who has never had any *real* contact with the black street community, yet he was trying to tell me how to help my race; it was just plain stupid. Then after the whole shit was over, making me twenty minutes late for class, he gave me a cut for my first period and said I was giving out leaflets during class time which was untrue.

Only when their empires are crumbling, only when their control is threatened, only when revolution and liberation of the students is going to destroy their mercenary way of life, their pay checks, and their reputations, do they come forward to be seen. When the violence, the violence that they themselves have created by their inability to work in the best interests of the people, is coming to the surface, the principals step forward to divert it. To divert it they will use any means necessary. They issue proclamations that explain how a small minority is causing the disturbance, how all the more "intelligent" students realize there are legal ways to do things and will have nothing to do with the revolutionaries. Their favorite story seems to be that it is not these students at all, but a group of "outside agitators" who are causing this violence. They pull fascist, gestapo tactics like suspending and sometimes arresting all the student leaders, and calling in hundreds of stormtrooper police to invade the people's schools. But when these methods don't work, when the violence and strikes continue, that is when the principals are up against the wall, and that is when they grant the demands of the students. But these demands aren't enough. They only appease, for they are only a "cup of milk for a hungry lion"; there will soon be more demands and more violence, and then more demands after that until finally the schools are liberated and are completely in the hands of the people. Any attempt by the reactionaries to stop this trend will be doomed to failure, for the stage is set for revolution and the revolution in the schools is now. The progress of liberation will not be stopped.

Violent Tactics

To discuss violent tactics in schools we first must go into what power is. Power is the ability to define a phenomenon and make it act in a desirable manner. In this country we basically have three types of power: feudal power, economic power, and military power. Feudal power is the power of the landowners, the farmers, big cattle barons, etc. These people have power by presenting consequences to Congress on the basis of crops. For example, they can have the price of corn raised because they can threaten to stop growing corn. Congress doesn't want corn to be taken off the market, so they will raise the price of corn. Economic power is the power of the rich financiers, the avaricious, capitalist pigs. They basically do the same thing as farmers, only with money instead of crops. They threaten Congress with their power to take money out of certain investments, thereby fucking up the economy. Also they control the government by financing Senators, Presidents, Congressmen, etc. Certain people control the government by financing both candidates. Thus decisions are made in *their* interests, more than in the interests of the people.

Then there is military power. Military power is the power of the gun, the fire bomb, the tank, etc. This is the power that must be taken by the people. Since the people have no land and no money, they are left with no choice but to get guns, cut the strangulating, parasitic hold of America by the capitalists, and set up a decentralized government that is truly of the people and by all the people. To be truly a government of the people, it must be socialist, with the people controlling the means of production. To stop the exploitation, the oppression, and the fascism that exists in America today, the people must grasp the power of the gun to overthrow the oppressor.

Since the control of the school is in the hands of the capitalists and not in the hands of the people, and since almost every member of the Board of Education of the City of New York is a director, member, or trustee of some corporate industry, the schools are working in the interests of the capitalists, not in the interests of the people. Thus the people must seize power in the schools on a community level, using military power. Firebombs, guns, explosives, riots, as long as they don't harm the people in any way, must and will be used by the people to liberate the schools. The people and the people alone are either going to have full control of the schools, and have education that expresses the true nature of this decadent American society, or the people will burn the schools down. If violence is the only effective way to take what is ours, then violence is the form that must be used, as long as it is not directed against the people in any way.

And don't say that violence is the work of few radicals because you know that's a motherfucking lie. Don't say that some outside agitators have instigated the masses of students to do something they normally wouldn't do, because that is calling the masses a bunch of idiots that will be led around like sheep. Don't think that someone has tricked the students into fighting for liberation on all levels, because the students aren't stupid—they know what's happening. Don't blame others for starting the violent revolution you yourselves created. You're the motherfuckers who bring pigs into our schools, you're the bastards that have a bureaucratic dictatorship over us, you're the ones that try to install a bullshit morality code and blind obedience to authority. You're the swine that stifle our creativity. You're the fascists that are turning people into mindless androids. You're the puppets that give us the fucked-up capitalist system's dog-eat-dog competition ideology by putting so much emphasis on good marks and pressure to be the "smartest in the class." You're the motherfuckers that herd us in and out of school every day like cattle and not like people. It's only a matter of time until the students realize the shit that's going on every day, and when they see it they move on it, and they move on it with any means necessary. Schools are closed, strikes are called, schools burn, violent take-overs occur, and riots take place. In the course of national revolution and liberation, the schools must be used by the people for the people's struggle, and not by the oppressor for his brainwashing counter-revolutionary fight. The pigs' schools will be destroyed unless they serve the people, and to serve the people the schools must be controlled on a community level by the people.

Keep On Pushing

by Paul Gayton

> *Paul Gayton is a seventeen-year-old black student from East High School, Denver, Colorado. He lives by himself in order to make things easier for his thirteen brothers and sisters. He is a member of the Black Panthers.*

I'm from Denver, Colorado, and I go to East High School. I'm eighteen years old, and I come from a family of fourteen. My parents are living together in Springfield, Illinois, but I live by myself out here. It's easier on them if I live on my own, and any money that I make I send back to them. My father is a construction man. He builds homes and things like that.

In East High School there are about 200 black students out of 500. There are about three blacks out of over a hundred teachers. I wasn't happy at the school. In fact, I wouldn't say that anybody is happy at the school. You go there and try to learn, but it's hard for the black students to learn. Most of the teachers don't want to learn you. They learn white people more things than they do black. If you're black, I guess it's concluded that you stay back. And the teachers don't help you to pass. A lot of the teachers are racists at East High School. You go to class. If you come in late, you have to go down to the office and maybe get suspended. And if you get two suspensions from there, you get kicked out of school for the week, until your parents can come in. And after your parents come in, the same thing next week. That's what happened to me. They kicked me out because I was late trying to get something from another teacher.

Well, see—you go to this class. If you have been out suspended or sick and you want to find out what you missed, you ask the teacher. Some teachers tell you to wait after class and get this information. After they kick you out of school they don't want to tell you what you missed. But it's different if there's a white kid who comes up and says that he was out of school sick, maybe like I was—sick for a long time. This white boy might say he was sick too, but really he just went around and didn't go to school. And he goes up there and asks the teacher, "Could you tell me what my back homework is, my makeup homework?"

She stops right in the middle of class and says, "Well, you do page 24, 25, and 26, and that's all."

I would go up there and ask her, "Could you help me with this 'cause I've been sick and out of school?"

Then she'll say, "Well, you wait after class and I'll give it to you."

You wait after class and probably the teacher has gone already. You wait. She say she has to run down to the office or something like that, and soon she's gone and you be late for the other class and you don't have a pass or nothing. And then you tell the next teacher that you were trying to get this stuff from Miss —— and that she said wait after class, and she says, "O.K. Paul. Why don't you go on down to the office anyway to see about getting an excuse."

They know it's hard for me to get an excuse. My uncle say that's why they send me there in the first place. I go down there and talk with Mr. C——, the assistant principal. And he say, "Paul, this ain't the first time you been down to the office."

And I say, "I know this."

And he say, "You're going to have to be suspended from school."

I say, "For what?"

And he say, "For coming to class late."

I say, "I told you the reason I come to class late."

And he say, "You still getting suspended."

I finally say, "O.K., I don't give a damn, I'm going." You know how they make me mad. I studied hard, but it seemed they were all out to get me.

They send me on home, and I tell my uncle about it. And my uncle say, "Paul, you're just going to have to go ahead and live with it because you can't help it. That's how the teachers are there." So he gets me back in school. And then for about a week, everything going smoothly a little bit. But before I know it, again they are going to kick me out of school.

You see, my aunt was sick in the hospital, so I called long distance to tell my parents about it. I got out of my class; this nice black teacher let me out of my class with an excuse. But Mr. C—— came up to me and said, "Why aren't you in class?"

I said, "I got an excuse to be out of class 'cause my aunt is sick."

And he said, "You shouldn't be taking up school time. You don't belong here."

"Well," I said, "I'm going to talk to my mother. I don't care what you say, because my aunt is sick and I got to talk to her."

So he said, "Well, I got some paper for you, so when you get off the phone, you just come to the office and get ready to go on home."

I got fed up again. I say, "O.K., I don't care."

The assistant principal got my uncle believing that I'm just messing around in school. My uncle gets mad. "Well, Paul, you know you're getting in trouble like this."

So I say, "I'm calling my mother because your wife is sick and you're getting mad at me about it." I went and asked my teacher to tell Mr. C—— that he gave me an excuse to be out of class. So the teacher goes and says that Paul was excused from class.

The assistant principal say, "Well he was out in the hall messing around outside and out front. I'm kicking him out for that." So the teacher now gets mad. This is a black teacher, and he gets mad.

He say, "We gonna see something about this."

The assistant principal say, "Well, you're a teacher. Why don't you agree on what we're doing?"

And the teacher said, "That ain't fair, because black students should have the same rights as white students do. They're allowed out in the halls with passes."

The assistant principal then said, "Well, we're still kicking him out anyway. We don't care what you say. We're paying you, and you do what we want you to do or get out." This is one of the ways they make it rough on the black kids.

Blacks also get punished worse than the whites. I remember when I got in a fight with this white kid. The kid knocked into me in the hall, so I said something like, "Hey watch it, cowboy!" He had his hair and stuff like a cowboy. The cat got mad and tried to jump me and everything. We fought, and after I done whopped the cat and everything, they wanted to kick me out. And this white kid got to go to class.

"You go on to class; we'll do with him. We're gonna make sure we get this straight." They took me to the office and let him go on to class. They didn't even bring him to the office. In the office they're asking me, "Paul, why do you do this and everything?"

I say, "You know, he bumps into me, and then wants to get mad because I call him a name. And it wasn't like the kind of names I'm always called."

They say, "Well you're getting kicked out of school."

I say, "What are you going to do with him?"

They say, "We'll take care of him."

Before I know it, some brothers came to me and said, "Paul, he's still in school."

I was kicked out for a whole week. And then when I came back, I can't make up no homework, 'cause they don't let you. When you go to a teacher and tell her you're behind because you were suspended, they say, "Well, that's your tough luck. You should do things right. If you don't get it, if you don't know how to get ahead in school, you might as well not learn anyway." Some teachers tell you what the homework is. Maybe one or two, if they're black teachers. Black teachers try to help you out whenever you want. But a white teacher says, "That's your tough luck." It's almost like saying, "Why don't you go on somewhere. Go in a corner and hide somewhere cause you ain't getting nothing from me. If you fail, that's too bad."

I say no black student has a chance of learning as much as a white student. The black student go into class and sit there ready. But the teacher jump all around. She be talking like in history. She'd be talking about a certain subject, and you'd have to write these things down; and then all of a sudden she'd jump to another subject in the book. "We gonna study about this now. You catch that other thing later." The teachers do this mostly just with blacks. They don't care. I don't see no white teacher care about a black person in school. They just don't care. If you don't learn, that's your tough luck. And most of the white teachers come here anyway and drink—you can smell it on their breath. The only thing they come to school for is to get the money. They're getting paid for this. That's good for them. But they think they don't have to teach anything.

You go to school and you try to learn. You learn what you can today, and get what you can, because if you don't get what you can you ain't gonna learn at all. But it's so hard if you're black. I remember there was this teacher in the seventh grade. I'd go there to her class, and she would always kick me out. I'd walk in the class and she would kick me out. She didn't like the looks of me. *You're out, you know. Don't like you. Don't like the way you look 'cause you're black*. That's the way it's been in all the schools for me. That's why I just say forget it. I want to go to computer school 'cause I think I could learn more there than I could learn in high school.

East High School is a regular school like any high school. They give vocational courses, but some people go on to college. Not hardly no blacks though. That's mostly whites. Like I know this one sister. She was making good grades. She wanted to see about going to college, and they said talk to the college office if you want to go to college. So she went up there and they wanted her to go to a lower level school. I can't remember the name of the college, but it was lower level—some kind of junior college. And she was making A's and B's like a real good student. Smart and had the brains. And they wanted to hold her down, keep her from going to a good school.

They always want the blacks to get bad grades. Like I was in History, and I was making what should have been some good grades in that. Every paper that I would bring in was good, and the teacher would put it down, like put back the grade. I remember that I was in one class, and the teacher made me so mad. I always went to this class and listened to the teacher. I'd try to get everything. One day the teacher says we gonna have a test. You know, you walk in and find you're having a test.

"What are we going to have a test about?"

"We're having a test. Don't worry about it." We have the test. The whole class was black students, and they don't know anything about it. This kind of thing never happened in a class where there were white kids. You take the test, and you fail it. You don't know what you are going to have a test on, and you haven't even studied. If you don't know what you're supposed to learn, and you don't read nothing and don't know what the test is gonna be about, then how are you going to get good grades?

For the kids who don't go to college, East High School doesn't help at all. They got these courses in woodworking —cutting wood, drilling, and stuff like that. I done learned that at home by my father. I can go into class and almost tell the teacher what to do in drilling. The kids spend all their time learning stuff like this, and then when they get out they find there ain't no jobs. Those kind of jobs aren't around no more. In this day, what you need to learn is how to read computers and stuff like that. There should be courses in these things. Of course even with them, blacks still gonna have trouble getting jobs. You go to a white man, say in a big company, and he looks at your diploma and says that's very good but why don't you come back tomorrow. And a white kid comes in with a diploma and he's got the job right there. The diploma don't even mean nothing anyway, it don't seem like to me.

There's some subjects I would like to learn. Like History I really dig. But you can't hardly learn anything in History because the teachers try to teach you only about white people: about Columbus, and Washington, and all the others. So we got ourselves together and said that we wanted to be taught Black History. We don't want to hear about Columbus discovering America and stuff. We want to know what's going on today, and like what's happened in our past life too. That other is the only thing we've been hearing about. This Columbus and all the other guys they're always talking about in white History. We told them we wanted to learn Black History. Black History wasn't given at all in a regular course, but they finally got it in a regular course. In one year you take one semester of Black History, and then one semester of white History. We say why can't we have Black History in two semesters? We say we want to know what black is, and they say why don't you learn what white is. Well, we say, we've been learning that since we were in kindergarten. You were brainwashing us and all this stuff. We finally got it in the second semester; we got Black History taught to us.

First they had some white teachers trying to teach us Black History. I had the course first semester, and I had a white teacher. I'd go in there, and the teacher would say the blacks were over on this side of the world, and stuff like that. She don't know what she's talking about. I don't want to be in this class. 'Cause this teacher ain't teaching me nothing. She done heard so much of this white stuff that she'd been brainwashed. I want to learn something that can help me. Something that will help me bring up all my black brothers and sisters. So I said, "Will you change me to Mr. Grauf?" All the black students were trying to get with Mr. Grauf. He's a black man. We got him, and he's very smart in Black History. He's been reading and everything. He started bringing us together on this, and we got very interested. And so did the white kids. They wanted to learn this too.

Mr. Grauf said, "We'll just let them come on in and learn this, because they been brainwashed too. They might just as well learn some things too." So we let them come on in 'cause they want to learn. We tried to learn too. Everybody's trying to learn. I went on in and I was learning, and he taught me more than I ever learned about Black History in my life.

Before, when I was in elementary school, and in high school before 1969, I didn't know nothing about no black man. I didn't know anything but about whites: white this, white that. I didn't think a black man ever did anything. I'd been brainwashed. I don't want my brothers and sisters to be brainwashed like I was, so we try to fight and get this stuff together. We can't gain nothing by thinking only white men did anything. The schools just started teaching Black History. I hear that in Illinois, where my parents live, they are this year—1970—gonna start bringing Black History out. But they still fighting. Some schools don't want it 'cause they scared of it. My principal's scared of it, like he is about the BSA. That's the Black Student Alliance, and we was learning in that before we had the Black History course. They don't want this around either, but it is what we need in the schools. The blacks need a group, so that the brothers and sisters can talk and get their thing together.

That's what's needed. I think we could probably learn more in these outside groups than in school. Maybe we can even get our own school of blacks together and learn by that, if we get black teachers. 'Cause I think a black teacher can learn me more than a white teacher ever can. He can sit down, and he can talk to us right. He can talk to us and communicate better. When I have a white teacher, all I hear is blah, blah, blah, this and that. They're always talking loud, and it gives you a headache trying to listen to somebody who's talking like that. And you can't hardly understand them. But if you have a black teacher, he can talk soft to you. You can understand him. He won't say, "Shut up over there." He will say, "Brother, do you want to learn? If you don't want to learn today, why don't you come back tomorrow." But if you come in the white class all you hear is, "Shut up! Don't say nothing! You listen to me! You write this down!" They tell you to write down some big words, and you don't hardly know how to write the first letter of them. They want you to feel stupid.

The white teachers are always doing that. Like, you come to class and they throw some words at you that you ain't hardly ever heard of. They could use little words, but instead they use these real big words, and then you can't understand them. Most of the black kids around here haven't been educated enough to understand these big words. Like me, I can't understand these big words. They have to come down to me. I say, "Can you come down a little more and explain to me more what you're saying?" I'm talking to white people, white teachers. They bring out some big-letter words, and if you don't get them, sorry. You just don't understand them. That's what happens because of these teachers today. You don't understand them, and you're not learning nothing. The black kids try to understand these teachers, but they just don't understand. Little by little they're getting it. They try, and they keep on trying and trying. That's the only thing you can do is try and hope that you can do it. I was praying, "Oh Lord, would you help me." I would pray, "Would you please help me to understand, and get through this day of school." It's hard. These teachers would throw something at you that you ain't ever heard of in your life. You look stupid, and they want you to look stupid. They go around criticizing us and all. You're dumb 'cause you don't know one long word. "You're dumb."

"Well why don't you learn us to understand you more. Why don't you take time to teach us." But they don't want to teach us.

If I had my way, there are several changes I'd like to see. First, I would like to see more black teachers in the schools. I believe black teachers can communicate with black students more. And a course in our Black History should be given. O.K., we are getting that so far. Slowly, but we will overcome. And in high school, I would like to see them bring in courses that students should be learning for the future. Bring things in like reading computers and other things like that. This would be better than woodworking, drilling, and stuff like this. We want to learn how to read computers and things like this, so we don't have to go and pay about $1,500 for a special course after high school. These courses would be better in high school. We wouldn't have to pay the money, and we could then learn something important in high school. When they get out of high school the students say, "I'm out of high school; now what kind of job can I get?" They're dumb. What kind of job can they get? They haven't learned nothing. But you go to these business schools, and that's what they are learning you for. You go and learn a trade. Like I'm going to learn a trade, 'cause I've had enough of high school. And I say, I'm gonna learn. I can learn more out of this trade school than I can in high school. I know that. 'Cause you know how I got messed up in high school, how they kept kicking me out. They just kept kicking me out 'cause the teachers didn't like me or something like that. So I said, O.K. I had this half semester to make up. I said, I'm going on to this computer school and make this up. That's the only way I can see out of it. That's what I'm going to do now. I would rather go to computer school than go on to high school and get my diploma. And I ain't going to get the diploma. It just doesn't mean anything—to me, or most other blacks.

Even though there was always these problems, I went to school and tried to learn. I would get tired of this, the teachers yelling at you every day and you're not learning nothing, but I'd get out of bed and I'd go there. It's just like a job: you get up at 7:30, you have to be there before 8:00 to go to class. So I'd just get up and go. And I go to work at nights. I got to make money to live. And I try to save money to help bring up my brothers and sisters. I would go to work at 6:00 in the evening and get off about 1:00 or 2:00 in the morning. I worked all night, and I was tired. But I'd still go to school. You go to school and you listen to those white teachers trying to tell you something, and you're not learning nothing. I kept on, and I just said, "Damn, I'm not learning nothing." But I accepted it. I thought that was the way it would always be.

But then I started hearing about the Panthers, and how they are moving, and talking, and learning. How they can communicate better and stuff like that. This was Junior year. I said, "Gee, I'm getting out of this other bag." So I got on some friends, and we got ourselves together. Most of them were also Juniors. The Panthers helped get us all together. We'd go and listen to these other brothers and sisters, listen to them talk about the schools. They told us what was happening—things I didn't think of before. And I say, well this is true. This is true, you know. Keep on brothers. I say, man, how stupid have I been. These years that I have been in school, I've been listening to all of this, been brainwashed, and now finally I'm learning the truth. I only wished I had learned it back earlier.

The older brothers and sisters in the Panthers said that we should do something about the schools. They thought, and we began to agree, that we shouldn't put up with the conditions there. They said, "Why don't you write petitions on the teachers who are not learning you nothing, who tell you to get out. Why don't you write this up and see about this?" So we got together, and we started writing these things up. Then we went to the office. And the principal sat down and listened. One of the things we wrote up was that we liked soul food. We'd been eating all this white food all our life, and we wanted some soul food. We wanted soul food put in the school 'cause all this white food doesn't give us nothing. The white students get their hamburgers and hot dogs and things, and why can't we be eating black beans, some corn bread, and some chittlings and things—some soul food. They said no at first. "You can't have this." Another thing we wrote was that we want our brothers and sisters who have been kicked out of school for no reason at all put back in school. We had some brothers and sisters who had been kicked out for the year for something that they didn't do. The teachers said they done it and they got kicked out. Then we had a list of demands to remove the teachers that we don't want in the school, the teachers who is not teaching us anything. They are putting white things in our heads and trying to put more white things in our heads. And we don't want that. We have to stay in school, but we don't have to become white.

They finally let us have soul food. But it wasn't until we had an argument and everything. We kept on, kept on. We say, if we can't have this then we'll have a walkout. And we had a walkout. Not all of the black students walked out though. You got some niggers who stand up in the window and look at you. Look down at you. Knowing that you're blacker than they, but saying to their white friends, "Look at them fools!" The principal say you ain't having this, you can't have this; so we got together and say we was walking out. The principal and teachers couldn't stop that. They tried to, but they couldn't. They called the police and then they had pigs all around us. The pigs even took their guns out. You could see them out in the seats of their cars. They think we gonna get real bad and try to tear up everything. Rowdy and all this. But we were just all outside, and we just talked. We was getting ourselves together, and we was talking and everything and telling about this list of demands. The principal finally came down. He wanted to run out there and turn off the speaker. He wanted to pull the plug so we couldn't make ourselves heard. But we ran in there, and we had guards around the plug so to make sure he couldn't pull it out. I guess he gave up, 'cause then he said, "Come on in to the auditorium, and we'll discuss this."

So we got in the auditorium. We got up there, and we was talking to him. We was telling him, "Well, you got some teachers around here who do not like black brothers and sisters." We was telling him just like that. The only thing he could do was sit there. He was stunned up in the chair. He just looked at us. And we said, "We don't like the attitude that you are putting down that if we come late to class two times we get kicked out of school. We don't want this. A white student come to school and he be late, and he come on into class. But if a black student do it, he's out. For a week." The only thing he did was sit up; he soaked it all in. And we just kept talking to him.

And he said, "We, wi-wi-wi-will try for this." You know, he stuttered. "We wi-wi-will talk to you. We will talk to you."

And we said, "We want to talk about this now. We here now, and we want to talk." And we said, "We done heard that all the brothers and sisters that walked out of school today are kicked out."

He said, "Nn-nn-nn-no. We'll let you back in school, we'll let you back, we'll let you in."

And we said, "Are we excused for this? We want to know this right now. If we're not excused, then we're going on a . . . you know." And he's knowing that if something that he says is wrong or something like this, the school's gonna come apart right there, 'cause there's brothers and sisters who want to tear the place apart right there anyway.

There was about 150 brothers and sisters in the auditorium right there. It was fulled up. Brothers and sisters all over. And the only thing he could do was to sit up there and listen to us. He said, "You're excused for this today."

And we said, "We want one of these discussions tomorrow because we have to get our demands down, and we want to talk to you about this." So he grabbed names. He

got everybody's name who was up there talking, and he got
in contact with them.

He come up to me when he saw me down the hall.
"Paul, come here, man. I want to talk to you." He say,
"What's going on? What's going on? Tell me please. Please
tell me."

I say, "You'll find out in due time. You'll find out." And
so he kept on doing this, and pretty soon they wouldn't kick
me out of school for nothing, 'cause they knew that something would come up about students getting kicked out
right now. They knew that something had to be done about
this 'cause the brothers and sisters are waking up. They
getting tired of this.

Not all the demands were met. We got soul food, and
we got some of the teachers kicked out. We got some racist
teachers kicked out. They were withdrawn to another
school 'cause they had to go. We didn't want this no more.
We was tired of it. But there are still others around. I say
that the brothers and sisters are still gonna have to keep
strong and keep on with these demands. Like in September,
we supposed to go back to the Board of Education in
Denver and talk about some more of these demands. We
gonna try to keep this together, and tell them that some of
these teachers around here are telling black kids to get out
of the way and everything. I can remember one time when
this happened to me. A white teacher came up to me and
knocked me out of the way. I was in junior high school, and
I can remember that he shoved me out of the way. And he
got away with it. The only thing I could do was get mad and
cuss him to myself, and then they knew you said something
so they'd grab you and give you ten swats for that. They try
to break the paddle they hit you with. I know some brothers
and sisters who got paddles broke over them. I got tired of
it.

I don't think something like this could happen now.
Today, if a white teacher came over and knocked me, or
any other black student, he might as well be ready to die.

The black student wouldn't accept it. The teacher would be blown away. That's how I feel. When I was home in Springfield, Illinois, last week, these white kids picked up by brother by the head. And I found out. My brother came home and told me that "a lot of kids jumped on me, Paul." Two or three big, husky cats. So I went down there with my '25 pistol. I wasn't gonna let them sit. But my father beat me there and stopped me. He knew something was going to happen. 'Cause I don't like no white person pushing around on my brothers and sisters, or any brothers and sisters in this world. I'd die for them. And I want my brothers and sisters to understand this. My mother and father try to talk to me, but they been around and heard so much white talk that they don't understand. The only thing I can do is just wait and hope that they will understand. Like, they don't understand what's going on in high schools. If they went to high school for just one day I believe they would understand.

The black students are getting together; that's for sure. But there still are a lot of Negroes all over. You can't help that. The only thing I can say is that the black brothers and sisters move on, and keep up, and try to help with the Negroes. You have to help them, and try to get them together, little by little. I know, 'cause I was a Negro once. I'm not lying about it, I was a Negro. It was just about two years ago. What changed me into a black was seeing what the teachers were doing to the black brothers and sisters. I said, "I'm not taking no more of this. I'm tired of it. I took all I can take, and I'm not going to put up with this any more." Also, some brothers and sisters rapped down to me, and they said, "Paul, we know you better than this. You're messing around and you're acting crazy and everything. Why don't you get yourself together?" I had to sit down and think about this, cause they hurt me. They said I played like I was black. I was going around saying, "I'm Black and I'm proud," and all this stuff. And they got down on me and started talking to me. And I woke up. I said, "This ain't good." Now, I don't like the James Brown record—he made some money off it—"I'm Black and I'm Proud." I really don't like it, 'cause most of the cats, the brothers and sisters who are going around here singing, "I'm Black and I'm Proud"—they are Niggers. They talk, but they don't do nothing. They come up and say, "I'm Black and I'm proud." They dance and all this stuff. But when something comes down, you don't see them. They're the ones who stayed behind during the walk-out. They're the ones who say, "No, I'm not with them. I'm not going to die for them. I'm not going to no jail." That's your Niggers. And we have to work with them and try to make them understand. We have to help them change from being Niggers to black men.

I now think that if some improvements in the schools are not made quick, say in the next semester or so, then there's going to be a whole lot of trouble. They are going to be shooting. I'm pretty sure, 'cause I know the black students. They woke up from what must have been a three-hundred years' sleep. I think that last year, 1969, the black students came up more than they have ever before. And I think they are going to push on. I hope the brothers and sisters keep on this, regardless of the problems. Regardless, regardless, regardless. If they shoot a person now, they don't care, 'cause they know they done it to help their brothers and sisters. That's what I say. The brothers gonna push onwards. They gonna push on, and this is beautiful. I like to see this. I want them to get their rights. And if I can do everything in my power, I'm gonna be with them. I'm going to stand up there in the front line, and if I'm gonna get shot down, I'm going to stand up there and go down.

I think the way the blacks at Cornell held the buildings with guns was beautiful. I think it was beautiful. The teachers and principals don't understand what's going on, and that's the only way you are going to get through to them. We want to learn our stuff today. We want to be somebody too. They don't understand this, so that's the way we can show them that we mean it. If we are going to have some violence, we will have violence. If they can't understand by words and marches, well they might understand by guns. And if they don't understand by guns, well then they're dead. So they might as well understand this. They're gonna die if they don't understand it.

If the teachers and them don't wake up pretty soon, they're gonna find themselves six feet down, deep down in the ground. So I think they better get themselves together. I'm saying this because I believe in the black people. They're coming up more and more, and they're gonna be powerful. They done heard so much of this white stuff that they're tired of it. Like I'm tired of it too. I don't want to hear somebody come and try to tell me something more about the whites. They might as well go ahead and talk to a brick wall, 'cause I'm not listening. They're not gonna brainwash me no more.

I want the brothers and sisters to keep on pushing. This is beautiful, and I want them to keep on pushing. They're starting to go forward, and if they keep pushing on, and keep all this stuff together, they gonna go a long way.

I say, "All Power to the People, the Black People, and Power to the Vanguards!"

My Teacher
Is a Racist

by Susan Snow

*Susan Snow (a pseudonym) is a sixteen-year-old
Senior in Academy High School, Erie, Pennsylvania.
She is an only child, and both her parents are politically conservative. Her father is a mechanic, and her
mother is a librarian. Apprehensive of their reaction
to her public statements, she prefers to remain
anonymous.*

What I first disliked about Academy High School was
its size. It is very big and very impersonal. The students are
in cliques, and they are generally apathetic about anything
outside of their own little groups. They're apathetic about
the world situation, they're apathetic about the problems
within their own community, and they're interested in
school games and sports cars.

The school building is very old and poorly equipped.
The study hall has only thirty chairs, and it is supposed to
hold fifty students. Twenty students have either to bring in
chairs from outside, go to the library, or sit on the floor.
Many of the desks are broken, and it's hard to write on
them because of the marks and names that have been
carved into the wood during the last thirty years. The
school board was supposed to replace them, but they never
got around to it.

The teachers at Academy are qualified in that they have their teacher's certificates, but in practice I don't think they're so qualified. I've discussed this with a lot of my fellow students, and we all agree that most of them are prejudiced against the black students. During one of the black-white disturbances at Academy, there was of course a lot of confusion. Kids were running around screaming, and it was very difficult to get to class. Both black kids and white kids were coming in late. Two black girls walked into class and the teacher would not let them in. She said she didn't want them in there, that they were "troublemakers," and that she knew their "kind." She refused to admit these black girls, but there were many white students arriving at the same time and she left them alone. Whenever there's a disturbance, the teachers think, "Ah, it's the black kids who are doing it." They are prejudiced in just about everything. If the white students are walking in the halls when they're not supposed to be, they can usually get away with it. The teachers don't question them. The black students are more apt to be questioned, and more apt to be punished. Of course neither is supposed to be out there, at least not without a pass. It used to be that if you went to the girls' room, you got a board. The board had the room marked on it in big red letters, and you walked down the hall with the board. It was like being back in sixth grade again. Now we're treated maybe like seventh graders. Kids were swiping boards, so they now have pieces of paper. Whenever you go out of the room the teacher in your class has to sign your name, the time that you left, and the reason you're leaving the room. When you get back, the teacher marks down the time returned, and sends it to the office. This is done allegedly so that if something happens (like a fire alarm being pulled) the principals can check on who was out of the room and determine who was responsible. I don't think, however, that this is the real reason for these passes. For some reason the teachers and principals think of seventeen- and eighteen-year-olds as children, and they think it's necessary to treat us like children.

The teachers show this attitude toward us also by the way they teach us, which is on a seventh-grade level. They have us memorizing by rote, and they never go into abstracts. In my English class, which was an honors' English class, we read *Hamlet*. We spent a week and a half on the play. We read it aloud, and we were tested on such things as "Who is Hamlet?," "What did he do?," "What happened in the First Act?," and "What happened in the Second Act?" We never went into the abstract qualities or literary aspects of the play.

The teachers are too busy taking attendance. Each class period is forty-five minutes long, and it takes some teachers I've had over twenty minutes to make sure they have the attendance correct. Teachers are rated by their supervisors largely on the neatness and correctness of their record books. The result is that they spend more time filling them out than they do teaching us.

Some of the teachers seem unqualified. My French teacher is a good example. Though she is retiring this year, she should have done it years ago. She was supposed to teach us French, but she did not know the language herself. She kept her book in front of her literally reading the lessons to us, and her tests always broke us up. She would copy exercises from the book, and then give us a test on them. It was really ridiculous because we would already have gone over all the exercises in class. It didn't challenge us at all. If you had memorized the exercises, then you passed the test. She copied words onto the board, often misspelling them, and she pronounced the same word in different ways. My sister had a good French teacher, and my sister speaks a totally different language than I do. My teacher's name was Samson, and the kids in the class used to say that we weren't learning French, we were learning Samsonese. No one who was French would ever understand a word we were saying. I got disgusted with the class and never took a book home after the first half of year, yet I kept an A average throughout.

There are many teachers at Academy who are as bad as

Miss Samson. I was in all honors courses. The teachers in the honors courses are supposed to be the best in the school, those with the most education, and those who are most qualified, yet I think that some of my teachers are unqualified to teach anyone—A or F students. You can imagine what some of the others are like. There is a teacher who comes to school drunk quite frequently. She keeps a whisky flask in her desk, and while she hasn't been seen drinking in the middle of class, she most probably does between classes, judging from the way she acts. One boy went up there and swallowed the contents of the flask when she wasn't in class, and when she came back, the bottle was empty. One day she could hardly stand up. She couldn't talk coherently, she passed out paper and then forgot why she passed it out, and the whole class ended up just sitting there wondering what to do. My girl friend, who is in the class, spoke to her and suggested that she go home, that she looked "sick." She just ignored her, and told her to get back to her seat. I heard about it and decided to go to the office. They told me that she "had indigestion" or was "on medication" or something like that. They didn't do a thing about it, and that is standard policy. No matter what happens at Academy, the teacher is always right. The administration will always back the teacher, regardless of the circumstances. This has been reaffirmed through the disciplinary code.

After we had a few disturbances in the fall of the last school semester (1968), the administration decided that the problem was basically that there was not enough discipline within the school. They felt that the teachers were being too lax in letting students get away with too much, that they, like our parents, were being too permissive. They gave us a disciplinary code, which was about five or six pieces of mimeographed paper with such rules as: You have to be in Homeroom by 8:30; You can't be in the halls unless it's absolutely necessary; You can't be insubordinate to a teacher. This last one is the catch-all rule: *insubordination* can be literally anything, anything that the teacher wants to consider it. Some teachers use this rule to punish students who haven't done anything specifically wrong simply out of personal dislike. And the student has no method of appeal if he thinks he's being wronged. The teacher writes on a piece of paper what you're being insubordinate about, and then sends it to the office. You can go and talk to the principal about it, but he will definitely back the teacher. He might not even listen to you, but that depends on your "attitude." If you feel that you've been wronged, and you go in there justifiably angry, then he won't listen to you. You've got to go in there docile, respectful, and almost go down on your knees before him. Even if you did, no action would be taken. Other students and I have seen this happen again and again. The administration will not help us against teachers we think are unfair.

After some disturbances in school, there were "Dialogues" or discussions held on school problems. One of the main issues raised was that of the relationship between teachers and students. It was mentioned that students are not allowed to go home for lunch, and that they cannot smoke on the school premises; yet if you go into the teachers' room you can't see because of all the smoke. I think it is unfair that students are denied the privileges of teachers. It should be a two-way street. For example, boys are not allowed in school with mustaches because mustaches allegedly "hamper the learning process." The teachers come with mustaches, so I figure that if they hamper the students' learning then they must also hamper the teachers' teaching ability. However, nothing is done about it by the administration. We just figure that there should be equal rights for all.

The courses offered are the basic academic subjects: English, Math, Science, History, and a foreign language. I've already mentioned how uninspiring and elementary they are. Many of the kids at Academy don't go on to college, and there are very few courses that will be helpful to them. There are some vocational courses given, but in skills that were useful twenty or thirty years ago. They teach drafting and metal working—things that are no good in

1969. I hear that some schools offer courses in Computer Programming, in which there are many jobs today; but Academy has nothing like that. When about 70 percent of Academy's graduates go looking for jobs right away rather than going to college, this lack of preparation speaks poorly for the school. A lot of the boys go right into the army after graduation, and it is there rather than at Academy that they learn trades for later life.

The teachers always seem to skirt certain subjects. For example, I've never had a lesson on Vietnam. Anything I know about Vietnam is through my own outside reading. There may be an occasional remark like, "We're escalating again," but we've never actually discussed what the situation was like before we got in there, and what's happening there now. They boys in my class will soon be asked to go over there, they'll be asked to kill, and they'll be asked to die; we don't even know what it's about—we're not told. We are told that Russia is "bad," but we're never told how the Russian society is different from America. I've never been taught what the communist doctrine is, I've never been taught about socialism or Marxism. Anything like this we have to find out on our own. It's not part of the curriculum; it should be, because it's part of the world picture. Some of our national problems are touched on in a course called Problems of Democracy, but even then everything is much too theoretical. For example, when learning about town government we learned about the different bureaus and agencies that make it up—how many councilmen there are, how long the mayor's term is, what the aldermen do. We didn't talk about how Erie's Mayor Tulio is the head of a party machine that controls the policemen and the firemen in addition to the school board in town. An actual case like this that contradicts the textbook is never discussed; and a teacher would never talk about what can be done to solve such problems as the war and Tulio's control.

Students should have a voice in decisions about curriculum. As of now, we are never listened to. Once, when it was requested by students that a course in psychology be introduced, the school board came back with: "There are not enough funds." They've done this every time students have asked for something, yet they seem to find funds very conveniently when they need them. Giving up on help from the teachers and the administration, a group of students took the initiative to get the materials needed for a certain subject. We wanted to learn about the history of certain minority groups so we went out and got eleven sets of magazines to be used in the History classes. The magazines were put out by a scholastic firm, so the teachers couldn't say that they were radical or anything. They were a condensed version of Negro History which the teachers could teach from, but they never used them. They said, "Oh great, we'll work these into our curriculum," but only one teacher out of eleven ever did. I think some of them didn't want to teach Negro History because they were prejudiced, and many of them are just too darn lazy to work it into the programs that they do have. Some of the teachers use the same study plan for five and six years running. I guess they think that the world never changes.

Within the History curriculum, there was no Black History course offered. A few of the black students got together and asked two teachers if they would start an after-school Minorities' History class. They suggested that once a week kids would come in for about an hour to study a topic which they considered important but which was not included in the regular program. The two teachers agreed, and they got clearance from the administration to have this after-school class, to be open to all students, black and white. There was a pretty big turnout for it the first few weeks, but gradually the teachers lost interest. Maybe they were too tired from their regular classes, but whatever the reason was, they stopped coming. The class was held Monday afternoons, and we began to hear almost regularly on the public address system the announcement that "Minorities' History will not be held today." The last few months of school we lost all confidence in them, and there were no classes held at all.

I think there definitely should be a course in Minorities' History introduced into the regular curriculum. But as it looks now there won't be such a course this coming school year. At the end of last year, I went to one of the teachers and asked whether we were going to have a Minorities' History class next year. He said that he didn't know, and I thought this was odd because he was the one in charge of it. I don't think it should take that long to organize a new course like this, but the school bureaucracy in Erie stifles any real changes in the schools. Any reform proposal must first go to the school administration. If the administration approves it, then it must be presented before a meeting of the school board. Board members have the final say in a matter like this, and they usually take their time considering things. If they want to spend six months discussing it, well then they'll spend six months discussing it; meanwhile, the course will not be taught in the high school. All of the members of the Erie School Board are white, and they have no interest whatsoever in any black issues or Black Studies program. Sometimes I don't think they have any interest at all in our education.

Feeling this to be the case I worked last spring to try to elect to the school board a man I thought was good. That was my first political campaign. I was working to try to get a Mr. James Wade elected to the school board. He is black, but I considered his race to be incidental because he was obviously the most qualified person running in the primary. He had his Master's degree, he had been in school counselling, prison counselling, and he had worked in the black ghetto. I thought he would be fabulous to have on the Erie School Board. However he only pulled a couple of hundred votes.

I now think that was probably my last political campaign. I don't want to do it again. First of all, it's a farce unless you're working within the two established parties, and we weren't. I don't have much respect for the two-party system, but I figured I should give it a try, or at least work alongside it, before I started condemning it. I know that if you want to get someone elected, then you have to make people aware of his qualifications. To do that we had pamphlets, we had leaflets, and we tried to pass them out. But we were kicked out of every place we went to. We went down to the Mall, which is a big complex of stores. We tried to pass them out there, and some officials of the complex stopped us and asked us what we were doing. We said that we were campaigning for Wade, and they said that we couldn't do it there because it was private property. It may be private property, but I've seen many people campaign there, at least for Republican and Democratic candidates. Later on I went to one of the town plazas and I was told that the police would be called if I didn't leave. Officials in Erie consider any party other than one of the established two, to be "radical" and "dangerous." Mr. Wade was running on the ticket of the New Democratic Coalition-Committee for Better Schools. It may not sound particularly radical, but in Erie "Better Schools" is a radical idea.

The "Dialogues" that I mentioned before were an attempt to improve some of the conditions in the school by discussing them with the teachers and administrators and persuading them to make changes. It had been suggested by a Vista worker in Erie that we get together a student-run organization within the school which would work for reforms. It was set up as a meeting which students could come to and talk about issues that were bothering them. We got this going and it seemed to work well, but it ended up just making us more frustrated. We found out that there really was a lot to be said, and the kids came and they said it, but nothing could be done. We were just talking among ourselves, and the teachers and administrators were ignoring us. We finally decided that we should have a confrontation with the teachers—that we should set a date, and that both the teachers and the students in "Dialogue" should go down to the auditorium and talk things out. We felt that the problems of teacher prejudice and teacher competence should be discussed openly with the teachers. A certain procedure would be established so that students would be given the opportunity to talk openly with any teacher. This decision was made almost unanimously by the students.

The administration and the teachers flatly rejected the idea. No teacher was willing to stand before individual students and be questioned. That in itself seemed to show that they had something to hide, but knowing it didn't do us any good. We beat our brains out trying to get some form of compromise, and what we finally got wasn't much of an achievement. We were permitted to bring in a panel of students who had something "specific" to say to a teachers' meeting. The students would be given ten minutes to talk, and that would be it. No questions of the teachers would be allowed. Talk. That's what we had done among ourselves and nothing was accomplished. That's what we did in the teachers' meeting, although here it was a monologue rather than a dialogue. Again nothing was done about the issues that bothered us. No action was taken.

Some students in Erie have gone straight to the superintendent of schools with their grievances, but that too has proven ineffective. A group of black students at Storm Vincent High School drew up a list of specific complaints and presented them to him. They complained about such things as no Afro-American program, no black teachers, teacher prejudice, and teacher qualifications. They were all specific gripes, and the students tried to talk them out with Dr. ——, the superintendent. A meeting was called and the news media were on hand. Dr. —— arrived, but he refused to speak to the specific grievances. He listened to the students for about fifteen minutes, and then in the middle of their presentation, he got up and walked out. The media got up and walked out, and the black students were left sitting there alone. The next morning, to protest this treatment, eighty-two black students at Storm Vincent quietly and nonviolently got up and left the school. Dr. —— suspended them for two weeks. They had done exactly what he had done, and certainly with more justification, but I'm sure that never entered his mind.

I don't know whether it was in response to the walk-out

of black students, but at about this time last year, in May to be exact, the school administration really started clamping down. They made a rule saying that any student participating in a school demonstration—a sit-in, a walk-out, an assembly, or a protest, either violent or nonviolent, would be punished. If the student is seventeen or under, he is immediately suspended, and if he is a Senior he is expelled for good. Any Senior caught taking part in a demonstration is thrown out and will not be accepted into any other Erie school. Thus Seniors working to change the conditions of their school will never get their diplomas, unless they move to another city and enter another high school.

This edict, which was passed down at the end of last year, will probably hinder protests in the school year to come. There are many students who are unhappy in the school and would like to protest to change it, but who also want to go to college. With this threat hanging over them, they will probably end up sitting still. But I'm sure there will still be riots and demonstrations of some sort this coming year. During the last two weeks of last year, after the rule was passed, there were many disruptions in school. Waste baskets were set afire, lockers were blown up, and fire alarms were pulled despite the edict, showing—I think— that students will continue to be active in the future.

I can't see the future of Academy High School as being anything but violent. The problems haven't been solved, and nothing's been done to change the situation in the school—if anything, the conditions are worse. For example, a lot of teachers were prejudiced against the black students, but their prejudice lay beneath the surface; it rarely came up. Now it's come to the surface and they're very hostile toward the blacks. Many of them are hostile to any student who's "acting out of line." Sometimes I think "acting out of line" means doing anything other than sitting quietly and speaking when spoken to.

This repression by the teachers and the administrators is bad because it frightens some of the kids from protesting against the conditions in the school. Even more unfortunate, however, is the fact that it has split up the student body. Whereas before, the black and white students were working together to improve the school, now because they have been completely frustrated by the administration, they are fighting among themselves. Some of the white students are now acting as prejudiced as the teachers. They may always have been prejudiced, but it just came out, and probably as a result of this frustration. I think that there will definitely be racial fights at Academy next year.

As in the past, these fights will be produced by some teacher or principal showing preference for a white student and treating a black student unfairly. Whenever there's a conflict between a white and a black student, and there's some question as to who's in the wrong, it's the black student who gets the ax every time. When the blacks feel they've been discriminated against, they act. One day at lunch they'll pull a fire alarm, and someone will start throwing chairs, or something like that. It has happened before, and usually we all get excused for the afternoon. The next morning when we come back, there are groups of white boys standing outside and groups of black boys standing outside. Sometimes they'll be taunting one another, but usually just eyeing one another. After one of these stand-offs, sometime in May I think, all hell broke loose. The black students had all gone back to class, but the white students started running around the school chanting "White Power." They tied white shoe strings to their jackets, and they ran around the school trying to urge the other students to come out and join them. They boycotted classes because they said the administration had not taken firm enough action against the black students who had rioted sometime before. About mid-afternoon, some of the black students started going out, and fights broke out in the halls. It was really bad. Teachers had to link arms across the hall to keep the two groups from getting at one another. This coming year I'm sure there will be a continuation of hostility within the student body in addition to friction between the students and the administration. It will be an interesting school year.

I've now reached the point where I'm tired of trying to improve Academy by making reforms—establishing "Dialogues" within the student body, speaking to the principal and superintendent about incompetent teachers, and trying to organize special-interest courses only to have them squashed at the last minute by teacher indifference. You can only talk, petition, discuss, and compromise so long. I now realize that a high school in Erie (and maybe elsewhere) cannot be changed in this way. The school system in this city is stagnant. It is standing there rotting, and it can't be changed piece by piece. More and more I come to the conclusion that the whole system is going to have to go. I know that the only way whole systems have been changed before is through revolution, and I have difficulty accepting the violence that usually goes with it. However, I really see no other answer. There are three things that a student can do: he can drop his hands in despair and say that he doesn't want to think about the school's problems, he can keep trying to work for change peacefully, knowing all the time that it's not doing any good, or he can resort to violence. I'm not really sure where I stand right now; but I do know that the third possibility seems increasingly more appealing.

III

CULTURE

High school students of both sexes wear hair down to their shoulders. They dress in clothing that is sometimes wildly colorful, sometimes purposely ragged. Whatever it is, however, it's different from the dresses and suits of their parents. With dynamic tastes in music and art, young people have brought about revolutionary changes in both fields. Rock and electronic music are widely popular among the young, though they still offend the ears of many adult listeners. Psychedelic art, with its colorful designs, can be seen hanging in many teenage rooms. In addition, the young in America are keeping their parents up nights with their presumed or actual explorations into drugs, and an apparent openness toward sex that shocks those over twenty-one.

What do all these developments mean? Is there really such a thing as a youth culture today, one that combines all these habits of the young? If so, is this culture in conspiracy against "traditional" America? Two students interviewed spoke about the "cultural revolution" in process today. A girl from St. Paul, Minnesota, discusses some of the elements of the youth culture. To avoid reprisals from her conservative parents she preferred to remain anonymous, and will be referred to as Jane Thompson. She spoke into the tape recorder. Fred Silber of New York City wrote about his experience at the Woodstock Music Festival, the huge youthful gathering last August that has been referred to by some as "Tomorrow's America."

Turn On, Lay Down, and . . .

by Jane Thompson

Jane Thompson (a pseudonym) is a seventeen-year-old student from Madison, Wisconsin. She is an only child. Her father sells used cars, and her mother is a housewife. To avoid possible reprisals from her parents, she preferred to remain anonymous.

I'm seventeen, and I go to Bryan High School in St. Paul, Minnesota. I come from kind of an upper middle-class background and I've always been fairly comfortable. My father is a salesman, and he makes a lot of money. I guess because I'm an only child, he and my mother always gave me anything I wanted: dolls, toys, and now records and books. Maybe you could say they sort of spoiled me. These things don't mean that much to me anymore though, and actually I'd now prefer not to have them.

I haven't always been politically very active or even politically very conscious. It's just been recently. In fact, two or three years ago I didn't have any political attitudes at all. Politics was very boring. I just didn't care one way or the other. I just wasn't there politically. That's not the way I feel now though. I've gone through some kind of change since then. Basically, the Democratic convention last year had a lot to do with it. I'd been working for McCarthy for part of the summer. The fact that he didn't make it was really disappointing. I was mad because I was really for him, though I don't remember exactly why. Some strange reason or other. I guess I thought he could end the war. But what happened in Chicago, the riots and everybody getting bashed over the head for no good reason, changed my mind about everything. I finally realized that the whole country's got to be pretty bad when they do that. When they beat whole crowds of people who simply wanted to sleep in the park because they had no place else to go, and when they attack demonstrators for what they're saying—they made me really disenchanted with the system, with any kind of Establishment politics. As far as I was concerned it just didn't work. The people, the majority, were left out. It didn't make any difference what they wanted.

After Chicago I thought a lot more politically. I didn't like the kind of politics I'd seen on television, and I guess it was then that I became sort of radical. I liked what the radical Movement was saying. Things began to make sense that I'd never heard of or thought of before: like revolution, or the idea that communism was not the worst thing in the world. I had never thought about these ideas one way or the other. The Movement exposed me to new ideas. I started hanging around a lot at the Draft Resistance Union. I listened to people talk, and talked to people there. That's when I found out what was going on, what was happening. And I decided I liked it and that I agreed with a lot of it. Anything seemed better than what we have now.

I didn't actually do much with the DRU, but I did begin to talk to other students who felt the way I did. We had meetings, a couple of meetings. It was just a group of kids, kids from the different high schools in St. Paul. The meetings didn't really do much. We talked about how the East High School kids were putting out underground papers and what the Bard kids were saying in their school. But we didn't do much of anything. We had lots of people come talk to us though, and two or three came out periodically just to discuss schools—what they were all about and what they were doing to students. One of them was a person who graduated from Bryan and then dropped out of the university his first year. He'd gone to Bryan for four years, and he knew what it was like. He knew the teachers, the principals, and other things like that. From the way he talked I guess the conditions were as bad when he was there as they are now. He said some things that I hadn't thought of before, things like how the school "programs" us and stuff. I guess in a way he opened my eyes. I don't know how much he did for the other kids at the meeting, but most of them did agree with him at least on things he said about the school. However, they didn't want to do anything to change school conditions. He made some suggestions, but they weren't interested. They were afraid of getting in trouble or they didn't care enough. Many of them said, "Well, we'll be out in another year." That's not the way I felt. I thought we should do something.

Aside from what happened at Chicago and my experience with the Draft Resistance Union, there have been other things that have helped turn me into what my parents and teachers call a "radical." I don't know if all of it goes under the heading of the "generation gap" they're always talking about, but there are a lot of things young people are doing today that make them different from their parents. Maybe you could call it a kind of youth culture. Whatever it is, however, the young people in this country have created a totally different society all our own. We think different things, we like different things than our parents, and we do different things than our parents. We're not hung up on some of their values like "money" and "success," and this all shows itself in various ways.

One way is through the drug scene. Almost everyone I know takes drugs: pot, speed, acid, even some harder stuff —though not too often. Drugs are an escape for some people. There's a lot of ugliness in the world, and some people want to make it pretty by taking drugs. There are only a few people I know who do that, and I don't agree with it. But I think most drugs are better than the liquor my parents drink for the same purpose. People rarely get violent with drugs, like I've seen my father get on occasion when he comes home drunk. They also don't get sick the next day. But most kids I know take drugs for better reasons. Like drugs really do help some people, if they don't overdo it. They don't do that much for me, only relax me and give me a pleasant feeling. But they do expand some people's minds. I know that they do help some people to get their thinking straight about some things. On occasions they have for me too. But not too often.

Another thing that makes us different from adults is the whole thing about sex. My parents have been telling me for as long as I can remember that "sex is bad, sex is evil, only sex between a husband and wife is all right." All this talk used to inhibit me when I was younger. I didn't like my body. I was ashamed of the feelings I sometimes had. I now realize that there's no reason for this shame. My friends think the same way. I don't know why my parents are such Puritans. Maybe it goes in with their whole idea about waiting for everything, waiting until we're older and "successfully" established before we do anything. Or maybe they always wanted to have control over me. Even if that's not the case, that's the way it turned out, at least for awhile. The first couple of times I did anything with boys I felt really uptight. My parents' teachings sort of haunted me. Fortunately I'm now able to ignore them, and I can do whatever I want. I guess I could say that I'm sort of freed sexually. I'm glad that's the case because I think sex is really enjoyable. When you meet someone you like and he likes you, there is nothing better than having sex together. It's fantastic. There's a feeling of comfort, of warmth, and of sharing, that sex gives you. I always feel so complete when it's over. A lot of other high school people feel the same way. We see no reason why we should wait to have a piece of paper in our hands before experiencing the pleasure our bodies can give us.

This interest in drugs and a natural feeling toward sex are attitudes that are part of the youth culture. This culture is very new. I think it began around 1964, probably with the Beatles, and all young people of today are affected by it, whether they're with it or not. The youth culture is something. The culture that this country supposedly has is nothing, at least nothing alive. The main attraction of the youth culture is that it is a culture of some sort. I think a lot of kids are attracted to it because it's something to belong to. If you're totally alienated from this society, as many kids are, you've got to have something to belong to. You've got to have people who believe the same things you do basically. It's a group of your own kind of people. The people in the youth culture are together on quite a few things. Most of them are from upper middle-class backgrounds, and they don't like the middle-class materialistic culture or whatever you call it. They don't like the fact that they're rich and there are a lot of people starving. They don't like being pressured at home to do well in school so that they'll be successful in later life. Things like that. Most of them realize that there are more important things around to worry about than money. Some people think they can find it in drugs, some people find it in sex, and some people find it in music or art. Some people can't find it in any of these things. It's hard to say what we're looking for really. We know what we don't want, but we're less sure about what we want. I guess some people are looking for something to believe in, some people are looking for something to belong to, and some people are looking for themselves.

Rock music, the kind first played by the Beatles and the Stones, and now by the Mothers and The Band, is an important part of this youth culture. It was, first of all, created by us. When the Beatles first came here we were the ones who screamed at their concerts and bought all their records. Maybe it was their long hair, maybe it was the fact that our parents didn't like either their looks or their sound. They then were exciting just to spite our parents. Whatever the reason, we helped them to survive. Since then we've enabled other groups to survive also. They belong to us. Without us they would never have made it. Rock music is intended for us. The song writers are generally not much older than we are, and rock groups are often our age. They sing about things that bother us. They sing about what it's like to be young today, and how we represent a change in this country—with our concern for individual freedom, drugs, and togetherness. Rock groups sing in our language. They talk to us. They take us seriously.

Art does the same thing for us. Stuff like the psychedelic posters is exciting because it seems to have been made by us and belong to us. With its wild, sometimes glowing colors, it's a break from traditional art. It's not traditional oil painting with trees in it and all that. It is a form of rebellion, but it's a lot more than that too. For the people who actually do artistic things, it's a method of expression, a method of releasing emotions. To paint something is emotionally healthy because you are doing something creative, especially when what you're creating is new and different. Some high school people I know do paint these psychedelic posters. Everyone I know likes them. They're also part of our culture.

Our clothes and the way we look are also part of our culture. Long hair, dirty jeans, sandals—all these are what we want to do, what we want to say. We dress this way for a reason. For one thing, people who wear sloppy clothes and go barefoot are often not high school kids. Poor people do it because they can't afford to do anything else. And high school kids do it partially because it identifies them with this group. A lot of them think: well, why should we go around dressing in the latest fashions, expensive clothes, when other people can't afford to? In quite a few cases I think it's a deliberate attempt on the part of wealthy kids to identify with the poor. They're rejecting their middle-classness, their affluence, and all their money, because they realize that they can be just as happy with one shirt. There also just seems to be something wrong with having money and spending it on expensive things when there are so many poor people around.

Some young people have rejected everything in their parents' world. They've even given up the idea of privacy which their parents taught them about. A couple of years ago the hippies started living communally, and there are a lot of communes now all over the country. People live together, men and women, and they share everything they have. Some of them raise their own vegetables, and even share the kids who are born there. At home I would very much resent a situation in which everything belonged to everybody and there was no privacy. But if I were living with a group of people I really liked, it wouldn't matter. Everybody would belong to everybody.

The youth culture, with all these things I've mentioned, had a pretty big effect on me. But I don't think it affected my politics that much. It just went along with them, getting them together. It was just a part of it. It was a part of changing my way of life. My politics and my way of life changed together. But I don't think they directly influenced each other, so much as they went along with each other. They fit together, but there's a huge difference. You can become a hippie and not become political. Or you can be a radical and still sit around and watch football on Sundays and drink beer all the time and do other things that middle-class people do. They usually do go together but they don't have to.

My radicalism gave me a lot of trouble at school. The administration and most of the teachers just didn't like my politics. One of them in particular, my art teacher. First of all, I have to say a little about the teacher so it makes sense. He consistently preaches racism. He thinks he's God. Everything he says is right. Nobody else knows about art especially. Nobody knows anything about it but him because he's had thirty-five years of experience. No, it's not true. He knows a lot more about it than us, but that doesn't mean everybody else's ideas are totally stupid and wrong. That's what he insinuates. He goes around talking about how black people are lazy and inferior and stupid. He says the same about the Japanese, which doesn't make any sense. Neither of them do. He's constantly harassing people about one thing or another. Another girl in my class, whom I like, sits next to me. We used to have all sorts of discussions during class. We had long political discussions about conditions in the country, about capitalism, and all this philosophical stuff. Naturally he thought I was totally wrong and he corrected me on my stupidity and my crazy communist ideas or whatever they were.

During one class I was talking about how we were going to leaflet the school about the Christmas assembly. The Christmas assembly is one of the yearly assemblies that they force you to go to. We were going to leaflet about why people had to go to assemblies. They're so bad most of the time, and they're totally administration-planned. Once in a while the students get to participate in planning them, but it's never anything that the kids want to do. It's an administration-planned thing. It has to be approved by an advisor before it even gets through. The Christmas assembly seems to be forcing religion on you in a way. We wanted to protest about forced religion, but more about the fact that we had to go to assemblies in the first place when they're so ridiculous and we have no part in planning them.

We had a meeting, and I guess about three of us were going to leaflet. Three at the beginning anyway. One of the kids refused later because his parents were really down on him. He practically got grounded just for associating with me, because I was a radical. So two of us were left to do it. We decided two weren't enough but we'd do it anyway, because we had the leaflets printed already. The day before we were going to do it, our art teacher overheard us talking about it in class. I'd asked one girl how many people she thought we could get to walk out of an assembly. It wouldn't have been this one but it would have been the next one. At the end of the leaflet we had something about how this assembly will be the last one we sit through, or something like that. The art teacher heard us talking about this, and I got suspended that afternoon. The official grounds were insubordination to a teacher. I suppose from their point of view I was insubordinate, and probably from my point of view too.

We had argued constantly with that teacher. You can't avoid him if you tried. At first, we decided the only way to get along with him was to pretend that he's not there. But you can't even do that because he will come in and enter into your discussions whether you want him to or not (nobody ever does). The insubordination charge may have been to punish me for my "crazy" political views, but I think it was more just to prevent us from leafletting the assembly. One person could never handle it alone, and they knew that.

The suspension was supposed to be for three days, but I'm sure it was an illegal suspension because I didn't come back to school for over a month. It happened two days before Christmas vacation which is really a great time to suspend anybody. It ruined my whole vacation with my parents. Christmas is a hell of a holiday to ruin. It doesn't bother me because I don't believe in it anyway. It's just a thing that's there, but it's not fair to ruin it for everybody else in the family. They said I had to come back after Christmas and talk with them. We went to California during Christmas, and while I was in California, I decided that I was not going back to that school because I hated it and there was no good reason to go back. I would have been happy to drop out forever from any school.

I do want to graduate now, but at the time I didn't care. I went back and the first thing the principal said was, "Well, if you want to come back to this school, you're going to have to go along with all the rules."

I said, "I want to come back." All of a sudden he got sympathetic. He said he wanted to help me "straighten things out," and that I should come to him for guidance. All I could think of was how he had acted when I was still attending the school. He was really a bastard about everything. He was always screaming and hollering and yelling about this and that. All of a sudden, I said I didn't want to come back. I still wasn't sure what I'd do, and I wanted to see how he'd react.

"Well, what's the matter? Why don't you like this

school? What's your problem?" he yelled. Real concerned and sympathetic.

I dropped out. I don't know whether I actually dropped out or got kicked out. I dropped out officially, but I also was kicked out. And I was away for over a month. I didn't know if I was illegally out of school or not. I finally talked to one of the DRU lawyers and he said, "Don't worry, legally you're safe." But I didn't know that. In Minnesota you have to be in school till you're seventeen. You can quit when you're sixteen but you have to have your parents' permission. I was sixteen and I didn't have permission. That made me open to legal action, or so I thought. At first they would have had to do it to my parents, whatever they were going to do, because of me being out of school. Fine them or something. But if they decided that I was uncontrollable, they could have done just about anything they wanted to do to me. I probably was uncontrollable, more or less.

I didn't go back to Bryan. I enrolled in Woodside, and I went there from February on. The conditions were better at Woodside, but nothing could be worse than Bryan.

I would like to get an education, but I know I can't do it in high schools without more or less reading about everything that we do in school from someplace else. You have to do a lot of outside reading on the same school topics to really get the truth. If one had discipline and really wanted to do it, I think he could get a better education if he stopped going to school at ninth grade and did outside reading all the time. I know a lot of kids who do things like that, do a lot of outside reading. I know at least two or three persons who could pass a High School Equivalency Test right now, and get their diplomas. I'm not sure if you have to be eighteen to do that, but I know at least two or three kids that could do it. One of them is fifteen and the other I think is sixteen. I don't know if I personally have the discipline to do all the reading on my own. And since by state law I have to stay in school, I'd like to see certain improvements made in the schools. I think one of the major things they could do is give the teachers the freedom to teach the way they want to. Also, I know one really good thing to do. A few classes do it now but not many: teacher and students come together and talk about what they want to learn and what they want to cover that year. It's experimental, or else it's done without the administration's knowledge. If a teacher does it, she'll usually say to the class, "Well, don't tell everybody about it because it wouldn't be that well looked-upon." I'd also like to see a complete abolition of any kind of dress code at all. I think people by the time they're in high school know how to dress themselves; and even if they don't, they still have a right to dress the way they want to. Besides, who's to say what is right or wrong to wear. It's ridiculous.

I think it's a good sign that high school students all over the country have been demonstrating and protesting about the conditions in the schools. But it's stupid to think that the radical High School Movement is going to be effective immediately. Right now it's not doing a damn thing. It doesn't do any good at all because you can't change schools with a bunch of high school radicals. It's not going to change the whole system. For one thing, you have school boards to fight, and in some cases you have state laws to fight. And what can the students involved, even if they are 50 percent of the high school students, do about a state law. They can't vote. All they can do is talk to their parents and talk to other people. It might do some good eventually though. It's good that kids are on the move for the first time. But at the moment, I don't think the Movement is strong enough to do a lot. It might change a few things like dress codes, and that's a good start. But to make bigger changes I think it's going to take a lot more than just a few high school radicals. It's going to take people who can vote, because there are these ridiculous state laws. They say you have to have Phys-Ed classes, they say you have to have a certain amount of History, they say you have to have a certain amount of English, Math, and so on. The rigid state laws have to be changed, and students can't do it by themselves.

It's going to take a lot more than just a few high school radicals. For one thing, a lot of the kids aren't with us at the moment. Like I know some girls who don't particularly want to wear slacks to school, and therefore they don't think you should change the rule—just because they don't want to. They think that girls should wear dresses to school. Maybe they should and maybe they shouldn't. It doesn't matter that much what they wear. They should have a right to wear slacks whether they want to or not. That's the argument I usually use in trying to convince them. They agree, but they still don't think you should change the rules. However, more and more kids are getting involved. Radicalism in high schools is very new. It's got to go somewhere. It's not just going to die immediately, because there are too many people unhappy with the schools. I think all the activity began last year because it had never before occurred to most high school students to do anything about their schools. It's occurred to them now though. The Movement is bound to get bigger. I'm sure it will, because I don't see how it can avoid it. Education is really outdated, antiquated. It's just not—I hate the word "relevant," because I'm sick of it—but education isn't relevant.

It should be said that some kids are participating in the Movement because demonstrations are fun. That's not the sole purpose of them—fun—although it is fun to demonstrate, walk around with signs, march a lot, and yell. It's fun. It's also like the thing about communes I was talking about before. In a demonstration you're doing things with other people. You're all together working for the same goal. There's something beautiful about doing things like that with a lot of other people. Like those other things in the youth culture, it sort of gives you something. But people don't always march just because it is fun. A lot of people really believe in it too. There's nothing wrong with having fun at a demonstration. But you've got to believe in what you are doing too.

There's all this talk about how the schools are part of the country and how you can't change the schools 'till the whole country is changed. I'm not really sure. But I don't think you can restructure the country until you restructure the schools, because the schools are what make people good Americans, or at least try to. I think you'd have to change the schools first, because the country's such a huge thing. There are about three thousand different things in the country that need improving. The schools are just one thing. If people would really make the school system good, then you'd have people who come out of the schools as reasonable, logical, intelligent, independent people. Oh boy. People who have enough sense to know this country's not beautiful, lovely, and wonderful at the moment. School just makes you apathetic. If people could only have an idea of what the school situation is like. You couldn't have an ideal school situation probably, but you could improve it a hell of a lot. And if you could do that, people who come out of the school system would be a lot more capable of doing something about this country.

Woodstock:
The Children's Crusade

by Fred Silber

Fred Silber is a seventeen-year-old Senior at New York City's Stuyvesant High School. He was associated with the underground newspaper, The Weekly Reader, *which later merged with the* Herald Tribune. *He has had two poems published: one in the* National High School Anthology of Poetry, *and the second in a book published by Random House last November called* In a Time of Revolution, *edited by Walter Lowenfels.*

> A long tail'd Pig, or a short tail'd Pig,
> Or a Pig without any Tail;
> A Sow Pig, or a Boar Pig,
> Or a Pig with a curling Tail.
> Take hold of the Tail and eat off his Head;
> And then you'll be sure the Pig hog is dead.
>
> —MOTHER GOOSE

In the early 1930's, shortly before the Nazis took over Germany, large numbers of German youth would go up into the Highlands and hold music festivals. In the years that followed, many of these same young people became willing recruits for the Hitler youth . . .

In mid-August of 1969, somewhere between 300,000

and 750,000 people "took to the hills" for the first Woodstock Music and Arts Aquarian Rock Exposition in Bethel, New York. Rarely has such an event received the coverage and exposure accorded that "lost weekend" (those three days) somewhere in the Catskills on Max Yasgur's dairy farm. Newspapers—straight and underground—radio stations, TV networks, feature magazines, the rock press, and every photographer east of the Allegheny made the hegira to the wooded Woodstock hills to report the proceedings as they unfurled. *Life* magazine thought the weekend "important" enough (meaning "salable") to issue a *Life* Special Edition, only the third ever—for those who count such events as the tokens of history.

It was early spring when the rumors first began circulating that a mammoth rock festival was being organized somewhere in upstate New York. By May, announcements on FM rock stations were giving details. The dates were August 15, 16, and 17; the place an otherwise undistinguished site called Wallkill. (It was originally supposed to be in Woodstock, but the Festival promoters shortly discovered that the town, with a chilling sense of precognition, was not about to help usher in the Aquarian Age with a "rock, drug, and sex" bash in its own backyard.)

Billed as "Three days of peace and music," the promised serenity of the Festival was upset almost immediately with the news that the "townspeople" of Wallkill had told Woodstock Ventures, Inc., "Thanks, but no thanks." The next location was at White Lake, near the town of Bethel, in Sullivan County, New York. A massive advertising campaign was initiated to inform people of the change, but as late as one week before the first concert of the Festival was scheduled to begin, a crowd of no more than 200,000 was expected, and that was a generous figure.

"The rest," as they say, "is history." More than half a million people (representing possibly fifty times that number) invaded the normally tranquil area of White Lake. Mammoth traffic jams tied up every possible route to the Festival. Conditions did not improve at the Festival grounds. With crowd estimates off by a few hundred thousand, at the least, a state of "emergency" developed almost immediately. Concession stands were out of food on the first day, water was in short supply, and the limited medical facilities were very quickly taxed beyond their capabilities as the number of "casualties" grew.

The lackadaisical optimism of the producers of the Festival was best exemplified in their preparations concerning possible adverse weather. Perhaps they thought that such an event could not be spoiled by something as trivial as rain; perhaps they figured we'd all be so stoned that we wouldn't particularly care. And if they thought about the rain, God knows, they certainly didn't think about the mud.

But if their preparation for weather stemmed from wish-fulfillment, their concept of adequate toilet facilities must have been based on an abysmal ignorance of biology.

Certainly the music helped quite a bit. Although the Friday night concert was quite erratic, mostly due to the rain, more than three hundred thousand of us sat and listened to the sounds of Richie Havens, Tim Hardin, Arlo Guthrie, Ravi Shankar, and Joan Baez, just to name a few. By Saturday those of us who were going to stick with the scene had begun to make our "adjustments" and things went more smoothly. Beginning at approximately 2:00 P.M., fourteen acts proceeded to play to more than 500,000 people for the next seventeen hours. Saturday night (including Sunday morning) was the high point of the Festival musically, with top groups such as Canned Heat, Creedence Clearwater Revival, The Grateful Dead, Janis Joplin's new group, Sly and the Family Stone, The Who, and The Jefferson Airplane playing while the crowd witnessed the breaking of dawn.

Sunday was anticlimactic, the crowd steadily dwindling in size, until finally no more than 20,000 were left for the last rites on Monday morning as performed by Jimi Hendrix. (Ironically, Hendrix was the highest paid performer of the weekend, receiving $18,000 for his services.)

The trip home was a little easier than it had been

coming up, but large traffic jams still prevailed. It was over. We had survived and what had started out to be a disastrous fiasco looked like it had ended up bigger than anything anyone had expected. A "success" by any standards?

Not according to the promoters of Woodstock Ventures, Inc. Although stating that they were tremendously pleased at what had happened at White Lake, John Roberts (the "money man") and Michael Lang (the "hype man"), the two main promoters of Woodstock Ventures, Inc., claimed they had taken a $1,300,000 (mud)bath on their Aquarian weekend. Acknowledging $1,400,000 in advance mail order sales, Roberts and Lang claimed that the Fair's expenses totaled $2,700,000. Included in this figure were $500,000 for moving the Festival from Wallkill to Bethel, and $600,000 to "provide helicopters, food, and medicine to the site plagued by inclement weather, excessive drug use, and overpopulation." Financial matters weren't helped any by the fact that by Friday evening, all the concerts were "free" (Lang and Roberts wisely noting that fences would mean nothing considering the size of the crowd already gathered), which naturally resulted in a large loss at the box office. Ironically, the newspapers seemed to be more fascinated by the Fair's bookkeeping than by its music.

But within three weeks after the Festival, some question was being thrown on the pecuniary aspects of the disaster. For instance, it *did* seem strange that Roberts and Lang tried to buy out each other's interests in Woodstock Ventures, Inc., at a reported $1,000,000, a considerable sum for a company that was supposedly $1.3 million in the red. Some observers thought that the $600,000 expense ascribed to helicopters, food and medical supplies was difficult to credit. *Variety,*[1] which usually knows what it's talking about, put it this way: "Eight helicopters at $500 an hour for three 10-hour days account to [sic] $120,000 which leaves $480,000 for food and medicine." "Both figures

1. *Variety,* September 10, 1969.

seemed unrealistic" said the trade newspaper. By now, most people believe that if indeed there was a loss, it was considerably smaller than the one publicly claimed. And when all the receipts are in, including film and recording rights, it is likely that Woodstock Ventures, Inc. will find itself with a nice little profit.

But the "mercantile aspect" of the Festival is only one part of the phenomenon of Woodstock. Four hundred thousand "mostly white, mostly middle-class young Americans" were indeed far removed from the commercial side of the weekend. There was something about the atmosphere created by the people who went up to Woodstock that made it different from similar rock festivals in Texas, Atlanta, Atlantic City, *et al*. Much of it was based on the image of "Three days of peace and music" coupled with the best line-up of rock groups ever. Not surprisingly, it soon developed into a social urgency of the teenage underground (if you weren't going up to Woodstock you just weren't "with it"). But the body of the image was to take shape that weekend. Since a majority of the huge crowd had arrived without tickets, a sense of unity developed almost at once. When the sheer chaos of numbers resulted in the "liberation" of music, when the box office became an instant anachronism, a sense of excitement began to take over. Something *real* was happening—maybe for the first time in many lives. People liked the idea that so many of them were there, with a power no longer defined by the dollar sign. They began to feel that they were working toward something, even though they didn't know exactly what it was. Each individual there could feel 400,000 other people within himself. Whenever announcements were made informing the crowd that it was the "Third largest city in New York State" or the "Tenth largest city in the nation," the audience was obviously pleased beyond words. One writer, Irwin Silber of the *Guardian,* explained it this way:

> And far from being discouragements, the rain, the mud, the shortages of food, shelter, clothing, the isolation and the

distances all contributed to the "groovy" atmosphere. For here was a generation which had shown its contempt for the plastic technology of the only modern day industrial society they knew. Here was a generation which had seen science and reason employed as the weapons of deception and oppression. Here was a generation which wanted desperately to believe in the justice of ecology, in the abiding truth of natural man and natural life.

If one were to scan the crowds at Woodstock, he could see the kids from Alice's Restaurant, college students, hippies, yippies, and more, all representing a variety of personalities and views but all fundamentally united in their rejection of and alienation from the "American Way of Life." And it was at Woodstock that they saw and felt something which was completely unlike anything they had experienced living in the U.S.A. Jon Grell said it for many of them in *Rat:*

> . . . i saw what i was fighting for. i was with my people. like the indian gathering on the plains to celebrate an annual peyote ritual, we were a people gathered in the greatest manifestation of our culture; our music. yeah baby, my dope was free, and my food was free, and honey, i was free, and that's what we're fighting for. we saw our revolution, and we built it, and we made it, baby, and i dug it so much that i'd kill to make it happen forever.

This sense of accomplishment, no matter how small or meaningless, was quite frankly the most real aspect of Woodstock. And, as Grell says, people were indeed quite free. Free in the sense that none of those inhibiting and forbidding organizations of society were there to limit or cripple free instincts. Isn't that the way it should be? Freedom, man, Freedom!

But is man naturally free? ("naturally" meaning the absence of social organization). Is freedom simply the absence of restraint? Or is such a concept of freedom one of those philosophical illusions which have outlived their usefulness? Christopher Caudwell, a revolutionary Marxist of the 1930's, said on the subject:

Freedom is the product, not of the instincts, but of social relations themselves. Freedom is secreted in the relation of man to man . . . Man cannot strip himself of his social relations and remain man. But he can shut his eyes to these social relations. He can disguise them as relations to commodities, to the impersonal market, to cash, to capital, and his relations then seem to have become possessive. He "owns" the commodities, the cash and the capital. All his social relations appear to have become relations to a thing, and because man is superior to a thing, he is now free, he is dominating. But this is an illusion. By shutting his eyes to all the relations between men that constitute society, and are its real stuff and substance, man has enslaved himself to forces whose control is now beyond him, because he does not acknowledge their existence. He is at the mercy of the market, the movement of capital, and the slump and the boom. He is deluded by himself.[2]

And then, almost as if he were writing in the wake of Woodstock:

. . . So far from being free, he is whirled like a leaf on the gales of social change. And all this anarchy, and impotence, and muddled dissensions is reflected in his culture. Productive forces have outgrown the free bourgeois and mercilessly crush him and his illusions.

According to Abbie Hoffman, that weekend saw the building of a new nation, "born from the seeds of the Woodstock Festival." In his book, *Woodstock Nation,* Hoffman talks about his maturity as a "cultural revolutionary" at the festival. To Hoffman, there are two nations and two cultures—"Woodstock Culture" and "Pig Culture." Yet Hoffman doesn't seem to realize that his culture, Woodstock Culture, is not only derived from but is an integral part of Pig Culture. It would be hard to convince anyone at Woodstock that what they were witnessing was one of the many long and last howls of the "Pig Culture." Woodstock

2. Christopher Caudwell, *Studies in a Dying Culture* (New York: Dodd, Mead, & Co., 1938), pp. XXI–XXII.

did not herald the coming of the revolution, and to consider it "counter culture" is simply to offer a retreat from reality as an alternative to the death culture of capitalism's dying years.

Woodstock is not that new culture, but in a certain sense it might very well turn out to be counter-revolutionary if it has the effect of diverting the energy for revolutionary social change in America into channels which do not threaten the fundamental tenets of capitalist social and productive relations.

Woodstock, along with hippies, the drug scene, and all the other formidable youth phenomena, may finally add up to nothing more than a comfortable "cop out" in the last years of American capitalism. It shows how easy it is for this, the arch-manipulative society of all time, to feed a whole generation the illusion that they are freeing themselves from an oppressive society while it neutralizes all of their efforts for meaningful social change.

On Saturday afternoon, at Woodstock, an incident occurred which somehow sums it all up for me. When the army helicopters began flying in the food and medical supplies so desperately needed, an announcer stepped to a microphone on the stage and said, "See. See that, the army's helping us. They're not the enemy. They're on our side." At which point the throng burst into applause and held up their fingers in the "peace symbol" (or was it the victory sign?) as the helicopter flew over.

> An army without culture is a dull-witted army, and a dull-witted army cannot defeat the enemy.
>
> —MAO TSE-TUNG, "The United Front in Cultural Work" (Oct. 30, 1944)

I guess it's all a matter of who's the enemy and who's the army. Strange how they can be so reversible. The most fitting tribute that could have been paid the Woodstock Festival was Jimi Hendrix' rendition of "The Star-Spangled Banner" on the final day.

. . .

Ellen Sander, perhaps the festival's most ardent publi-
cist, wrote afterwards: "The way I figure it, the next pop
festival should be a million people and last for a week, the
next one should be 8 million and last for a whole summer
and the next one should be everyone on the whole planet
and last forever."

> Hush a by Baby
> On the Tree Top
> When the Wind blows
> The Cradle will rock
> When the Bough breaks
> The Cradle will fall
> And down tumbles Baby
> Cradle and all.
>
> —MOTHER GOOSE

Oh well, God bless the child . . .

IV

RELIGION

What role does family background play in determining which high school students become radicals and which do not? Michael Marqusee has already spoken about what influence his family's class has had on him. Besides class, do other things such as a student's religion, play a part in making him radical? It has been noted by other writers that a high percentage of radical college students are of the Jewish faith. Is this also the case for radical high school students? Richie Cohen from Greensboro, North Carolina, talks about his experience as a Jewish high school student in Christian territory. Are students from other religious groups prone to becoming radicals? Mary Ann Kennedy from Erie, Pennsylvania, talks about her Fundamentalism and her school. Both Richie and Mary Ann spoke into the tape recorder.

IV

RELIGION

Jesus Says I Should

by Mary Ann Kennedy

> *Mary Ann Kennedy is seventeen years old, and lives*
> *in the black ghetto of Erie, Pennsylvania. Though*
> *she is mulatto (her mother black and her father*
> *white), she is dark-skinned, and identified by her*
> *Academy High School classmates as being black. Her*
> *parents could afford to live outside the ghetto, but*
> *they prefer to remain near the people they serve.*
> *Mrs. Kennedy is the principal of a new private school*
> *for poor blacks and whites who need individual*
> *attention. Mr. Kennedy is an engineer. He and his*
> *wife are missionaries of the Pentecostal faith.*

I am a Fundamentalist. Both my parents are mission-
aries, and I have always been taught to follow the ideals and
values that Christ represented. (I have also had a personal
experience with Christ, which gave me what years of teaching never could. Religion *has* to be, ultimately, an individual experience—"your own thing.") I am also a student in
Academy High School of Erie, Pennsylvania, a school that
was racked by student disturbances for the past two years.
The conditions there, and in most other schools in the Erie
school system, are really bad; they run contrary to the
purposes of my faith.

I think my Fundamentalism makes me very sensitive to
conditions around me. To use a cliché, I think that it

opened my eyes and helped me to see how bad things really were and to see that something had to be done to change conditions. I can't use violence to change things, because I've been taught to love my enemy. How can I love my enemy while I'm hitting him over the head with a brick? However, though I won't use violence, there must be some change. The school system as it stands is not accomplishing much good, and this should be the aim of everyone—to accomplish as much good as possible.

I feel that as a Christian I should try my best to understand everyone—to "love the unlovable"; and to understand others, I have to understand myself. If you understand people, you realize that everyone has problems. In trying to understand these problems you try to understand the causes; and when you realize that the causes are often terrible and sordid, you decide that you have to do something about them.

As a high school student I have been close to the problems of an ineffective, even destructive school system. My Pentecostalism would not allow me to sit back and do nothing; I felt an overriding responsibility to work to change bad conditions. I tried to effect some change at Academy; I don't know how successful I was, but I did what I could.

The deficiencies at Academy with regard to black students are the same as those throughout the country: there are no Black History courses and very few black teachers. There are also problems for every student, black and white, in every school in Erie: poor teachers and poor facilities, not to mention unfeeling administrations. I am not dismissing the question of prejudice, which is indeed present. For instance, if a black student is walking in the hall during classes with a white student, a teacher will confront the black and demand to see his pass—not the white's; the black will be told to return to his class, and the white will be left alone. These incidents are not isolated; they happen often. They are not really thought of as something wrong, but rather taken as a normal part of life.

I think that some teachers at Academy are prejudiced. They are not racist in that they have an open hatred for all blacks; they just seem to think, either due to earlier training or sheer ignorance, that blacks are inferior to them. There are some good teachers at Academy, and they do their best to help black students—but sometimes their desire to help backfires. Some go overboard in their desire to help blacks and end up being patronizing or unfair to whites. This tends to antagonize white students and blacks end up in worse shape than they were to begin with.

I happened to be placed in accelerated courses with mostly good teachers. However, for the average black this is not the case. Blacks are lumped with slower students and automatically (especially if there is a record of previous "troublemakers" in the family) placed in a class—or a room, for they are not fit to be called classes—where nothing at all is taught. They are forced to sit still for forty-five minutes doing nothing. The teacher comes in for five minutes to hand out "busy work," and then goes down to the teachers' room to smoke, drink, and relax with his friends. There is nothing creative for the students to do; there is no stimulation.

The majority of prejudice seemed to be along disciplinary lines. Admittedly, more black students than white ones seem to have acted up in school and consequently gotten in trouble; but I think that the school itself is largely to blame for the bad behavior of many students. The school system offers no challenge for most students; there is nothing for them to do except sit and chew gum. If the school had really good teachers, teachers who would do their best to motivate their pupils, I believe that there would be a very small disciplinary need. But as it stands, the Erie school system is the state dumping ground: many times we get the old and incompetent teachers whom no other city wants, but we have to take them because not very many young teachers are willing to work in the Erie school system. If we had some new and enthusiastic young (or old) teachers I believe that the disciplinary problems would be solved and students would become interested in school and in learning once more.

Most of the issues directly relevant to our lives as students are not mentioned. Only occasionally is the question of poverty raised in class, and I rarely heard any teacher allowing a discussion of racism in his class. In a school that experiences open hostility between races, I think it's strange that the issue is overlooked. It's as though some teachers are afraid of the whole matter. And as far as the Vietnam War is concerned, a war in which most of my male classmates will be fighting soon, there is almost no coverage of it at all —except for routine papers when a student may choose his own topic. All that is said is the same that is said about any American war—that it is great and right and glorious. The few discussions that there are probably serve to spread propaganda more than they encourage the formation of individual opinions. Many teachers are like government agents, insuring that we have the United States' opinions instead of our own. (This is probably because of a desire to keep their jobs—there is a great deal of pressure on teachers from the administration to conform, and this pressure comes to students from the teachers.)

I am fortunate in having obtained a fairly good education so far. But I must honestly say that the Erie school system deserves very little credit for my education, except for that fact that they gave me a piece of paper certifying that I had "satisfactorily completed the course . . ." Rather, it has been my parents, both college graduates, who have encouraged me to learn and who have provided me with an atmosphere conducive to learning. You have to have some sort of motivation from somewhere, and I received mine from my parents. I am lucky to have parents who are concerned with education and who inspire me to learn, because I certainly would never have received such motivation from the public school system. Friends of mine, whose parents are too ill-informed or too busy to take an interest in education, are left out. They get nothing from school, nothing from home, nothing from anywhere. Unin-

spired to learn, they see no point in working in school; they
usually end up in jail or on the streets.

A good example of what happens when there is no
motivation is the series of disturbances that have plagued
Academy for the last two years. There was much dissatisfaction, considerable boredom on the part of those unin-
spired students whom I mentioned, and a desire to change
things. The result was a major explosion. The initial disturbance began after a white teacher got uptight with a
black student and knocked him down. The black student
got up and struck the teacher back. It seems that this was the
signal for an eruption of tensions that had been growing in
the school for some time. The boy was temporarily suspended, and the administration said that he might be expelled. To protest this action a group of students (both
white and black) started a petition and presented it to the
principal. Officials say that the principal was out when the
petition was brought in and that he never saw it. I don't
know whether that is true, but the petition was certainly
taken to the office and no acknowledgment of it was made.

After nothing happened about the petition the situation
became even more tense. There was a disturbance to get the
suspended boy back in school (he was readmitted). Two
black girls, who were supposed to have thrown bricks at
policemen (actually they were taunting the policemen and
being disrespectful) were arrested and later given harsh
sentences—I think six months in jail. When they were sentenced there was another disturbance to protest the sentencing. It turned into a rather ludicrous chain reaction
situation: a disturbance to protest sentencing, a sentencing
of the participators in the disturbance (usually blacks were
sentenced), a disturbance to protest the sentencing of the
participators . . . At first the student body was united
against the administration, despite the lack of homogeneity
among the student body—Academy was composed mostly
of lower classes and upper-middle classes; there was a very
small middle class. But after the continued disturbances,
many students (black and white) felt that the riots were

getting idiotic. Some of the more militant whites developed a white backlash: after blacks rioted, the whites would riot —perhaps to prove that they were just as strong. At the end of the school year there was definite friction between races at Academy.* There has already been at least one riot at this writing (October 1969) that was far bloodier and more vicious than ever before. And the tension has spread to other Erie schools.

Not very much was changed this year at Academy. Black History is supposed to be taught next year in the Erie school system, but it's just token and won't really amount to much. I think, and most blacks in Erie will agree with me, that there should be a really comprehensive Black Histories Program instituted in the public schools. Blacks of college age have been advocating that such programs be established in colleges, but I think that the programs should start earlier. Black History courses must be introduced at the high school level, if not earlier. Blacks are a part of American history. One can't get away from that fact: they helped to build it, and they are helping to sustain it. Blacks are an integral part of American society. You take blacks and their culture out and you lose something tangible. Whites have to learn about black history because they have to live with blacks, whether they want to or not. Blacks need to learn about black history because there is an obvious deficiency of racial pride among some blacks. Today's "Black is Beautiful" slogans and concepts are helping to develop black pride; and courses in black history and culture will enhance

---

* I was right in the middle of the turmoil—literally—because my mother is black and my father is white. I am grateful for my inter-raciality because, although I can see neither side completely, I can see both sides partially. My friends are worried that I will become involved in role conflict: they think that society sees me as one thing and I see myself as something else (that society sees me as black and I refuse to see myself that way). I find it impossible to ignore the heritage that I have received from my father. I feel that my unique situation has helped deepen my insight into the problems at Academy, and I would not want to change.

the pride that is already there. When each race truly has pride in its own race *and in the opposite race,* then our racial problems will be over.

Many people have asked why high school students, for the first time, are demanding the same programs as blacks in college. Are they led, they ask, by the same "black militant" groups? No. High school students have finally come to recognize the need for black pride and for black-related courses. Actually, these courses would be best started on an elementary level. It's far better to start with the idea that "I'm something worthwhile" than to start with "I'm terrible" and then later on, in high school or college, try to change the idea. Black courses early in education, for both black and white children, amount to something like "an ounce of prevention."

Black courses are certainly important for all students, but course offerings are only one element in the over-all school experience. Other things will have to be changed before presently hostile and/or apathetic high school students ever become enthusiastic about school again. I think that the most important thing that must be done is to get rid of incompetent teachers. At Academy and at least one other Erie high school there are some alcoholic teachers who remain on the faculty year after year. When the superintendent of schools came to Academy we asked him why something was not done about these alcoholic teachers, and he said, "Well, you can't really have proof unless you give them a blood test." (How many high school students are equipped to administer a blood test?) Then he said, "And if you don't give me proof, then I can't prosecute them." We asked what would happen if there were a flask in the teacher's drawer, and he said, "Well it doesn't really matter, it might just be an accident." That is the kind of run-around that we get from the school system. They refuse to risk the publicity that looking at their teachers would generate. They refuse to make or even recognize waves, but rather advocate and encourage stagnation and conformity. Nothing at all is being done to get rid of the bad teachers. When they get good teachers in the schools, then the motivation problems that I mentioned earlier will be solved. From good teachers comes motivation, and from motivation will come good students.

It really angers me when I think that such bad teachers are condoned at Academy and at other schools. Considering that there are at least thirty students in every class and five class periods in a school day, every teacher comes in contact with a minimum of 150 students a day: 150 students, given a bad teacher, are wasting their time; their dislike of school and learning grows. And then the superintendent tells us that his hands are tied and that he needs more proof! At times like this I am greatly tempted to resort to violence, despite my pacifistic beliefs, because violence seems sometimes to be the only thing that will make people sit up and take notice. But then I feel (idealistically, yes) that there must be a better way. I am fully in favor of sit-ins and other peaceful protests; an organized student strike might be an answer for Academy this year. There was an attempt last year to organize a mass boycott of classes by black students and to establish freedom schools, but the black community in Erie is notoriously "not together," and the idea fizzled out.

For something—*anything*—to be done, the young people must join forces and work together. We have to form a movement of students: whites, blacks, everyone. We realize that we can't rely on most adults any more because the majority of adults have betrayed our trust. We have inherited a world that's really messed up, through no fault or desire of our own. Since we have received this world we must do our best, and the only way is through a concerted effort of young people. Such an effort is coming (that is not a threat, but a promise).

The basic thing that I look for in a teacher is understanding. I think that a teacher should be sensitive to the general problems of being young, and sensitive to the problems peculiar to any one student—be they racial, financial, environment, physical, or educational. I realize that this is a big order to give a teacher, but I think that it's necessary. After all, if teaching is a profession, it's reasonable for us who are being served to expect certain standards from these craftsmen. At Academy, which has a faculty of about eighty teachers, I came in contact with only ten faculty members who had this understanding. I didn't have all of these as teachers, but I knew of their attitudes. They were the ones who stuck their necks out for what was right. They were the ones who, after a disturbance, tried to find out what was wrong, and who tried to do something instead of just sitting back and condemning all students. That's what most of the other teachers did. Some of them were so blind to what the problem was that they threatened to punish the entire student body if there was another disturbance. (There were enough teachers to have done it, too.) They said that they would change the school day schedule from the present 8:30 A.M. to 3:00 P.M. hours to a 7:00 A.M. to 1:00 P.M. schedule. There would be no assemblies, no lunch period, and no other time for any sort of relaxation; no chance for students to get together with other students outside of the classroom. The few teachers who did oppose a "teacher backlash" and really did try to understand (the advisor to the school newspaper was one of these), tried to say something against it, but they were too few to have any great effect.

The failings of Academy High School can easily be read in the small number of students who go on to higher education after high school. This is not a reflection on the students or on Academy itself, but rather on the entire school system. Here we get back to the subject of motivation: many of these students, whom most teachers consider stupid, are really intelligent. One boy who was removed from the public school elementary system because he was getting D's and E's, was placed in a private Christian school where personal attention is emphasized—and got A's and B's. This improvement was not because his I.Q. changed overnight, but because he received personal help and realized that his new teacher really cared for him. A lack of love holds these students back, and that (plus motivation, which comes with love) is what the school system should, but doesn't, provide. Right now it seems that some teachers and administrators at Academy are actually discouraging students—black and white—from learning and developing intellectually and socially. One assistant principal in the school system would call a student into her office and say, "You're sixteen now, and you aren't getting anything from school. Why don't you quit?" Instead of making sure that every student *did* benefit from school, it was easier to suggest that the student simply quit. She probably figured that the less students there were, the less work there would be for her. Thoughts of future employment or personal fulfillment for these students probably never even entered her mind. To her, teaching was a job, and the less work the better—regardless of the consequences to the students.

That's the point that things have reached in Erie, at least in the inner city schools. Obviously unqualified teachers and administrators remain in schools almost forever, as long as they don't antagonize the Democratic Party, whose head is the present mayor (hopefully not for long), Mayor Tullio. Any teacher who wants to keep his job had better not do anything that goes against the mayor's grain. Tullio, head of a powerful Democratic machine (Erie is a Catholic/Democratic city) also seems to have racist tendencies. A manifestation of these prejudices is in his actions during the school disturbances. When about twenty-five white boys were arrested (after the Erie Police Department finally seemed to become partially color blind) fatherly Mayor Tullio came down and told the boys gently, "Now boys, I want you to realize that what you did is not really right, and this is a warning. You may think that you were justified in what you did, but next time I might not be so nice. Be good, now." He let the boys go free right then. At another disturbance they arrested some black boys, and Tullio didn't even begin to show such "sympathy and understanding." All the students were forced to stay in jail, and many of them were given harsh sentences without fair trials.

Tullio was once a school board member; many public office holders were once teachers or administrators. They all help each other—it's "one big happy dictatorship." Not many serious politicians would criticize the Erie school system. (There is now a new breed of school board members who are not afraid to speak out for what is right—and surprisingly, they still survive politically. Soon there will be more outspoken leaders, who will not be timid about uncovering the truth.) The standard policy now is a smooth, no-change policy. Students must make the necessary changes in our schools. No one else may care, but we certainly do.

I consider myself a pacifistic radical. I think a drastic change is necessary in the Erie school system. But I am sorry to say that people who are devoted to affecting change are in a distinct minority. Most of the students realize that there is something wrong, but they either need motivation or they just don't care. Some say, "Well, I'm in the honors courses and I'm doing very well, so why should I care? Why should I worry about someone else?" But there are students who will follow if there is a leader—good or bad. After the first few disturbances a friend of mine and I got together with a group of other students and started "Dialogue," a confrontation session between blacks and whites. We tried to get all the racial tension out into the open, in the belief that verbal fire was better that material fire. Once the program was organized there were quite a few students who participated. The program proved that there were students who wanted to help.

The "Dialogue" program itself was only moderately successful. The first few sessions were excellent as far as discussion was concerned: each side gained a deeper understanding of and insight into the other side. But the discussions eventually got stale—we ended up talking about the same things over and over. Attendance slacked, and when there was yet another disturbance we wondered if discussion and understanding really were the answers; I still don't know. To keep up interest and to be doing something constructive about the racially tense situation, we eased the discussions into a lecture/discussion series. Speakers ranged from black racists (a Black Panther advocate) to white racists (the afore-mentioned superintendent of schools). Our program provided us with a free, unrestricted discussion period and with insight that could not be obtained during the regular class day. That this program came out of the racial disturbances seems to suggest that such agitation does pay dividends. It's highly unlikely that the school administration would have approved of "Dialogue" and permitted it to be held in the school after the regular classes were over if there hadn't been such turmoil, and I'm sure that there would have been fewer students interested in attending. While I find it difficult to support violence, it sometimes seems to be the only thing that will arouse the apathetic and produce necessary changes.

High school students have just begun to find themselves this last year, at least in regard to their potential power in the schools. It's been a long time coming, but I think that many of us are finally realizing how bad school conditions are and how poorly most students are treated. Students were experimenting last year with discussion and disturbances, with conversation and with violence, to see which worked better. Students won't continue to put up with alcoholic or unsympathetic teachers and administrators; they won't put up with boring and irrelevant courses. I foresee the high school movement getting stronger in the future. Students will continue to seek change in school conditions, and change will come.

"'Jewing down' South"

by Richie Cohen

> *Richie Cohen is 18 years old, and just graduated
> from high school in Greensboro, North Carolina. He
> was a football player in high school. He now lives
> in Berkeley, California.*

For Allan, Sara, and Lew

I am from Greensboro, North Carolina, and I just got
out of Grimsley Senior High School. I'm eighteen years old,
and I moved to Greensboro at eleven from Baltimore, Maryland. I come from a Jewish middle-class home. I consider it
middle-class, although there is a difference between the way
my family lives and the way the other Jewish families in
Greensboro do. Most of them live in a fairly rich section
(the really rich section is for the old tobacco families), and
we live in an apartment. My father makes about $10,000 a
year. He's a travelling salesman and isn't home very much.

Until I moved to Greensboro I never even thought twice
about being a Jew. My mother is fairly religious (we're
Conservative rather than Reform), and she always put a lot
of pressure on me to hang around Jewish kids. All of my
friends back in Baltimore were Jewish. While I did resent
my mother's pressure, and became sort of a hell-raiser just
to spite her, the whole question of Jewishness really didn't
affect me. It was only after I moved to North Carolina and
started to go to junior and senior high school there that I
saw "being Jewish" as something else. There were very few

Jewish families in Greensboro, and virtually no Jewish kids in my classes at school; for the first time in my life I began to feel strange just because of my religion and background. I always felt that I was treated differently by the Christian students, like I was some kind of outsider. They all had stereotyped ideas about what Jews were, and what they did. You didn't gyp someone in Greensboro, you "Jewed" them. I guess I thought it was all sort of amusing at first, what with the attention and all, but after a while it really started to bother me. I didn't like being considered different from anyone else.

As a result of all this, I went through a process of what I would call Christianization. While I don't think I was particularly conscious of it at the time, I can see now that I tried to release all my identification with "being Jewish." I wanted to be as much like the other students as possible, and that meant being less Jewish and more Christian—both in looks and in attitude. Thinking about it now, I realize how bad this kind of self-denial can be. You try to imitate the way the "other" people act and look, and it even gets to the point where you try to get the kinks out of your hair, you wish your nose would move up on your face, and that kind of thing. I never actually said, "I want to have a nose job," although I must admit that I did think about it many times. But my last name was Cohen, an obviously Jewish name, everyone knew I was Jewish, and despite what I might do to my looks, everyone would still consider me Jewish.

I still attempted to make myself as non-Jewish as possible so that I'd be wholly accepted by the people around me. I took less and less interest in Jewish things at home. And I stopped going to synagogue altogether when I was about fourteen. The Christianization process kept me from Judaism in this way. But what upset me even more was that it kept me from being able to free my head—from doing exactly as I pleased, from letting my emotions go the way I felt they should.

This Christianization process really was a process of

oppression. I was being subtly forced by the Christians, who predominated in Greensboro, to give up my thoughts and beliefs. I did it then in order to be accepted by people my age and not be considered different; I now see it as a force making me conform so that I'd be less of a threat to the Christian society. And it worked. As I said, I felt bothered about being Jewish, and I always talked about it. But now I see that it doesn't make any difference anymore. I'm through worrying about whether I am or am not Jewish, and I've come around so that I'm no longer ashamed to identify with it.

The anti-Semitism in Greensboro wasn't a surface kind of thing; it was a basic part of Southern culture. Jews are thought to be inferior to pure white Christians (I guess we're sort of "white niggers"), in a really stereotyped way. All Jews are money-grabbing and big-nosed; there is no difference between any of them. There's never much real thought given to any of these ideas. That's just the way the kids are brought up and expected to think. The Jews are really a different kind of people, and no one can be so different and hope to become one of "us." I like some of the people in the South, but I hate its institutions and attitudes.

I finally did make friends and go around with some of the people in the "cool" (and Christian) crowd. But even then, after I was sort of accepted by them, I had to pretend to be someone I was not. For example, I had to do and say things I honestly didn't feel, things that went against basic values I had learned at home. Growing up in Baltimore, I had learned from my parents that you should love everybody. You should love Negroes too, but just never marry a Negro. That's what my mother and her Jewish friends would say. Well, obviously that's not what most of the whites in Greensboro believed. To them a Negro was still a slave. The high schools are fucking racist. You could talk to Negroes if you had to, but to have one as a friend or to think of them as equals was out of the question. This situation presented quite a conflict for me. All my friends, both the "cool" ones and the others, referred to them as "niggers," and I still called them "Negroes." That made me stand out, and I was known in school as a liberal; but since I was going along trying to lose myself in the Southern Christian culture, I didn't want to be considered a liberal so I even stopped calling them "Negroes." But though I stopped acting like a liberal and appearing different than my friends, it still bothered me inside to do the kinds of things I had to do. It was really cool to buy a six-pack of beer and go riding around in a car, but it would bother me when one of my friends would lean out of the window and yell, "Nigger," or be really nasty to the black people we passed. I'd feel really bad inside, but of course I'd never say anything about it. That would have shown me to be an outsider.

Sophomore year was when this whole Christianizing thing was at its height. I was then at Page Senior High School, which is made up of kids from the richest families in town and kids from the poorest families—the working class kids whose fathers work for one of the big textile mills in Greensboro. The Christian conformity seemed to be greater at Page than at any other school I ever went to, and therefore so was my non-Jewishness. It was the whole shitty scene —debutante-date-shit-clothes. I was asked to leave the school at the end of the year because I was a troublemaker.

I now see that besides affecting the way I was socially, this whole Christianization process influenced my attitudes, especially in school. I think my often disruptive behavior in school was to some degree caused by it, and I'm now glad I misbehaved. I was always trying to get the attention of the class, either by making wisecracks or by just fooling around. My ninth grade principal wouldn't even let me go to graduation because he thought I would disrupt it. I now think this need I felt for constant attention was the result of the Southern cultural oppression. I wasn't allowed to be me, so I had to get attention in other ways, like by fooling around. It actually seems sad that I was forced to act up and get in trouble just to be free.

But I think in the long run this Christianization process

actually benefitted me. Where I am now as a person, and particularly politically, is due, to a great extent I think, to what I had to go through as a Jew in the strongly Christian city of Greensboro. I wasn't allowed to be myself, and I was forced to follow certain established cultural rules which I had no say in making. I could ignore them and assert my own Jewish identity, but if I did I was bound to be rejected and isolated. I now see the popularity and acceptance which I wanted, to be the very subtle rewards that Southern society holds out to you in order to make you conform. I guess acceptance was very important to me at that age, and I chose that rather than being completely true to myself. I don't consider myself hypocritical, though. I was really too young to see what was happening to me, how the Christian South was oppressing me, and I do consider it a good sign that I was such a troublemaker. I'm not just trying to justify myself when I say that my defiance of school rules and my surly, disrespectful behavior was a kind of protest against the Christianization process that was forced on me. I'm certainly no psychologist, but I do think I was objecting to what the school and the community made me do. I do know that I was never really happy at school.

I said that this Christian oppression has actually benefited me, because I think it has helped make me much more conscious about how things like cultures, societies, and even schools, function. I've learned this by comparing my experience as a Jew in Greensboro with my experience as a political activist in Grimsley Senior High School. I see many parallels between the way I was treated as a troublemaking Jew in the ninth and tenth grades, and the way I was dealt with as an activist sounding off in the eleventh and twelfth grades. In both cases I was thought to be an outsider, an agitator, someone who *had* to be different. All of my principals since junior high school have disliked me. Two of them thought I was crazy and should be committed someplace; one of them, the principal at Page, just suggested that I go elsewhere. One thought I was crazy because I made trouble, and as I said before I think this was caused by my reluctance to conform culturally; the other thought I was crazy because I raised political issues that the school wanted to ignore. It seems obvious to me that if you don't accept everything that is imposed upon you, either in a community or in a school, then you're a "troublemaker" or you're "crazy."

During my Junior year in high school I first started to change politically. I had been asked to leave Page, and this was my first year at Grimsley. Though I had always been interested in politics, I had never been personally involved in them, and it was at this point that I started becoming more involved. A lot of my change is the result of my friendship with a certain Greensboro family. The T——'s are a very liberal family in town. In fact they were the first ones to push for school desegregation in Greensboro. My sister had known the older daughter in college, and through her I became friendly with the son, Alan. He had dropped out of college and was in the process of getting a C.O. classification from the draft board. Alan is one of the most creative people I have ever known, and I guess he started getting me politically involved. The whole family was very involved in liberal causes. They were working with poor black children and actively organizing antiwar vigils when I first met them. In the last year I've become fed up with liberalism and have become a radical, and now we can't even talk politics anymore. But at that time, two years ago, Alan and his family helped open my eyes and get me more personally committed to politics.

I did not completely approve of the Vietnam War, but I felt that since we were there we might as well support it. I even told one of the T——'s that I thought it was stupid to have antiwar vigils. But they urged me to read different things about the war, and the more I read the more I began to agree with what they were saying. The country really didn't have a need to be over there, and it seemed to be a tragic waste to kill so many American boys as well as Vietnamese families. This feeling of doubt about the war resulted from all the reading and thinking the T—— family encouraged me to do. It marked the beginning of my political change.

During my Junior year I became much more personally involved in political activities. Twice a week I helped tutor black children, and in February of that year (1968) I first stood in a peace vigil. I had become so opposed to the war that I felt obligated to stand in the vigil, but I was still scared shitless. I had never done anything like it before, and in the South it was not a small act. In Greensboro, once you cross the line you can't come back. And standing in a peace vigil is really considered radical in Greensboro. While I was standing there I kept thinking to myself, "I don't mind if that guy over there sees me, but what if someone I know comes by and sees me in the downtown vigil."

My personal involvement in politics continued after my Junior year. During the summer I was active in the McCarthy campaign and I kept working with the black kids. Then, when I returned to school and the fall, I brought my new politics with me. There was a lot of shit going on at school that I opposed, and I wanted to do something.

Grimsley just started to get a Marine ROTC program at the beginning of my Senior year. My hatred for the war had grown to such a degree that I felt anything having to do with the military was immoral and inhumane. And I thought that a MROTC program in the high school was particularly corrupt because it was used to recruit students for the war, and to give them the American Eagle Brainwash—students who would be especially impressionable when sitting in a regular school classroom listening to a so-called teacher-officer. I was totally opposed to the program, and started to organize an anti-MROTC campaign in school. But none of the other students would join with me. Those who were interested in changing the school were more concerned with the Honor Society than with MROTC I was alone, and I really wasn't able to get much accomplished. I made up some hand-written anti-MROTC posters and put them on the walls, but they were taken down right away. Try as I did, that movement died almost before it began, at least as far as the other students were concerned. But my attempt to make an issue out of MROTC was not lost on the administration.

Someone must have told the principal that I had put up the anti-MROTC posters on the walls. I was called down to see him in his office, and we had a long argument about MROTC and the war. I was dealing with an ex-Marine, and regardless of what I said he answered by saying, "Richard, you just can't trust them communists." That's the whole thing. That's where he stood, and that's where all "liberals" stand as well. He didn't give a damn about what the war and MROTC programs were doing to young people like myself. I kept telling him that they're now teaching us to kill in high school, they're teaching us to kill right underneath the auditorium. What kind of shit is this? The whole country's going military. I kept trying to tell him what the whole thing implies: that they now have mini-MROTC, that there's green in our schools, and that high school students are now marching and shooting guns. Physically they might not be going to Vietnam, but physically they are promoting this terrible war and the military nature of this country. And they are extending the military to younger and younger levels. Fifteen-year-old kids now pick up guns. But all this talk was wasted. The principal was more worried about "trusting the communists," than about corrupting the minds of young high school students.

I should have known that the principal was going to be rigid about the military. But what I'm sorry about now is that I didn't join MROTC myself and then work from the inside to abolish it. I would have been in a much better position to talk to the kids in it and possibly organize some kind of mass effort against it. Also I would have learned a lot of things. If I had been in MROTC I would know how to clean a gun in the dark, how to pull it apart and clean it without even looking, and also how to shoot properly. Because I didn't want to be associated with it in any way, I didn't learn any of these things. They would be good to know.

I didn't do anything else politically at school during the fall and early winter; not until February. The war was still going on, MROTC was operating in full force at school, and I decided that we, as students, had to do something to show where we stood. Whether or not we opposed the war and the military didn't really matter because we hadn't done anything. So I decided that we should have a peace vigil at school. I decided on Monday; I went around and talked to a lot of kids, and we organized it for Wednesday lunch time.

But before we even had it, all hell broke lose. Wednesday morning came and teachers were up in arms about it; angry parents were already calling the school to complain. Everyone knew that I was responsible for the planned vigil, so the principal called me down to his office first period, second period, and third period. For over three hours he yelled at me and threatened me. It was just like the old days in ninth and tenth grades. He even accused me of working with some international communist plot to overthrow high school principals. Really incredible things. Fourth period, just before the vigil was to begin, he started pleading with me. He begged me not to go through with the demonstration, saying that politics had no place in the school, that this kind of thing belonged "in the streets, not in a school where you are supposed to learn." I seemed to be in a strong bargaining position, but I knew that was not true. I asked for the abolition of MROTC in exchange for my cancelling the peace vigil, but I knew that he would never do it. He didn't. So I refused to cancel the vigil, and it was held.

It was held from 1:00 to 1:30. Forty of us, and my mother (she got pissed at the principal) stood there silently in the front of the school to protest the war, but from the way things looked you'd think we were preparing to kill someone. There were cops all around, and the whole school was looking out windows at us. The MROTC guys at first didn't know what to do, but after yelling at us they started to circle and threaten us. The assistant principal

came over and stood between us so there was no violence.
The vigil came off very well, but I was suspended for the
rest of the day. It was funny to me, because it was just like
when I was a real troublemaker in the ninth and tenth
grades. All the principals know how to deal with kids who
mess up, have fights, or even skip school and get drunk.
These are the kinds of things they can understand, because
they probably did them when they were younger. But politics in the high school is brand new to them, and they don't
seem to know how to treat someone who acts politically in
the school. My principal couldn't identify with me, or try to
talk things out. He could just punish me, and that's what he
did.

But he didn't stop me or any of the other students at
Grimsley who were interested in peace. From then on 'till
the end of the year in May we had a peace vigil every
Wednesday during the lunch hour. The principal tried to
suppress us by reading rules over the loudspeaker about
how it was illegal in North Carolina to disrupt school and
that guilty people could be sent to jail. But we knew we
were not disrupting school at all, and therefore continued to
have them. In fact, to make sure we were not breaking any
law, I went to the Police Department and got a permit; from
then on we held the vigils off school property on the public
sidewalk next to it. The American Civil Liberties Union
had heard about my being suspended, and was now representing me. The ACLU is pretty powerful in Greensboro,
and from then on the principal was afraid to do anything as
unconstitutional as suspending me for organizing the vigils.
Students do have a right to demonstrate their political beliefs as long as they don't interfere with the normal functions of the school. We weren't interfering with anything,
and we were doing what we as students could do about the
war. The principal knew that he would lose the case if he
punished or interfered with us again, so he just left us alone
during the remaining vigils.

But these vigils were unusual and thus they were unpopular in the community. So while we were still permitted to

carry on the vigils, we were treated like outlaws. For a month I wasn't allowed to go to my Geography class. The teacher even told me that I was being kept out not only for what I had done, but for what I believed and said in class. Anyone who opposed the war was a communist in his eyes, and he didn't want any "communists" in his class. I was also known at the police station. I was there to pay a ticket one time and this cop I had never seen before came over and said, "Cohen, what are you doing now?" They all thought that I was a member of SDS and that they were behind the vigils. No one believes that high school students are capable of doing anything by themselves. They also thought that I was an "agitator" bent on making trouble. There happened to be student strikes at the Greensboro branch of the University of North Carolina just about this time. I did have a part-time job there, but it was pure coincidence. I had nothing to do with the student strike, but no one in Greensboro would believe that. There were two FBI agents who followed me. I used to ride my bike home at night, and when I passed a certain place they'd come out in their car and follow me home. They'd sit around for a few minutes and then leave. This, in addition to tapping my phone, shows that they all felt pretty threatened by my politics. And what was I doing? I was just demonstrating for peace. But I sure dug the trouble I was causing.

The MROTC assembly marked the end of my political activity at Grimsley High School. There is an assembly at the end of the year to honor the MROTC. For a week before the assembly I was called down to the principal's office almost every day. He kept saying that he didn't want anything to happen during the assembly and that if something did he would kick me out of school and wouldn't give me my diploma. He didn't scare me because by this time I didn't really care that much about the diploma. The assembly was held in the stadium, and I went up there with over one thousand anti-MROTC leaflets, ready to pass them out. But they were ready for me, and I got kicked off the campus with the leaflets. I put the leaflets away and just went into the assembly, along with the forty other students who wanted to demonstrate. We all wore black armbands. Several of us refused to stand when they sang "The Star-Spangled Banner," and another student and I walked out just when the principal was about to speak. I got in trouble for that.

What I saw outside showed me more than anything else how little political freedom high school students have. Standing outside the stadium were eighteen cops with helmets and clubs, several police wagons, and all kinds of riot equipment. It was really strange to see all that at my own school. It was the first time it had happened in the high school. Seeing all the cops there to stop protests got me really mad, and I went and got leaflets and handed them out in front of the school. I then was told to get off the street, and threatened with arrest. I knew I was in the right, and I could have made a case out of it, but I decided not to.

They were other school protests in Greensboro at the end of the year. There was a lot of trouble at the black high school, Dudley, which ended in riots. The National Guard occupied the city for four days—with helicopters, tanks, and the works. An MROTC assembly was cancelled at another high school because of me. Later, when I put out a petition demanding that the National Guard get out of the schools and the city, I was threatened with arrest for inciting to riot.

I did receive my diploma from Grimsley High School, though, I didn't really have enough credits to graduate, but they wanted me out so they gave me a diploma. I was a "troublemaker" they'd had enough of.

The United States of America is a bunch of shit. All the institutions you come in contact with fuck you up; families, schools, and the government put you into categories and packages. They don't let you be yourself. By the time you reach five years old you can't show natural emotions. You're so manipulated that an honest relationship with yourself is impossible.

What it all boils down to is that you have to attempt to control your own destiny. You have to use yourself as your first, middle, and last security, depend on yourself, and have confidence. YOU ARE THE REVOLUTION (from Abbie). You have to learn to share, to be free—competing doesn't mean shit. The American way puts you down for running away from problems, and tells you that you waste time if you don't do what it tells you to do—like go to college or have a job. I'm out of high school and I'm not in college, and I don't feel bad about sleeping late . . . the sun is warm in California. There's this funny idea that radicals can't be happy, or smile, or enjoy themselves.

The Movement is changing. At this point the New Left is very old. It's mostly made up of civil rights workers and college heavies with their words: "Support Someone Else's Struggle." SDS is an example of this. It supports all black, brown, and Third World struggles, and says white people aren't oppressed. I think we are all oppressed. The new Movement I'm talking about has started in the high schools. It is made up of kids who turn on to their own trouble. They want to start an underground paper, print a leaflet, start their own classes, and demonstrate, and they get shit for it. For me the Movement was a change from anti-authority and misbehavior to political issues and political misbehavior. The mistake that I made was equating what I was doing politically with intellectual ideas. That is wrong. When eighteen riot-equipped cops come to a high school ROTC assembly because one kid threatened to pass out one thousand leaflets, there's nothing intellectual about it. It's just plain trouble. I didn't have to read Marx to find out that something was wrong. I looked at my teachers, the President, the alienation of two hundred million people afraid to walk out at night, over a million Vietnamese dead, 137 brands of underarm deodorant, and last but not least at my parents, to find my own oppression.

When people turn on to their own oppression they can relate to other struggles without paternalism or liberal bullshit. Your politics and your life style have to be the same: the way you eat, sleep, talk, fart, love. Becoming a revolutionary means changing your whole life, not just your politics.

After I moved into the High School Commune in New York City, I realized that I never really made a friend in high school. I said "hi" and smiled to a lot of people, but it never meant anything. When I moved into the Commune I started opening up to people, and I said things that I had not said to my psychiatrist in four years of visits. One of the things that happened was that I started talking in "we's" instead of "I's." It's great working collectively.

I think the technology that the United States and the world have at this point could give every child, woman, and man a decent place to live, good food to eat, more time for creativity, and a world in which men control machines. Right now machines are controlling men. Ralph Nader proved that two cars going 50 m.p.h. could hit head-on without injuring anybody, if certain changes were made. But General Motors and Ford still make unsafe cars that break down every three years so you have to buy a new one. Tires work the same way. They could be made almost perfect so there'd be no flats or blowouts. But corporations get richer while fifty to seventy-five thousand people die on American roads every year. Capitalism must go, by any means necessary.

When it does go, the next step will be to divide up the control of this society among the people. We have to smash a system that controls people's lives. We should be able to enjoy life.

In closing, let me say that I really love all of you; read Abbie Hoffman's book; if there is another Woodstock, go to it; and enjoy life.

Love and Changing,
RICHARD COHEN

V

JUNIOR HIGH RADICALS

The protests occurring in high schools have surprised teachers, principals, and parents alike. Rebellious students have become commonplace on college campuses, but high school students have been traditionally docile, obedient, and silent. Where, the adults ask, did all these active, radical students come from?

Many of the high school radicals are themselves the formerly silent. They have become radicals just recently, after looking at their schools, their country, and their world. But conversion to radicalism in high school may not be the trend for long, since future high school students, those now in junior high, are also becoming radical. Seventh graders participate in antiwar demonstrations. And eighth and ninth graders are protesting the conditions in their schools.

What is it that leads twelve- and thirteen-year-olds to rebel? Are they merely imitating the actions of their older brothers and friends, or do they think for themselves? What do they think? Joshua Mamis and Jim Gardiner of New York City answer these questions. Joshua spoke into the tape recorder, and Jim wrote his statement.

V

JUNIOR HIGH RADICALS

The Right to Petition at Eleven

by Joshua Mamis

> *Joshua Mamis is a twelve-year-old student at I.S. 44 in New York City. He made history last year by filing a suit in federal court for the right to petition in his school. His whole family is involved in radical political activity, and Joshua is supported in his actions by his parents.*

I am twelve years old and am in the seventh grade. I go to Intermediate School 44 in New York City. I'm not really happy at the school. I had pretty good teachers my first year there, but off and on other things there would really get on my nerves. For one thing, we have "silent passing" in the school. Every morning between homeroom and first period, and every afternoon between last period and homeroom, we have to walk through the halls without opening our mouths. We have to be perfectly quiet. Every once in a while at the end of the day the principal gets on the loudspeaker and says, "That silent passing was terrible. I want you to go back to your other classes and do it again." He did things like this every once in a while. It wasn't even that we were too noisy at silent passing; probably he was just annoyed with someone else and wanted to take it out on us. He really seemed to punish us unnecessarily. You can't expect kids to be quiet at the end of the day anyway, especially in the early spring and late fall when we've been cooped up in a hot school all day.

We had regular school for two days between the first and second teachers' strikes, and that's when I saw how the principal acted. The second day he told us that the "silent passing" was terrible. The silent passing may have been terrible, but what does that have to do with anything else? You come to school to learn, not to learn how to shut your mouth and walk in the hall. That got me really mad. And during the strike he joined the teachers in closing the school. I remember seeing him in the building. He wouldn't open the doors. He finally just got out of the building, ran to his car, and left. He didn't show up again.

We eventually did get the doors open. A school was set up by the teachers who broke the strike, and we had a really nice guy become acting principal. Nelson Harris, who had been just a regular science teacher before, went down to the superintendent's office and got permission to be the acting principal. For the next six weeks, until the strike ended, he was principal. The school was really nice. It wasn't just because there weren't as many kids and the school wasn't overcrowded or anything. It was just nice. Hardly anything went wrong. The day went smoothly, and we didn't get things over the loudspeaker like, "Do that silent passing again. It was terrible."

After the strike was over we got back the regular principal. He went right back to his old ways: "silent passing" and other things. He just refused to listen to anything. A girl went in to him with a petition to wear slacks, and he told her to "get out of the office," he "was busy right now." There were things like that. And the "O" period. The "O" period was the extra period which kids who had stayed out during the strike could use to make up the time lost. It was part of the strike settlement. The "O" period was held in the morning, before school usually opened, and you didn't have to go if you didn't want to. In our school there are the front doors, some stairs, and then the doors leading to the main office. The kids who weren't going to the "O" period had to wait in between those two doors, and there were about five hundred kids who weren't going. Five hundred kids had to be squeezed into about a 3 x 5 yard area. Half the kids ended up outside because they couldn't fit in, and in winter they'd freeze out there. The principal could have let us into the auditorium. No one was using the auditorium this early in the morning. I think he was just punishing us for having come in during the strike. He's that kind of principal. A few kids went into his office and asked him, "Why can't we use the auditorium? No one's using the auditorium in the morning. It's as easy as just letting us in." He said, "Well, we have some people rehearsing in the auditorium in the morning." I know that isn't true, because the auditorium is locked every morning when I walk in. And the lights are out. How could anyone be in there? The principal just makes excuses, as well as giving orders. He gives us all this stuff and says, "Here, do it. Just don't ask any questions, and do it."

When I saw how the principal acted after the strike, I decided to continue something I had started earlier. This regular principal wasn't too good (to say the least), and the principal we had during the strike was really good. During the strike I had begun this, but I felt I'd wait until things calmed down. But the regular principal was not improving by refusing to listen to this pants' thing of the girls, and there was the "O" period problem—so I decided to carry on with my petition.

I was just trying to see how many people in the school also thought the principal we had during the strike was better than the principal we had regularly. I didn't really think to myself at the time that maybe this petition is going to get me somewhere. I wasn't really trying to get our principal kicked out and knocked away. I typed up a petition. It said that:

> We the students of I.S. 44 think that we need a change in principal. Mr. Harris our acting principal during the teacher strike has done such a good job during the strike

that I think he should be our permanent principal. Sign
hear [sic] if you think so.

There were lines for kids' signatures. During the strike, at
lunch time, I went around to different tables asking kids if
they'd like to sign the petition. Kids did. Kids didn't. Kids
said I was crazy.

After the strike ended I decided to quit it for a week
until things got back to normal because there was so much
tension. As I said, the principal didn't improve, and if
anything he got worse. So I started again, and went around
to different tables during lunchtime. One lunchtime, a
friend of mine came up and said that he knew of a table
where there were a few kids who wanted to sign the petition
and could he go over there and have them sign it. I said,
"Sure," and I took out the petition and gave him a pen. He
went over to the table and got the kids to sign it, and just
then our assistant principal came over and asked him
whose idea this was. He told her that it was mine.

The next period, directly after lunch, she had the guidance counsellor call me into her office. Our regular principal was sitting at the desk, and he started asking me all
kinds of questions. Things like, "Here I am, you've only had
me for a month. How do you know what I'm going to be
doing?" He started saying all these things to me, like, "How
dare you," and stuff—trying, I guess, to scare me. I must
admit it was a little frightening. I had never been shouted at
like that before. He also took away the petition. It only had
about one hundred names on it at this point. Unfortunately
I hadn't really gone too far with it. I had only covered our
grade, and about three or four people from the other
grades. That's all. I'm just wondering how many more sign-
ers I would have had. The principal went on to say that I
had no right to do this. He said, "If you weren't a minor I'd
sue you." He also said that he might sue my parents. I kept
my mouth shut because I didn't want to make things worse.
But I just kept thinking to myself, I do have a right to do
this. What's he telling me that I don't for?

When I got home my mother was there. Nelson Harris, the other principal, had called her at her office and told her what had happened. The regular principal thought that Nelson Harris, who had returned to being a science teacher, had put me up to this. This wasn't the case at all. He had seen the petition, because I thought he should see it before it was circulated, but I guess he thought it wouldn't be taken seriously. I wasn't calling for the principal to be fired or anything, but I was serious. I did want to find out if other kids felt the same way I did about the regular principal. The principal also felt, and I think still does, that my mother encouraged me to write the petition. She helped keep I.S. 44 open during the strike, and has generally been against the administration of the school. He may hold her and Nelson responsible, but it was really my idea. I don't want to sound like I'm bragging, but they had nothing to do with it.

My mother really got mad at the principal, I remember that. She got angry when she heard that he had yelled at me and had been so mean to me. She thought he shouldn't have treated me that way. I do too. When she got home she immediately tried to call the principal to discuss it with him. He wasn't around so she called the district superintendent and asked if he would investigate. Later, my father reached the principal and tried to discuss what had happened with him. It was impossible. The principal refused to discuss it, and said that I had no right to do what I did. He also asked my father if "he knew what kind of son he had?"

Afterwards, my mother called a lawyer and asked if we had legal rights to sue the principal; not only for the way he treated me but because he took away the petition. The lawyer said yes. The principal, by taking away my petition, violated my First Amendment right—the right to free speech. We sued him, and the case is still going on. The Corporation Council of the City, which handles Board of Education cases, wanted to settle it out of court. The way our lawyer explained it, an offer to settle meant that they thought we were right. The settlement was unacceptable to our lawyers, because the settlement would mean only that "Joshua Mamis may circulate a petition." We felt that we may as well make it a case for all students, not just me. Children do have the right to petition, even against their principals, and I'm sure we'll win. In the meantime, however, my principal was kicked upstairs—possibly as a result of this—and we had a new principal for the second half of the year.

The reaction on the part of my teachers to the court case was very interesting. Most of them came up to me and said, "Good luck." Even one of my teachers who didn't come in during the strike and who felt very strongly about the strike made a special point to come up and wish me, "Good luck." I guess maybe they feel that students do have the right to free speech in school and are on our side. I had one or two teachers, however, who didn't say anything to me and who you could tell thought I was crazy. I don't know whether this is true or a rumor but one of my friend's teachers supposedly said to the whole class that she thought I needed a psychiatrist.

A lot of the students didn't like what I did. I think that's because their parents told them that I was crazy. They never came up to me and started screaming at me or telling me that I was disgusting or anything like that; they just booed me when I came up to speak about running for second vice president. It didn't bother me that much.

In addition to the "silent passing" thing, there are a lot of silly rules at my school. You can only cross the halls at the arrows that are marked on the floor, and you only have a minute and a half to get to your next class. You have a minute and a half to get from one end of the school to the other, and you're not allowed to run. Some of us had a schedule which gave us a class on the ground floor, then a class on the third floor, and then another class on the ground floor. Our teacher on the ground floor was all right, and he let us go a minute early. Even then we'd get to the class just on time. The late bell would ring just as we got there. But the teacher up there often held us in a minute because we got so noisy saying, "Can you let us out a minute early? We have another class on the ground floor and it's going to be as hard as anything getting down there." She'd say, "No, and another peep out of you and you're staying in another minute." She'd finally let us go, and by the time we'd get down there everyone would be marked late. And the teacher down there didn't help it any by saying, "Three lates is a cutting card." The teachers send the cutting cards to the office; with three cutting cards you get suspended from school for five days. Everyone in the class probably had at least two lates on them, even though we always ran up and down the stairs as fast as we could go.

For lunch we have a little over half an hour. During the winter you have to stay inside for the entire time. It's really not such a large cafeteria, but we have to stay there with all the noise and the flying food. The only way you're allowed out of the cafeteria is if you have a library pass. During the spring and fall you have to stay in the school yard. (In the fall of 1969, students were allowed out for lunch.) We're always on the school property, we're always under the school's rules, and we don't have one free period during the whole day to do what we want to do: go outside, get some candy or something. We can't do anything. There was a campaign on the part of many of the students to win the right to leave school property during lunch time. This was defeated however. The principals prohibited the kids from leaving because they were afraid they'd all cut, that they'd just leave school and not come back. Well so many of the kids are bored in their classes that they cut anyway. They play tag in the halls, they go in the bathroom to smoke, or they leave school through the holes in the fence. I'd say that well over a third of the students in the school cut regularly. The cutting increases as you go up in grade. As you get used to the school you learn how to get away with cutting without being caught.

Many kids cut because the classes are really boring. Some of the teachers just put stuff on the board and make the kids do half an hour of writing. You usually get about fifteen minutes of learning and thirty minutes of copying. Some teachers only say maybe one or two words in the whole period: "Shut up!" I was lucky to have fairly good teachers this year, but that's rare. My homeroom teacher next year has the reputation for being one of the worst teachers in the school. She's supposed to be really boring, and she's known as a "writer." She puts stuff on the board, says, "Copy it!" and then sits down at her desk to read the paper. When you have a good teacher, a class is really interesting. But when you have a "writing" teacher, you might as well fall asleep at your seat.

I'd say that a little more than two-thirds of the students in I.S. 44 are bored. That's why so many kids throw food during the lunch hour. The food stinks anyway, so if it's too bad to eat they might as well throw it. You end up getting hit in the head with applesauce every day. The kids don't know why they're doing it. They just do it for excitement, because they have a whole day of boring classes. Everyone laughs when someone gets hit with applesauce. You need some excitement in a school like this.

Even the kids who don't cut or throw food in the lunchroom are bored. These often are the kids who are brought up just to sit, take what's given them, and not ask any questions. They've been taught by their parents to listen to their teachers and to obey all the stupid rules. They don't really like the school, but they just do it because they're scared to do anything else. Even they might start cutting and throwing food in a while when they get really fed up. I'm fed up already.

I'm not really looking forward to going back to school. I have freedom now, and you don't have any freedom at that school. I sometimes wonder why I go.

Growing Up Radical

by Jim Gardiner

Jim Gardiner is a thirteen-year-old Sophomore at New York City's prestigious Bronx High School of Science. A brilliant student, he went through a three-year junior high school in two years. He lives in Morningside Heights, that part of New York's Upper West Side that borders on Harlem. His father is a Professor of Literature at a near-by women's college. Jim has been active in political demonstrations since he was eight. In October he was with the Weathermen in Chicago.

I live at 121st Street and Amsterdam Avenue in Manhattan, four blocks from both Harlem and Columbia University. Here I have lived since I was eight, in the summer of 1964—through riots, droughts, boycotts, strikes, snowstorms; through long, hot years and short, cool ones.

The immediate neighborhood is a pattern of small grocery stores, bookstores, and bars. Morningside Heights, as the area is known, is torn between the two extremes of America: the affluent and the poor, the cultured and the deprived, the overeducated and the subliterate. Each new construction seems to push it one way or the other, but every June the students leave and Harlem is victorious. Harlem, it seems, will always be victorious, for it is a huge, black constant, unchanging, eternal. It has survived the promises of liberals and conservatives alike, the rampages of police, and the actions of radicals, wars and peace. It bears silent testimony to the guilt of the white man.

Just up the street from my home is the Riverside Church. Riverside is a Protestant, non-sectarian, largely white church. Here Martin Luther King spoke, and here James Forman delivered his Manifesto. There aren't many black people among the congregation. Sundays, they are to be found at the local Baptist, Methodist, and Lutheran churches. The community meets under these circumstances for catharsis and to retain hope.

Religion is an integral part of Harlem, as it is of most black ghettoes. For many years the black clergyman has had a strong influence on his parish, been ignored by the white Establishment, and must now be reckoned with. I spent three years at Public School 125, which is still 15 percent white, 50 percent black, and 35 percent Puerto Rican. To be white in a black school would be frightening to many, I suppose, but I was not frightened. At eight, I entered the fourth grade of P.S. 125. That was in the fall of '64, immediately after the first major ghetto riot in decades, in Harlem. Nearly all of the faculty was white, largely Jewish, and in most cases scared.

Even at that early stage in urban education, racism had been perpetuated. Tests had been given determining which students would be placed in the ostensibly smarter classes and given the benefit of the best teachers in the school, and which students would be placed in the inferior classes, consigned from the first to an educational career doomed to repeated failure, frustration, and a future as black as their skin. Typically, these tests concentrated on reading comprehension, vocabulary, and word usage. The wording of the selections and problems was directed solely to pupils with the background of a middle-class white, leaving blacks and Puerto Ricans, culturally deprived by White America, in a position of apparent ignorance. How can a child to whom words like "banker," "phonograph," "painting," or "airline" are mere imaginings possibly contend with children whose parents can spare the time to help educate them?

My black classmates exhibited no prejudice toward me, nor do I feel that the teachers favored me visibly because of my race. Rather, the length of my hair (very long for that period) caused me to be hounded and teased incessantly. The faculty, good Americans all, seized upon every opportunity available to insult, embarrass, and downgrade me on the basis of my "haircut." This placed me in a situation similar, if more individualistic, to that of the black kids. My well-being was handled with the same disinterest, my education treated with the same lack of care, my future plotted with the same boredom.

To my eternal discredit, I contradicted the carefully formulated plans of the system for me by exhibiting signs of intelligence, that most dangerous of diseases among the masses. I remember commenting in fourth grade that the stories in our *Dick and Jane* reading book, a never-ending saga of a WASP family growing up straight, conservative, and thoroughly indoctrinated, were propaganda. This being true, and incontestably so, the teacher intimated that it was good propaganda, designed benevolently to instruct us gradually. Bullshit, I proclaimed then; and, five years later, bullshit I proclaim still.

In those days, the formative years of decentralization, one of the first battles for community control took place. During the 1966–1967 term, the Parent's Association of the elementary school, having broken off negotiations with the Board of Education, declared a boycott of all grades until the Board, as repeatedly promised, would allow the community to choose four candidates for principal, with the superintendent of schools retaining the final decision. One-third of the faculty and eighteen hundred of the school's two thousand pupils participated in the boycott, and many of them attended the Liberation School set up at the Riverside Church. I dug the free spirit of learning that was the medium of expression there. When both teacher and student are involved in a common protest, the gap between them is easier to bridge; and simply by virtue of our presence we all had made a commitment to ourselves and to our community.

Liberation School was taught by many of the regular teachers, sympathetic Columbia and Barnard students, and by parents. The community was very much into this scene; food was provided cheaply, gym facilities offered, materials donated, and people involved.

Eventually, the boycott was successful, and we went back. Reluctantly, I returned to a world where knowledge was a lifeless, stagnant mass of impersonal data, where human students are mere receptacles for the prejudices of whomever has been selected to instruct them.

The community of Harlem, or more specifically, Manhattanville, is extremely difficult to become familiar with. I have lived for five years within it, spent three full terms at one of its elementary schools, played in its playgrounds, and shopped in its stores. The people there are those one reads about in Riot Commission reports, front page stories in newspapers, third-rate novels, and books by urban sociologists. We are bombarded by a stream of misinformation and analysis; the words of men who have forgotten what it means to live in a ghetto, or in the shadow of one.

Our cities are dying, New York is crumbling; yet Harlem is not unlike a dormant volcano, which erupts as soon as his flame is forgotten, his rage ignored, his torment unlessened. Rats and cockroaches don't please suburban Americans, so they change the channel when the conditions in the ghettoes come up; when reports are given of children who cannot learn because their teachers are on strike, not teaching, and not interested; when pictures of looting, rioting, burning, and the rubble are shown. They change the channel because Harlem, Watts, Roxbury, Detroit, Cleveland, Miami, Flint, Bedford-Stuyvesant, and Ocean Hill-Brownsville are America's asshole. White America brought the black man in chains from Africa, subjected him to 250 years of slavery, preyed upon his illiteracy, terrorized him in his so-called freedom, denied him his manhood, refused him his rights, and sentenced him to virtual economic slavery.

Every American President until Lincoln owned slaves, and every one since has played politics with the rights of black people. Less than twenty years ago the U.S. government sanctioned by its silence (and until 1954 used none of the institutions at its command to condemn) the open, public, and state-empowered discrimination against and segregation of blacks in the deep South.

Racism in our institutions, no matter how deeply it runs, can and must be uprooted—even if the institutions must be uprooted with it. Black people will have their rights, or we shall level the earth in our attempts to get them.

Not quite three blocks from Union Square in Manhattan, there is a squat, four-story building, looking as if it didn't have the money to retire in Florida and is therefore condemned to the fortunes of summer, rain, and snow on a New York City sidestreet. Every four months or so, its environs are breached by a horde of students, radicals, revolutionaries, G.I.'s, and perennial volunteers. On the third floor is the office of the Fifth Avenue Peace Parade Committee.

Sometime in the early spring of 1969, perhaps in that very office, the Peace Parade Committee decided that it was time to remind Nixon of his extensive promises of peace in Vietnam, and to remind the American public that despite soothing words from the President and his Cabinet, talks in Paris, and a lull in the fighting, Vietnam had recently exceeded the War of Independence and become the longest continuously-fought war in the nation's history, and that 33,000 U.S. soldiers had died and were continuing to die at the rate of 150 and 200 a week. April 5 was appointed the date of the demonstration, and permits for a march up Sixth Avenue and a rally in Central Park were obtained.

At about 9:00 A.M. on a Saturday morning at the end of the third week in March, I walked out of the Union Square subway station to the Committee's headquarters. Mark, a coordinator of volunteer activity, put me to work as soon as I had stashed my jacket and made some coffee. I was assigned to a folding machine: feeding leaflets in, stacking them as they came out folded in half, and placing the stacks in boxes. The next day, there was more work—stuffing, sealing, and stamping envelopes.

It is my experience that a successful march is made not by the publicity it is given, but by the people working it and shaping it, by their activism and their attitude. A march or a demonstration is a beautiful, esthetic entity: it can be a fair, fickle woman, lovely in expectation, orgastic at its frenzied peak, and feminine in its acceptance of failure. It is a thing of beauty for a single instant.

With vivid memory I recall that spring of '69, memory mixed fondly with nostalgia. Then, like the Movement, I was at a political crossroad: poised uncertainly at a point somewhere between liberalism and radicalism, wary of either course; almost afraid, whether of a wrong decision or of my very indecision in the face of what I was sure must be an obvious choice, I know not.

Working, and working hard, as I did, precluded active pursuit of this eventual choice. Morally committed to efficient performance of my functions as a marshal, I found a substitute for ideological dogmatism in blind faith. Faith, that is, not in some forgery of duly constituted authority, but rather in those who labored for my own ideals with a positive sense of conviction in their tactics.

It was not quite early spring. Eating, sleeping, laughing, working—somehow each of these acts fit in with the March we were shaping—as if creating a painting on a blank canvas. Our canvas was a shameful awareness within America, the solemn knowledge of Vietnam. By exhortation, publication, education, and constant reminder, we must extract the painful guilt of America-Vietnam.

April 5 at 5:00 A.M. I awoke, dressed, and left, as dawn rose over Harlem outside my window. Walking through Union Square at six, tired and cold, past the sleeping statues, the weary buildings, I thought, finally, of myself. Of the six years I had before I came of draft age, of the war, and of peace.

The Central Park bandshell, under a drizzle, echoed with the sounds of the first few marshals rigging sound systems, pinning on the yellow armbands that were our only identification, ignoring the many uniformed policemen and the few undercover detectives, briefing each other on assignments, contingents, and responsibilities, and eating quietly. We ate matzoh and drank a good deal of coffee, joked a little bit, and replied with the laughs of guerrillas before an action. The park filled up slowly, until there were one hundred of us, carefully hoisting speakers to the tops of telephone poles, inflating huge balloons, unloading microphones, placards, and bullhorns from the van containing the borrowed equipment.

My group commander assigned me to Contingent G, which formed in Forty-third Street at Sixth Avenue. After about an hour and a half of waiting for the other groups to go by, we moved out. As I walked, keeping the pace orderly and uniform, watching out for attacks by right-wing fascists, doing the countless things a good marshal must do simultaneously, I was aware of the political decision facing me being made, almost on a subconscious level, by an entity which was not quite me.

Here were thousands of people with a massive potential for revolutionary action passively marching in docile submission to the limitations set by the power structure. Rather than offer violent resistance to the fascist, imperialist pigs whose malevolent acts perpetrated poverty, fear, and death on masses of oppressed people, they marched pointlessly past scores of policemen bordering their path. Yet I was one of them; I presumed to lead them. The total futility of mere nonviolent demonstration became clear. The rain came down, baptizing me. I was a radical.

Those of us within the public schools of large cities such as New York who are radically inclined have often encountered some form of obstruction and administrative interference, be it over matters of hair-length, attire, publicly expressed opinions, leaflets, petitions, or injustice. We strain to move aside the dead weight of authority blocking our path, but are either overcome by the bureaucracy, or are forced to use violent means.

When I was eleven, I entered the first half of a two-year Special Progress program at Intermediate School 44, Manhattan. Since I had just come out of the sixth grade at P.S. 125, the prospect of entering tenth grade in two years— provided I passed both terms—was an entertaining one; at the time I was sold on intellectualism as the ultimate trip. I.S. 44 was a cool school from this standpoint; it had a few excellent teachers, whom the office naturally assigned to the smartest, furthest advanced, S.P. classes. These Special Progress classes were almost completely white, the system having done its job of segregation well. The school had five different levels, or "tracks," ranging from the S.P. X track down through A, B, C, and D. Predictably, the lower the track, the higher the proportion of non-white students. Apathy dominated the scene, along with the burgeoning social awareness of adolescence.

The teacher strike of Fall 1968, affected us in a weird way. About half of the faculty stayed out, and the rest attempted a reasonable facsimile of normal operation. Not many students showed up, but this lack was more advantageous than detrimental, for in effect it served to weed out the motivated pupils from those who came simply because it was required of them.

Emotion over the strike ran high; animosity between the union teachers and the "strike-breakers" was continual. This polarization left its scars on the rest of the year; when an extended session was proclaimed by the Board of Education, a number of faculty members refused to participate in it on the ground that they had put in the required extra time during the two-month strike. The racial connotations of a work stoppage called by a primarily white, Jewish union against a black and Puerto Rican community are strong, so that it was a tense, uneasy peace which overhung 44.

During the 1968–1969 term, I became engaged in an effort to obtain administrative permission for the student body to exercise a basic right: leaving the physical school grounds during lunch. We also requested amnesty for five students who had done so contrary to official policy and had been threatened with suspension when caught. We formed an ad hoc Action Committee, printed and circulated leaflets, set up a meeting with the principal, and drew up a petition which was signed by one hundred members of the eighth grade. A nucleus of natural, unappointed leaders coalesced—which sounds very romantic, almost divinely inspired, until one considers that no one else gave a damn enough to lead what was mostly a group of uninterested faddists.

Our little quintet of leaders met briefly with the principal, and we were unenthusiastically told off. The threats of suspension were silently dropped, and another meeting scheduled; the Lone Ranger had ridden again. No mention was made of our grievances, nor of the possibility of instituting a non-captive lunch, a promise which had been made and broken on many occasions in the past.

I recall a very good friend of mine, a Mr. D—— of the Social Studies Department, voicing, among his praise and approval of our actions, an emotion which neighbored on awe but retained a degree of wariness. He is ideologically from that portion of his generation which has, after the diversion, patronizations, and eventual failure of the New Frontier crusades, at last yielded in principle to the ruling powers. Their philosophy died in Mississippi with Evers, in Dallas with Kennedy, in Nashville with King, and in L.A. with Bobby. They are morally afraid to become radical, too young to be conservative, and too "progressive" to be liberal. The immediate successes of radical youth in provoking change and drawing attention to its causes alienate these people and make them unpleasantly aware of their ages. These are the people who will be forced to stand with or against the oppressed masses when the revolution comes

For the second time, we met with representatives of the

administration in a vain attempt to persuade them that our program was a valid one. They gave us one week to design a foolproof, inexpensive plan for the entry and exit of students under a non-captive lunch, one in which they might go home for the meal or remain at school. With late hours, a lot of sweat, and help from parents, we fulfilled this requirement. Then the administrative office insisted that assurances of police protection of pupils at large in the neighborhood be gotten from the precinct. The leadership made four separate visits to the police station—a place where we were unlikely to be found voluntarily. When at last we spoke with the commanding officer, he said that his men would cooperate with I.S. 44 on the program. Our beloved warden, that is, principal, was undaunted by our success; she responded by telling us that the recommendations could not be acted upon unless fifteen parents could be enlisted to act as assistants to the teachers who would be responsible for the operation. Most of the families of the students were poor, many fatherless and on welfare, and there were very few in which the parent(s) did not work. It was impossible for fifteen of these adults to spend an hour a day working in the school as volunteers.

We had asked for nothing more than a basic student right. We had outlined a simple, cheap method to operate our plan effectively. Our efforts had wound through the bureaucratic maze and resulted in police support. We had the backing of faculty, parents, and one hundred members of the Senior class. Had we taken violent action to achieve our aim, tactically impossible because of lack of sufficient numbers, we would have been justified.

The United States enslaves, oppresses, silences, and murders to extend the scope of its power, its empire. It is often an ogre, a horrific beast who will suffer not the slightest defiance, the merest of disobediences. Nowhere is this attitude more evident than in the classrooms of the nation. Colleges, universities, and public school systems are jails. The educational Establishment has the arbitrary power to fail, suspend, and expel any student with the merest of justifications.

We are segregated, forced to pray to an All-American corporate-blessing God, denied knowledge of sex and evolution, restricted in our "inalienable rights" of free speech, petition, and protest, made to conform to puritanical standards of attire and appearance, and used as pawns in petty, racist power plays. If we dare to question, or worse, to protest, our leaders are squashed and our causes banned. No longer.

The pig power structure is going up against the wall. At Berkeley, Columbia, San Francisco State, Cornell, Wisconsin, Harvard, the battle lines are being drawn. We shall be free.

The Radical-Hippie-Yippie-Black Panther-Militant-Anarchistic-Subversive-Anti-American-Ultrafanatic-New Left-Communist Infiltrated-Moscow-Peking Controlled-Drugridden-Takeover-Conspiracy-Plot, in short, the revolution, is misreported, distorted, disregarded, underestimated, and INEVITABLE.

V I

PRIVATE SCHOOLS

The protests in the public high schools of this country have received considerable publicity. Teachers have been attacked in New York City schools. Demonstrations have been staged in suburban schools. These incidents have become well known to newspaper readers and television watchers.

But what about the private schools of America? Have they remained unscarred while the public schools explode all around them? Are private school students remaining contented and still while their public school friends are up in arms? What are the conditions in the private schools of America, and what do private school students think of their country? Three private school students address themselves to these questions. A student from the prestigious Phillips Academy in Andover, Massachusetts talks about the conditions there. To prevent expulsion he must remain anonymous, and will be referred to as Thomas Doland. Paula Smith talks about the conditions in her Catholic girls' school in Chicago. She also has very definite political beliefs. Eric Oakstein, (a pseudonym), from one of New York City's finest private schools, speaks about himself and his school. All three of these students spoke into the tape recorder.

Andover: Even the Best Are Bad

by Thomas Doland

Thomas Doland (a pseudonym) is a sixteen-year-old Senior at Phillips Academy, Andover, Massachusetts. He comes from Philadelphia, where his father is a businessman. He has a younger brother who is now in the same pre-prep school Tom attended before Andover.

I'm sixteen years old. Most of my life I've lived in an apartment building in a good section of Philadelphia. My family is upper middle-class. My father is an executive officer of a company, and he went to an Ivy League college and an Ivy League law school. My first eight years of school were spent in one of the richest and most exclusive private boys' schools in Philadelphia. I was overprotected there for eight years, so I had no fears about being kicked out for anything I did. My relationship with my teachers and deans was one in which I was their friend rather than merely their pupil. Thus from an early age I was allowed to voice my political feelings in the class, regardless of how immature they were, without being seriously reprimanded. I was put in the corner or maybe sent down for a nice little chat with the headmaster. But the school protected its own; and because it was a school of affluent children, it didn't want to get them into any trouble. And it wanted to preserve its image as a school that could get you into the boarding school of your choice when you graduated from eighth grade.

I went to Andover in ninth grade, or what they call there the Junior year. My whole family comes from Andover and when it came time to choose a school, it was really between going to Andover and staying at home. I was attracted by the mystery of Andover. I knew what it was like to go to a day school, but I didn't know what it was like living at boarding school. So I went to Andover, and I am now going into my Senior year.

Andover is a large, probably the largest, prep school in New England. It has 850 students, and a large faculty of over 120. It differs from schools like Groton and St. Marks in that it accepts a large number of students from underdeveloped areas all over the world. Nevertheless it does maintain a very high tradition and a set of values which it tries to impose on all of its students. Andover's history goes back as far as 1778, from the early days of the Boston aristocracy. The Adams family, the Holmes', and George Washington all had connections with Andover, as have countless diplomats, generals, and financiers. The school still considers itself to be a training ground for America's leaders. An "Andover man" is expected to continue his education at one of the Ivy League or military schools, and eventually to carry another Andover banner into the respectable fields of law, business, or government. Returning to the school to prepare the next generation of Andover men is also acceptable of course; but it has generally been said, and I think quite truthfully, that Andover considers itself residence before Yale before Wall Street. The school's admissions policies are liberal—in that 40 percent of the students are on scholarship—but the educational policy (what Andover seeks to do with the Harlem, Park Avenue, and West Virginia students) is quite conservative. Andover tries to mold a diverse student body into its own image.

The first or second day I got there we had an assembly for all new boys to explain the extracurricular activities.

Older students represented the different extracurricular activities at Andover, and were pushing all these activities and saying, "Join this, join that." When we went back to the dorm, the first thing the housemaster said was, "Don't join anything. You're here to work, and we don't want you to join anything." That was the first thing I was told: that I shouldn't join anything. They said you had to get involved with the school first. But I didn't pay much attention and ended up joining a political union, sort of like a congress. At the end of the year my housemaster wrote on my report that it was unwise for me to have joined any extracurricular activities, and especially that one. He said when I joined it that the political group was headed by "a bunch of radicals," and that was bad for me. I could tell then that they really didn't want you to be free at Andover. They wanted you to stay in your own class and not search for yourself. Let them search for you and make you what they wanted to make you. I saw the boys in my class fall exactly in the pattern of what the school wanted them to do. That wasn't what I wanted. I sort of knew what Andover stood for, and I didn't want to be molded. I had gone there for the experience of being away from home, and I also wanted to learn from going to the school. I didn't want the school to teach me.

Because I had done well in junior high school, I had gotten into some tenth grade courses, though I was only in ninth grade. I was busy working hard in these, when after about a month or two I got mono and they put me in the infirmary for three weeks. While I was there, the school doctor urged me to drop out of the tenth grade courses and to take only ninth grade courses. He wanted me out of these courses because he thought I would be influenced by the older people in my classes. They had been there one or two years and knew what Andover was really like; and he was afraid they would turn me against it. When I got out of the infirmary I remained in the older classes. When I came out I didn't really know many of my classmates because I hadn't seen any of them for two or three weeks. That was a pretty long time since I had only been there a little more than a month. They were all formed into little cliques: all they talked about was what they had done in the dorm the night before, who had stayed up late, and what sports they were taking. I noticed that they were doing all the little things that I had envisioned as prep school life at its worst. They were all dressing in the same acceptable way—with tweed jackets and weejun shoes—and they all seemed to drool with admiration over the housemaster's every word. The housemaster himself was a product of another New England prep school and then Harvard. His return to the prep school life without any interim experience on the outside, epitomized the limited background of most Andover headmasters. He was, as you might expect, quite narrow-minded, to the point where he would refer to the local citizens of Andover as "townies," different from "we up here on the hill." Though I considered him hardly worthy of respect, he had succeeded in winning the esteem of most of my dorm-mates. Uncritical respect for housemasters was also an expected Andover reaction.

The separation of the younger students from the older ones, which the doctor was aiming for with his advice, is done so the new boys will be more susceptible to Andover's indoctrination. It's easier to convince impressionable Juniors (ninth graders) of something if there aren't any "cynical" upper classmen around to contradict. Physically, most of the Junior dormitories are isolated from the upper class dorms, and the Juniors are separated in other ways as well. Juniors can only participate in sports with other Juniors. Everybody else is eligible for the Varsity in every sport, but no matter how good they are, the Juniors can only play on the Junior teams. Sports is a big thing at Andover, and they want to get all the Juniors together in this area so they can start shaping them. Start shaping them in the Andover way. The assistant headmaster actually came over to me once to say that he didn't want the Juniors getting influenced by the people who know the school. He said that so far I hadn't fit into the Andover way and that our paths may soon part because I continued to hang around with older boys. Also all my friends had long hair and that made them somewhat short of ideal "Andover Men."

While I did object almost immediately to the way the school tried to mold me, my objections were kept silent, and consequently I had very little trouble with the rules at Andover. The first year, I got a demerit from my basketball coach for cutting a basketball game, but that was about it. However during my second year, I started getting bored with classes, and I began cutting them. Students are allowed sixteen cuts a year, five and a half for each of the three terms: I took eighty-one for the year. I worked this by switching courses several times during the term and confusing the records. I then could take a cut but miss having my named called from the class list for a cut. I was able to have only nine cuts credited to me for the whole year, while I had taken eighty-one. But it was always nip and tuck because I would end up taking one or two cuts too many: I would then have to go in and check with the excusing officer, and work out some elaborate excuse so I wouldn't get Posted for overcutting. Fortunately I was lucky and was able to take many more term cuts than I should have and still survive. Rather than having to attend boring classes and athletics I wasn't interested in, I was able to spend my time in my room, reading and listening to music.

My second and more important involvement with the school rules had to do with smoking marijuana, which started out gradually in the fall and winter of my Upper year (eleventh grade). What first inspired me to take drugs was basically curiosity, and the fact that most of the other kids in my dorm were doing it. The first time I ever took drugs was at Andover, and the first drug I ever had was hashish. I smoked it in a pipe, and I liked it a lot. I took it with about six or seven other kids in a dorm room. One chick and five or six guys. I wandered into the room, and there was a pipe being passed around. I decided to join in just for the hell of it. That was in the beginning of the Winter term. I smoked more as the Winter term went on, but not very much. However, when spring came I decided to abandon all my studies and just try to pass them. That's just about what I did.

I spent most of my time taking drugs. A friend and I regularly went up to his room on the top floor of the dorm to smoke. We would smoke pot beginning at about eight o'clock, when study hours began. Sometimes we would smoke in the fireplace. We would lock the door, close the windows, and light up a pipe in the fireplace. Once, in a kind of a cruel way, we went down to the room of a kid who hadn't used dope before and asked him if we could use his fireplace. While we were smoking and rapping easily, the kid was really getting scared. He kept opening the door to see if the housemaster was coming, and telling us to keep quiet. He finally ended up having some dope himself, and he really enjoyed it. The other place where we used to smoke was in the attic. Getting to the attic involved boosting my friend up to a window enclosure in the ceiling right above the stairwell. He would fumble around in the dark, passing crates and mops, trying not to touch a thing. Then he would climb down a ladder in the janitor's closet, open it, and let me in. Getting back out was very dangerous. We would have looked pretty weird coming out of the janitor's closet at ten o'clock at night. But while we were up there we were in no danger of being caught. We could sit up on the rafters and smoke without worry.

We got into marijuana and hash very deeply. In fact at one point last spring we smoked up to forty or forty-five nights in a row. We disregarded our homework: did it in the afternoon if we did it at all. We'd go up into the attic to smoke, and then go back to my friend's room and listen to music. Music really sounds great on drugs. We usually ended up falling asleep exhausted at about one o'clock in the morning in a chair or on the floor. During the Spring term I hardly ever slept in my own room. Both our studies went completely out the window, but we did enjoy ourselves. And we became experts on the different kinds of drugs around. We got so we could distinguish good Acapulco Gold from bad New Jersey stuff. We rapped a lot about it. In fact most of our conversation day and night was about drugs. Our housemaster knew that we were using drugs. It was obvious: the whole dorm used drugs, and we were going around stoned—laughing all the time and doing really strange things. Fortunately, however, the housemaster didn't do anything about it.

There are a hell of a lot of drugs pushed around Andover. Very few of the ninth graders take them, but the number increases by grade. There are several reasons for this rather extensive drug use. I think all adolescents want to get intoxicated, because it's a hard time to live in. You have all sorts of conflicts within yourself, and you can forget them for awhile by taking drugs. People drink for the same reason, and there are still a lot of young drinkers around. Drugs are better though, because they don't depress you like alcohol does. They also don't make you sick.

The use of drugs has also gotten to be a status thing. The more you take, the more you can brag about it. People say, "Whoa, look at that!" There was one Senior last year who won a good deal of respect in some circles because he set records for taking acid. He took more than anybody else. And one legendary Senior a couple of years ago supposedly took a week-long STP trip. Drug use is very much a status symbol, just as drinking many cans of beer used to be.

The need for social acceptance and the desire for escape are the main reasons for drug-taking at Andover. Most fifteen- and sixteen-year-olds want to escape at one point or another, but at Andover the need is particularly acute. Andover is a very depressing place. In the middle of winter there are six feet of snow on the ground, and the paths are merely tunnels between the drifts. Anywhere you walk it's depressing. They only let you out of the place a couple of times a term. Many students experiment with drugs to help them escape: some people take whole semesters of classes stoned just to see what it's like. It's an escape to a different world. You get away from a depressing one.

It's impossible to talk about any boarding school and especially Andover without getting into sex. While sex really covers everything, it's the least talked-about subject in the entire school. There is for the Freshman class a little sex lecture given by the medical department every year. Everyone snickers about intercourse, and that's about it as far as authorized sex education goes. Nevertheless, sex colors everything at Andover: the faculty, the students, and the administration. Andover is a closed, private, boys' boarding school, and there's very little sexual satisfaction for students or teachers there. There are not many really attractive faculty wives around Andover, and the few that there are have scandalous reputations. One teacher went home and found another member of the faculty in bed with his wife, and lots of faculty wives flirt with other faculty members as well as students. There was one faculty wife who actually pulled a black kid into her house. He had to run out the back door to get away from her.

Poor sexual relationships obviously affect the faculty, because faculty members can't assert their masculinity at all unless they go out for athletics. Athletics at Andover has always been considered a good substitute for sex. It's on the gridiron that you're supposed to get rid of your physical desires, not in a bed somewhere. The sexual dissatisfaction of many faculty members affects their attitudes toward students. I sometimes get the feeling that I'm competing against the faculty members in everything: in athletics, in the classroom, and displaying wit before their wives at dorm parties. It's not the healthiest relationship to have between a teacher and his students.

In the past year, there has been a big move at Andover toward coordinate education. Abbot, which is the girls' school next to Andover, and has about 250 students, has now started to take courses with us. We also do lots of things like eat meals together, without sharing the same campus. The administration felt that the thing to do was to go slowly toward coordinate education. Everyone else is doing it, and if we don't do it we'll obviously become stifled and staid and we'll die out. So it was done. They started out with coed dining and some coed classes.

Sexual relationships between Abbot girls and Andover boys have actually grown over the past five or six years. Before that there were very few sexual relationships because most of the Andover boys who were respected were the athletes; and athletes had very little time for sex. They were too busy playing football and knocking their brains out. But now that drugs and new art concepts have come along, the long hairs and the artists are being respected. Drugs and art deal with sex, and the emergence of a new kind of Andover student has been a major reason for the better sex between Andover and Abbot.

Basically sexual relationships with Abbot girls run along two levels. First there's the level of going steady, which is kind of traditional in America. But going steady has faded out, because it's impossible to do anything with a chick up at Andover—at least legally. You can't take her into Boston. You can't take her around town, and there are very few opportunities to be alone together. Hence you can't have sex in any ideal setting. You can't go into a room where there's privacy. But this type of private relationship isn't big anyway. The type of sexual relationship which is now prominent between Andover and Abbot students is happening all over the country: communal relationships. A bunch of chicks and a bunch of guys will go off together in a group, on a kind of picnic. The group will go off to the Sanctuary, a large nature refuge on campus, and have a good time for the afternoon: smoke dope together, make love, and generally relate together as a group. The sex is not communal, but paired off. Being in a group removes the hardship of having to meet a chick, go out with her, and go through all the traditional rigamarole which you can't go through at Andover anyway because you can't take a girl out anywhere. You can't go through the talking and the other stages in the development of a normal relationship because you can't see a chick that much. So you have a rushed relationship, sort of like a sailor who has just gotten off a ship. You have all the fun you possibly can right away. In the last few years sexual relationships have become more and more rushed, especially because the younger Abbot chicks are sexually available and willing to go through any type of affair. So it's this type of communal sexual life that is growing at Andover. You do the most in the least amount of time without going through the bother of going steady.

The reason that sexual attitudes of Andover and Abbot students are changing is very simple. Free and abstract expressions of life—art and music—have become respectable and admirable to most of the student body. Any abstract, creative expressions in which you let yourself go—drugs, art, plays, communal things, and sexual freedom—fit into the model of the person who is admired at Andover, both by other boys and by girls at Abbot. Drug use is very rare at Abbot in comparison to Andover. I would say that only about fifteen girls at Abbot are deep into drugs at all— they may smoke dope once or twice a week. I also think that girls between the ages of thirteen and eighteen, even though they may be very intelligent, have a yearning to be dependent on the kind of creativity which an Andover student can develop. Because they don't have the ability or the facility around school to be particularly creative themselves, and because Abbot girls basically aren't into drugs and other liberating things, most of them have a very large sexual need which they transfer to the Andover student who is creative.

The Abbot girls are really good chicks. They're nice, and they have this built-in desire for sex, for freedom, and for just getting involved. After spending time with a guy in one of these communal experiences, they sometimes go way out to show their affection. I know of girls who spent the entire night in the Sanctuary with Andover guys. They'd stay out there, smoking dope and balling, all night. And it's not uncommon for them to come and stay in the Senior dorms. I'd say it happened in about 20 cases last year. Girls at Abbot who had good relations with their house mistresses and didn't see them often would come up and sleep with guys in the dorms. They have unlimited weekends (although we only have from three to five a term, depending on the class) and sometimes go off with Andover guys. I knew one chick at Abbot who used to take a couple of guys up to a farm shed in New Hampshire every weekend last spring. The guys took off illegally after their alloted weekends were up. I guess it's sort of mutual assistance. They help us, and we help them, to survive at school. I don't know how we'd do it without them.

The need for creativity and self-expression on the part of students my age is, as I said before, one of the main reasons why sex and drugs are so important at Andover. I'm not exactly sure why my friends and I have this drive for creativity and self-fulfillment, but I do know that drugs and sex are among the few outlets possible at Andover. Sports used to be the main outlet and the main source of prestige for the boarding school student. Sports provided a certain amount of controlled violence, group involvement, and organized educational structure; in other words, if you're a half-back you do this, if you're an end, you do that. Sports was the alternative which the school administration wanted because they didn't want an outlet in sex. Now, however, the students have discovered their own cultural and political outlets. Deep, intellectual people rather than strong, athletic people have become respectable as students. For what reason I don't know. I think a lot of it comes from the music and art of the late fifties. But whatever it comes from, the new outlet is definitely alienated from the Andover establishment.

Creativity is almost by definition an anti-Establishment thing at Andover. Teachers would try to refute that statement by claiming that they always encourage creativity in the classroom—in papers and on tests. That may very well be so, but classroom learning is a small function of the over-all Andover institution. The purpose of Andover is to process young men, turn them into "Andover Men," and channel them forward to a blandly orthodox life style and choice of professions. Andover tries to mold, groom, and refine its students; it cannot allow for true creativity which might be a threat to the school. Going to Yale and Wall Street is not creative; at least not if it's imposed on you by your school. You are strapped to an assembly line, unable to climb off. The sophisticated generation that is now at Andover is searching for creativity and identity, and dislikes being forced to do uncreative things. Playing football is not a creative thing. That's why other things than football are now respected at Andover. Art groups and musical groups are very popular among students. The new Art Center, which was built because our rival school Exeter had one, has become a gathering place for many of these anti-Establishment Andover students—and a worry to the administration.

There has developed over the last two years a group of about fifty people involved in the arts and together in outlook. There's a very strong bond between us, for which the school itself is responsible—primarily through one of the new interdepartmental courses it has instituted. In the last three years, Andover has managed to evolve a few interdepartmental courses that are experimental and quite free. The only reason they are approved was because everyone else was doing them—why shouldn't Andover make some token gesture to what is happening in education throughout the rest of the country in colleges and in some prep schools? So some art-English departmental courses have been started, a specific one being Contemporary Communications. This course is conducted entirely differently from any other course at Andover. The classroom is obsolete, and attendance requirements and grades are also obsolete. You get an automatic five at the end of the year unless you don't do anything at all. (A five at Andover is an honor grade.) The Contemporary Communications course has become a resting place for the alienated and artistic intellectuals who want to get together and work together. They have formed a very strong block.

Most of the people in the group are bright and independent, and are opposed to the Andover kind of manipulation. I think this is the first time the school has felt threatened from within, and the administration is uptight about it. Dr. G——, who is the head of the infirmary, made a report to the administration saying that Con.-Comm. was an unhealthy course. He said it divided the community. It brought together one group of people, the creative people, and restricted jocks and other people from joining. Dr. G—— was admitting that Con.-Comm. was a focal point for alienated people at Andover to get together and organize. As a result, the administration has started to make it harder for these students to meet. When Contemporary Communications came up for renewal this year, plenty of people applied for the course. (You have to have only ten people apply for course in order for it to hold, and there were thirty or thirty-five students interested in it.) But the administration announced that there were not enough people applying for the course, and Con.-Comm. was taken out of the interdepartmental category and turned into an art course. They decided not to eliminate it altogether because that would cause an uproar with the students; instead, they changed it so people would be discouraged from applying. Andover couldn't stand the subversive scrutiny that meetings of its students produced.

All the things I've mentioned so far—the use of drugs, the need to break rules in order to have sex, and the emphasis on creativity—have tended to alienate Andover students from the administration. This alienation, or general feeling of detachment, can't help becoming political. If a student takes drugs, whether he is a jock or an artist, he automatically becomes a lawbreaker and Andover becomes the enemy. Whether he is radical, liberal, or conservative doesn't matter, because once he becomes alienated from the school through drugs he becomes politically alienated as well. The same is true with creativity. When a person joins the artistic group at Andover, either because he wants prestige or because he wants to use his creative faculties, he automatically becomes part of a political opposition. There were artists last year who never had had any real political involvement in their lives, but who by the end of the year were getting deeply involved in demonstrations. They started off just being intellectually detached from the school, and ended up opposing certain concrete conditions and policies. When you join the artistic establishment, even though you may not have any political views at all, you become a member of the political opposition at Andover.

Besides the large number of students at Andover who become politically alienated from the school and can be considered potential radicals, there is a significant group of students who are actual, avowed, political radicals. I consider myself one of these. I think that U.S. government has shown itself to be totally ineffective in solving the problems of this country, and that it has—through such tragedies as the Vietnam War and the token welfare system—worked to perpetuate poverty, injustice, and national conflict in the world. I am in favor of a revolutionary change in the government and the society of America, and for this reason I am critical of Andover. Andover is a handmaiden of the Establishment in this country. As it processes students, imbues them with its traditional values, and prepares them to assume "respectable" roles, it helps perpetuate American society as it's presently constituted. It doesn't encourage its students to think critically of the country, but rather helps them adjust to its presently corrupt form.

The Andover administration also remains an active tool of U.S. government policies. At a time when the excessive military influence in American life is termed unhealthy by even moderate journals, Andover continues to pay homage to the warmakers. Housemasters receive extra benefits if they've had military experience, and our headmaster, a West Point graduate, forever praises the military for the "sound character" it produces in men. And last year Andover refused to honor Dr. Spock and Rev. William Sloane Coffin because of their opposition to the government. An annual award is given at Andover by the trustees to an alumnus for outstanding service. There was a proposal to give the Peace Award to Dr. Spock and Rev. Coffin for their work against the Vietnam War. Both men are Andover graduates. To avoid giving them the award, the Headmaster changed the wording of the award to say that it was for those who have actually been in government service. Most students felt that Spock and Coffin were technically serving the ideas of good government because what they were doing was right. To counteract that, the trustees made a decision not to give the Peace Award to anyone. The headmaster went along with them. He stated that since Spock's and Coffin's convictions had not been reversed yet, they were criminals, and Andover couldn't give the Peace Award to two criminals. That was a disgusting thing to say: here were two alumni who deserved the award, but since they were opposed to the war, Andover not only refused to honor them, but felt compelled to defame them. That incident was a perfect example of Andover's inflexible alignment with the government. I am opposed to such a connection on the part of Andover or any other school. It's like Columbia students protesting their school's tie with the Institute for Defense Analysis. If we want to change this country, it seems we have to change the schools first.

There are certain school issues that almost all the students at Andover agree upon. One is their desire to be given more freedom. At Andover we have to go to breakfast, we have to go to classes, we have to go to athletics. And up until last year we had to go to chapel twice a week—Wednesdays and Sundays. Many students objected to the forced chapel, for in addition to being another requirement, it was against free religion. We had heated arguments about it, and finally the administration made Wednesday chapel voluntary. All students are also in agreement on the tyrannical rules of the school. For example, disobedience to a faculty member is a major crime, and makes you liable to dismissal. In other words, if you just disagree with a faculty member you can get kicked out. The housemaster can have a little squabble with you when he's drunk, point to that rule, and have you kicked out. The rule really angers a lot of students. It angers me because so many things that the faculty do are wrong. And you can't tell them that they are wrong. These are the kinds of rules that aggravate both the moderate and the radical students at Andover.

There are about forty or fifty active radical students at Andover. And as I mentioned before, there are a lot of potential radicals. If things can go right, if things can be done anonymously, I think that about three-quarters of the student body can be counted on to support radical actions. An example was last year's election. Since 1789, every time the three upper classes elected presidents they were straight guys: football players and things like that. This year they elected three black students. In order for those three black students to be elected, they had to get at least 125 votes from each class. So you can figure that there are 400 to 450 students in the whole school who voted for what was basically a radical platform. They voted for avowed black militants against guys who had been presidents of their classes the year before. Then, in the Student-Faculty Co-operative elections, three white radicals were elected to the Executive Board. And both the black and white radicals had made their positions very clear. Over all, I would say that up to 500 Andover students [out of 840] could, if there were strong radical leadership, back a radical group, as they did in the Co-op. They would have to do it anonymously, but they would lend support to moves taken to change the school—moves whose means would be considered less important than their ends.

The Left at Andover embodies two different elements. There are those who are politically active on the Left, and those who are artistically active. The artistically active students resist the administration by attacking its values and beliefs through their artistic expression. Through plays that they write, poems that they recite in chapel, and paintings that they hang in the Art Center, they disturb the administration just as much as someone who gets up in Co-op and talks. The artistic people aren't going to start a radical activity. They are the ones who will lend creativity and inventiveness to it after it's been initiated. Therefore the political and the artistic radicals both contribute toward the radical movement at Andover.

The radical students believe, and I agree, that you can sit around and change specific rules at Andover all day without doing any good. Liberalizing course requirements and offering more weekend privileges doesn't amount to much. You have to change the basic attitude and structure of the institution. It's that attitude which, while liberalizing the admissions policy and admitting more black students than most prep schools, still provides a fairly rigid educational experience—one in which a student enters, goes through a maze of courses and rules, and comes out an "Andover Man." It's that structure which gives the student a certain amount of freedom of choice to pursue different interests, but limits him to conventional, unradical opinions. It's a Nixon-conservative, conformist structure, and it's that structure which must be changed.

The radical student movement really started at Andover in the spring of 1968. At that time, the chairman of what was then the Student Congress put a few small proposals for rule changes to the faculty. All were turned down. He felt (and I think rightly) that he wasn't given enough chance to speak out on the issues and present his side. The faculty simply took his five or six small proposals and automatically turned them down. At that point, one student got really angry and planned a demonstration to support both the student views and the abolition of the Student Congress in favor of a more meaningful group. The administration was so incensed by the idea of a demonstration that they got out and stopped it and delayed response to the proposal. But the demonstration did force them to act, and at the beginning of the 1968 Fall term a new student-faculty Co-operative was established. Anyone can come in and discuss any relevant issues with the Executive Board, which is made up of three students and three faculty members. The Co-op has improved faculty-student communications, but not to the degree that is necessary. The students still play a subordinate role, even on this purely consultative body:

everybody can vote for the students on the Executive Board, but only the faculty can vote for the faculty. However, students can at least speak up now, and largely as a result of the spring demonstration.

In the Fall term last year the Co-operative spent all its time discussing the religion issue. It was a bad first choice for an issue because it was very complex and abstract. But during this time the members of the Co-op became more and more alienated. Certain radical speakers began getting up and denouncing people like K——, the headmaster. Even though this did us no good, the fact that it was tolerated was a significant step. But there was vast disagreement on school changes, and nothing was done. So as Winter term rolled around we started getting really frustrated.

A disciplinary incident that occurred about that time got more students fed up with the school. Jim L——, one of the radical and artistic leaders in the Senior class, was turned in by a student for blowing his nose on a replica of the American flag. It was a scarf that he had worn in History class. But the faculty members on the discipline committee showed how narrow-minded and superficially patriotic they were by putting him on probation. There was a big faculty meeting about it, and four young teaching fellows—who had just gotten out of college and who sympathized with us—went into the faculty meeting wearing American-flag ties. They waged a fantastic fight for L——'s rights, and the campus was put in an uproar. The incident added a national issue, desecration of the flag, to local campus issues, and the students now were really agitated. Editorials in *The Phillipian* became more and more radical. The headmaster was criticized week after week. And there was great fear on the part of the administration. I remember talking to one of the deans in January. I was talking about the drug scene at Andover, and he was very scared that there was going to be violence.

In the spring there was a coat and tie demonstration. We have to wear coats and ties at Andover every day until April 30. In May and June we can take them off, but we don't want to wear them at any time. We organized a protest by circulating petitions, but it was a failure in terms of numbers. There were only about seventy or seventy-five students involved, and a lot of student skirmishes. But even small things like that really alarm the administration. They're not used to any kind of protest, and even a coat and tie demonstration drives them up the wall. One of the deans got very angry at *The Phillipian* for giving the demonstration front-page coverage, and he threatened to sanction the paper. He wouldn't be so stupid as to begin controlling the paper, but he could take away certain privileges—use of the press rooms and things like that—and make it very difficult for the paper to function. After this there was a violent protest which I was involved in. One night, some other students and I broke the windows in George Washington Hall, the administration building. And one student in the group broke some windows in Samuel Phillips Hall, the classroom building. We did it to dramatize student discontent, and to show how serious we were about the issues.

There wasn't any cohesive philosophy behind all the student discontent but there was a cohesive movement. By the middle of Spring term, there was an alliance created between the fifty radicals and the rest of the students. Coming from a depressing winter into the spring, when male sexuality demands freedom, the students were particularly irritated at the administration for clamping down on them so much. Consequently, by May there was a kind of union between the radicals and all the students who were discontented with the administration.

In May and June came the crowning blow, which convinced the students how rigidly conservative Andover was and how little regard was paid to their opinions. To give students the feeling that their ideas were valued, the administration called a special day on which classes were cancelled and students met together to discuss changes in the school put forth by the Discipline Committee. The faculty got together in groups to hear what the students were saying, and then they held their own faculty meeting. They ignored almost every student suggestion. Things like unlimited Senior cuts, and hair and dress regulations were not approved. Even weekend privileges were slighted. And then the headmaster showed just how much be believed in school democracy and in listening to students. On the next to last Sunday at school, the headmaster got up and announced the final decision about the hair rule. He said that "long hair was destroying Andover's image." "From now on," he said, "I will decide whether or not a boy shall have long hair, sideburns, a beard, or mustache." The students now were really bitter, and they showed it in the question and answer period. First, there was booing and hissing, and no applause from anywhere. The headmaster's reasoning went like this: If a boy's record showed any honor grades, he could have a beard. If it showed him getting less than honor grades, he couldn't have a beard. Honor students could have beards and non-honor students could not. He said that right out in the open. He also said that students could not have hair styles in the extreme, and there were lots of sarcastic questions about that. One student asked him, "Well, does that mean that a guy who has shaved his head has to go around wearing a wig until his hair grows back?" K—— didn't like that question. He had just made an announcement denouncing blue jeans, saying, "We don't want any blue jeans around campus at all." One kid way in the back got up and said, "Everywhere I see gray jeans, I see green jeans, red jeans, orange jeans, and white jeans. I'd like to know what Andover has against the color blue." And of course, since blue is Andover's color—blue and white—this brought the house down; and it embarrassed K—— tremendously. By the end of the assembly people were really angry. A whole bunch of students got up and started singing "The Royal Blue," which is the Andover theme song, in a very sarcastic way. That was the note school ended on last spring.

I personally am fed up with Andover. I want to change this school even if I have to do violent things and take part in violent demonstrations. However, I can't afford to get kicked out. I really don't care what it will do to my status or future, but my father does pay for me to go there, and getting booted certainly would hurt my relationship with him and the rest of the family. While still working for change, I have decided to stay at Andover. I don't want to disappoint my parents by quitting or getting kicked out, but I'm also staying for other reasons. I came because of my ignorance of the place, and I've stayed because I feel that Andover is merely a reflection of this civilization and this society. There will be no better place. And there's the added incentive that the people at Andover are among the most remarkable I've ever encountered. They are from all walks of life, and some are really extraordinary. I have developed some very deep friendships, with other students and even with a few faculty members who are truly outstanding people. I know other students who feel the same way about the people at Andover, but they are generally disappointed with the school.

Most of the students at Andover, I'd say more than half, are dissatisfied. They feel that something's wrong with the school, that something isn't right. I don't know what the reasons are for all of them, but I think the basic character of the school has a lot to do with it. The regimentation and restrictions that students suffer, the lack of meaningful administrative responsibility given them, and the feeling of being groomed and manipulated to fit a preconceived mold, all contribute to an alienation from the school that can easily grow into hostility. The growing strength of the radical movement is a good indication of the degree of disenchantment. Last year the influence of the group of forty committed radicals grew as the year went by. The other disenchanted students were looking for a banner to get under, and they picked that of the black and white radicals. Thus by the end of the year the radical movement had quite a large power base, as seen both in the class elections and the demonstration against the headmaster at the assembly.

At Andover right now, the movement is just as good as

it was last year. It still involves a continuation of effort by the small group of hard-core, self-avowed radicals. In the past, things usually faded back to normal soon after a demonstration. But with the election of radicals to the top six offices of the school, there's a good possibility that the pressure can still be kept on. And because the radicals have infiltrated the establishment organization, we don't need to form any new organization ourselves. In other words, we can use the establishment organization for our own purposes. We can turn it against itself.

A major issue this year will be the dope issue. The school is divided into two factions over dope: the student faction using dope, and the faculty faction which supports the Nixon view against dope. Students who are using dope can't admit that they're using it, and the faculty who are against dope don't want to admit that they're trying their damnedest to bust the student users. Each side wears a mask in public confrontations, and the issue is going to come to a crisis. Whether or not it's going to be forced into a political thing is questionable, but there is going to be a definite struggle about it. With Nixon's Operation Intercept, dope is now a national political issue. And Andover's position, like Nixon's, is that marijuana and LSD should not be studied—their users should just be booted out. In the confrontation over drugs, I think the headmaster is going to revert to a hard line, especially since it has become fashionable with the Nixon Administration. The backlash that came at the end of spring last year will come this much earlier.

We will be waiting for issues like this. You see, radicalism works at Andover because a small number of radicals are very together. They work politically to mobilize mass sentiments. The mass student body moves in a cycle: it goes from being contented to being discontented, and then back to being contented. It's up to the radicals to rally the mass student body at certain strategic points during the year. Unlike public school radicals who bring up certain issues to inform the student body and win its support, we can't make the first move. At Andover we can't do this simply because we have to let the administration raise the issues first, and then react: the only way we can get the majority of students on our side is through their discontent. Unfortunately, most of the students at Andover are basically cowards. They don't want to be left out in left field opposing the administration—therefore we radicals are not going to start a basic confrontation. If twenty-five radicals started a confrontation over an issue, we would be isolated in terms of political influence. We would be a minority among minorities, and we could be dealt with very quickly.

For example, if we took a position on an issue that we had brought up but the administration hadn't brought up or discussed, most of the students wouldn't have the courage to get up and stand there with us. They would leave us alone as a minority, and we could be disciplined immediately for any demonstration we had. But if an issue came up and there was a discussion and proposals made through parliamentary procedure, and after about two or three weeks the faculty had hashed around and nothing had been done, the discontent would be bred and at that point we could make a move. At that point the disenchantment of the majority of the students could propel them to come to our side. We choose this reacting rather than initiating tactic because it's more practical. At a private school like Andover you're always one phone call or one signature away from being out the door. And if we want to change the school, we must consider this factor in our strategy. How effective would we be if we were kicked out?

An incident that occurred just last week is a good illustration of the present student mood at Andover. An honor student and a member of the radical camp, F——, was placed on probation at the end of last week after he was caught coming back from Abbot twenty-five minutes after the normal sign-in time. The specific charge against him was "general bad attitude toward the spirit of the rules," a trumped-up charge. Many students became aroused, and the dean of students and F——'s housemaster petitioned the

Discipline Committee to reconsider the case, something which has never happened before at Andover. The Discipline Committee turned down the request, without even granting the housemaster an opportunity to state his views. A student demonstration on the steps of Samuel Phillips Hall occurred the next morning, with about 200 students and a few faculty members participating. The dean and the housemaster were there, but unfortunately the dean reverted back to the position of defending the Discipline Committee. The encouraging thing was that over 100 students signed a petition asking to be put on probation because their attitude was as "bad" as F———'s. *The Phillipian* broke with its tradition of silence about Discipline Committee cases by giving the incident coverage, and black and white student radicals held a forum over the radio station. More demonstrations are planned, and the exciting thing is that many new preps are respectfully following the examples of militant Seniors, in the same way that we followed the football players two or three years ago. With this kind of beginning, it should be an interesting school year.

Andover is not the only prep school that has dissatisfied, radical students. Students at Choate, Lawrenceville, Exeter, and other schools are similarly disappointed with the education they're receiving. Because of this, several organizations have developed to unite the different radical students and try to effect radical changes on all the prep school campuses. One such organization is the National Prep School Union. Organized by former Andover students, the Union works under the assumption that students should realize that radical action, thought, and philosophy are the key factors in changing the political and educational character of the prep schools. It's basically an effort to change the heads of prep school kids into thinking radically rather than liberally or conservatively. The basic educational philosophy of the Union is that specialization is a key factor in discovering your identity as a student. In other words, by specializing in one particular subject area, one with its own values and philosophy, a student can grow in that area to the point where he can really discover his identity.

The Union believes that the prep schools should provide background rather than influence. They should offer a large available ground on which students can discover themselves. To this end the schools should offer courses—majors —in specific areas. For example, if a student were interested in something like playing the cello, then he would give up all the other courses he now has to take in the pursuit of that. He should be given the opportunity to work on the cello as much as he wants. Students would pursue one or two subjects over a period of eight or ten years, in prep school and college, so that they could become experts in their fields.

Adult reaction to the National Prep School Union philosophy has been critical, as one would expect. "How," conservative teachers and administrators always say, "can fourteen- and fifteen-year-old kids make these highly specialized decisions for their lives, at such an early age?" They don't realize how harmful it has been for American society to push back the age of specialization to twenty-two or twenty-three as it has done. It is at the age of fourteen that a student's creative urge is at its height, and it is at this point, not later, that educational structures (rules and requirements) should be at their fewest. Admittedly, certain students may not be ready for this kind of early specialization; but the many students who are can become stifled by having to wait till they're older. The Union believes that secondary education should be redefined to provide the educational experience that certain progressive colleges and most graduate schools do today. These higher levels of education would be redefined accordingly to continue the specialization students need so desperately today.

The National Prep School Union has representative radical students at many different prep schools. Thirty some-odd prep schools, including Choate, Pomfret, and Lawrenceville, have been addressed by members of the Union, and some constructive results have already been

produced. Some of the schools have instituted teacher-eval-
uation programs, and others have introduced off-campus
studying projects.

The Black Prep School Students' Union is an organization for militant black prep school students headed by a
black at Mount Hermon. It is quite powerful, and has
already brought about some radical changes at Choate.
Like the National Prep School Union it seeks to rally students at the different campuses to the radical movement.
Through the work of these two organizations, along with
the efforts of unaffiliated radical prep school students
throughout the country, the basic character of American
prep schools may change. Ideally, the schools will begin to
treat students like mature young adults, and rather than
process them uniformly toward traditional futures, begin to
allow them—even encourage them—to develop as creative
and independent men and women.

The Headmaster's Word Is Law

by Eric Oakstein

Eric Oakstein is a sixteen-year-old student at a New York City private school. He is Editor of the school newspaper. His father is a psychiatrist.

I am a high school radical in that I march for causes most radicals of today are in general agreement on. However, unlike some of the other students in the Movement, I believe in strengthening certain areas of radical thought and playing down others. I live in New York City, and during the past year many of the public schools in New York exploded—quite literally. In my school however we didn't see any of that. I go to a private school in Manhattan, and for reasons that I'll go into later, no riots occurred there. I must admit that I was glad to learn of the riots in the public schools. They have been long overdue, and now that they've occurred I think they mark the beginning of the development of a conscientious, ideological High School Movement. While Marxists might term these actions "infantile disorders," I believe they can be turned into quite positive and forceful demonstrations of power and will on the part of high school students.

It's very understandable that the public high schools in New York City blew up this past year. I'm just surprised that it took this long. The high school system in New York is archaic. Students, eighteen and nineteen years of age, are required to get passes for the bathroom; they must show program cards when found walking in the halls. These things are small but are nevertheless ridiculous, and just add fuel to the general fire that brews in the high schools. New York's in a mass school system, and the students, reduced to numbers on booklength organization sheets, are fed up.

Principals, teachers, and critics of the young who think that this Movement is a mere burst of adolescent energy bound to burn itself out, are deluding themselves. What they forget, and what I think is the most promising thing about the radical High School Movement is that today's high school radicals are going to be tomorrow's leaders—of the world, or at least of the country. And I'm convinced that my fellow students, like myself, are going to remain radicals, and it's as radicals that we are going to lead and change this country. Another aspect of the Movement that's very encouraging is its increasing size. Radicals are being turned out by the day and by the minute, and the ages at which people become radicalized are going lower and lower. In my school there are quite a few radical students in the seventh and eighth grades. I am sixteen and entering the twelfth grade, and even though it's only been a few years, these even younger radicals are much smarter than I was at their age. When I was that age I had never read *The Quotations of Chairman Mao,* and I hardly knew who Lenin was. I was more interested in the traditional past-times of seventh and eighth graders.

I have always attended private school in New York City, and I am now at a very progressive, coed, junior and senior high school. It has many facets and sides, one of which is the headmaster's image of it as a training ground for New York's intellectual, academic, and artistic community. The people who come out of it are extremely well read and well versed in the major intellectual traditions of the world. That is something that I haven't come across in speaking to other high school students, as a general trend anyway. I've met various individuals from other high schools who conform to this type of intellectuality, but never on the scale that exists at my school. Whereas in other schools students compete among themselves in athletics and so on, in my school students compete intellectually. Perhaps the highest goal is that of intellectual and artistic achievement. Having read the entire works of Hermann Hesse is an accomplishment equivalent to that of driving a sports car or being captain of the football team at other schools. I don't want to give the impression, however, that everyone there is solely interested in intellectual activities. Drawing mainly from middle and upper ruling-class families, the school has many students who are primarily concerned with clothes, parties, and the social whirl of New York's Upper East Side *nouveau riche* society. And then there are the radicals. There are few of us at my school who are seriously involved in the radical High School Movement. There is only a small vocal group that is consciously together on issues, but as I said before, the ranks of radicals are growing rapidly. It came as a surprise to me when I learned that my immediate friends were not the only radicals in the school, but that there are students in the grades above and below who share the same political ideas my friends and I have. We did not know of one another because we concentrated our energies on separate but equally relevant issues. Hopefully within the next year these presently unaffiliated radical students will join together to enlarge the student radical movement. Possibly then, as a united radical front, we'll be able to gain the kinds of changes we think are necessary for even this, the most progressive of private schools.

Academically, I am happy at school. I realize that in today's "switched-off" generation it is unusual to be contented with one's school, but I must admit that I am more than satisfied with the possibilities for intellectual inquiry. One thing that produced this contentment was our success in expanding our seminar program. We have a seminar History course for Juniors and Seniors with the option of suggesting our own courses. Anyone who comes up

with a well-presented course suggestion is able to establish a new course, provided there is someone to teach it. My
faith in the system of seminars was confirmed after my
friends and I suggested to the head of the History department a course in Marxist studies. At first they refused to accept it for several reasons. It was claimed that
there was no one to teach it, and that it was not relevant to
our intellectual scheme. We had taken the initiative to draw
up an outline of the course with a list of suggested readings.
It was stated at the time that there would be no propaganda
course in the History department; but eventually the course
was passed because of our persistence and because there
was someone to teach it. Thus this year there will be a
course, for half-credit, in Marxist studies. This I consider
to be a real intellectual achievement, at least within the
given limited scope. In the over-all scheme of things I don't
think a small reform in a private school curriculum counts
for much, since half the world doesn't even get a grade
school education. However I was satisfied with the outcome:
this kind of intellectual freedom is what I enjoy.

While I am academically happy, I definitely think that
some administrative changes must be made. Our headmaster, a noted educator in New York City educational
circles, described the school's administrative philosophy
in a remark he made to a school assembly. He stated that
they allowed us complete freedom of mind even if they
don't allow us freedom of body. By freedom of body, the
headmaster was referring, among other things, to the dress
regulations. The dress regulations are, in my opinion, para-
doxically oppressive and juvenile for a supposedly progressive school. These rules require boys to wear coats and ties,
girls to wear long dresses and skirts, and both sexes to wear
what the administration considers "neat, well-groomed"
hair. As you might expect, these dress codes have been extremely unpopular among the students. And we've tried to
translate our discontent into a change of school policy,
using as a vehicle an established school mechanism—the
assembly.

There is a tradition at school whereby every week the entire high school meets in one body (with only 350 students in the high school it is possible to hold such a meeting). At these assemblies we are free and even encouraged to present any motions we desire, allegedly to help legislate school matters that concern us. The headmaster stands before us, listening to the expression of student opinion in a pretense of democracy. Our experience with the dress codes proves that it is a pretense. At a regular school assembly, when motions were in order, I took the floor and presented a motion that several of us had drawn up. It was a motion to abolish the dress codes, and it was passed democratically. We won. The vote was overwhelmingly for the motion.

People at school have a strange habit of blowing events way out of proportion, and thus making what was originally a small show of sentiment into a cataclysmic upheaval against all rule and authority. "Student Power," or the ranks of the "masturbatory ego-gratifiers" had descended in an attempt to ruin this respected junior intellectual community. One side started accusing the other side of making a mountain out of a molehill, and the other side responded with the same charge; before long the molehill was a mountain—the biggest controversy of the school year. Most students who voted for this proposal were not interested in taking over the headmaster's office; they simply didn't want to be told how to dress.

The headmaster got up on stage and explained his policy in one of his usual harangues, purposefully avoiding dealing with the motion. Afterwards, however, he confronted me and said, "If this was a referendum, or if this was an expression of the students' feelings, then I've heard it. If this was a motion, one with some legal intent, then I veto it." I'll never forget the quivering Freshman who came up to our headmaster after the government assembly and said: "But—but that isn't democracy?" He, with a broad grin on his face, replied, "That is right." That is the main trouble with the school student government. The headmaster does have the power to veto all motions put to him by the students, regardless of the force behind them. Such power is of course undemocratic. We are treated as the cream of the crop of our generation—the Einsteins, Lenins, Joyces, and Renoirs of the future world—and yet we don't know how to dress ourselves properly. This assumption also contradicts a school policy of "freedom of mind." What good is a school government if you can't use it? We cannot be satisfied with abstract notions of democracy. We want to put them into effect and see their concrete implications for our lives. That is how we'll really begin to learn about such concepts. Otherwise they remain irrelevant.

However, even without pretending to offer a school democracy, the administration should listen to the voice of its students, especially when that voice is almost unanimous as it was with the dress code motion. The headmaster chose not to listen, but instead criticized the methods by which the motion was presented. He also ignored the sentiment of the mass student body and decided instead to confer with a few handpicked students on an issue affecting all of us. Eventually I'm sure the dress codes will be abolished; but then the headmaster will probably present the change in regulations as an example of his so-called sensitive understanding of young people. The last thing he or any other administrator will ever admit is taking action in response to student opinion. Even in an allegedly progressive school like mine, students are relegated to secondary status. We are there at the sufferance of the administration, taught to think though not to act democratically. How, I wonder, are we to be expected to act responsibly after leaving school if we are denied the practice of responsibility now as students?

While as a student I do feel a responsibility to work to make my school as truly democratic as possible, as well as relevant to my life as a student, my major interest is not in the school but in the larger problems that affect this country. At their worst, our troubles result from the idiosyncrisies of the administration and to some degree the students. It may be to the school's credit that I've become as politically conscious as I am at the age of sixteen. Politically aware young people seem destined to become radicals these days, and in that sense I'm not sure my school would be proud of its achievement.

Without a doubt the most radicalizing influence on me was the Vietnam War. When the war began to go in the direction that it did in 1965, I was in the seventh grade. At that time I already felt that something was evil about the war, and I marched in those first major peace demonstrations up Fifth Avenue. At that time most of the spectators on the sidewalks were still pro-war, and they were out there shouting "Commie rat, go home!" I didn't understand this, for all I wanted to do was end the war. I certainly didn't want to have any kind of a revolution. However once I became involved in the antiwar movement, I also became sensitive to many of the other wrongs of America. I saw that while America spent millions to "Bring Democracy to Southeast Asia," democracy was being forgotten in our cities and in our rural areas. It became logical at that point not only to oppose the war but to oppose American racism and poverty at the same time. "End the War! End Racism!" then became the shouts of numerous young people like myself. I want to emphasis once again that during all this I did not identify myself as a "radical," a "liberal," a "commie," or anything. I was just opposed to the war and—by connection—racism. Many people, however, began to label me a "radical," and place me on the Left just because of my involvement with these two issues. My new category interested me, and I was eager to explore the various implications of "being on the Left"; coincidentally, I began to move toward what is considered a "leftist" position, but again by logical extension. I was doing a lot of political thinking, and I began to see that in addition to opposing the war and opposing racism, I also opposed the exploitation of tin miners in Bolivia, and migrant farm labor in California. There seemed to be a basic relationship between all these issues. The struggle of blacks who rioted in the ghettoes seemed related to the destitution of miners in West Virginia, and these two examples seemed related to the Vietnamese people who were fighting for their independence. From my concern with one or two issues, I began to see the numerous interrelationships involved and to evolve for myself an over-all political philosophy. My analysis drew me to a position that can be termed "on the Left," and I am now avowedly on the Left.

America is probably the most democratic country in the world, but that isn't saying much. At least America's concentration camps are so far unoccupied. The documents that sustain the government are not necessarily corrupt and not necessarily a blessing. They stand alone. The problem lies with the government's failure to live up to those documents, or even to follow them as closely as it could. If the government is still open to change (and I'm not sure that it is), then when young radicals grow up—if they retain their beliefs—there are going to be some mighty big social changes. If the government will not accept these changes, and if the number of radicals continues to swell at its present rate, then the government will be overthrown. I don't think that the electoral process of America is necessarily invalid. It's only that legislators and other people in the government deal with a military-industrial complex that is so vast and intricate that it can't possibly have the interests of the people at heart. That complex is only interested in making a buck—an interest shared by most of the powerful forces in our society today. To alter that trend will require a radical change. If it comes to revolution, then that's the way it will have to be. Thomas Jefferson said that we should have a revolution every twenty years, and it's been almost two hundred years since we had one. I think we're about due for one. Yet I'm a pacifist, both by upbringing and by being somewhat of a chicken. I would find it very hard to kill a policeman, who is basically not the most evil part of the complex of America but just a lackey for it. It would be dreadfully unfortunate also if he had to kill me.

He's not the person I'm really on the opposite side of any-way. I find myself on the opposite side of President Nixon and the heads of the five hundred corporations. And actually it's not so much even these 501 people. It's rather the systems that they've built—the vast complexes that can send a man to the moon while leaving people starving.

If I were old enough to vote I would vote, I suppose. It wouldn't mean that much to me, and I don't want to make a big thing about saying that I refuse to take part in and condone the capitalist system by voting for it. I don't really give a damn about that. However I don't think that the man we elect makes that much of a difference. How many politicians have we elected only to see them go in the opposite direction from what they promised? A great number of Americans voted for Johnson in 1964 because they were afraid of Goldwater. Look what happened. Johnson turned around and ended up worse than Goldwater. That's just an example. I think people should vote, but they shouldn't delude themselves into thinking that the outcome is going to change anything. Decisions are, after all, not made in the chambers of Congress. I don't believe that. I think decisions are made where power is held. On the campuses this past year many students did try to get their grievances heard and their proposals passed through legal channels. They found that the administrators just wouldn't listen. Once the students took over buildings and turned the proposals into "demands," then the administrators were outraged and then they listened. They had to, because for once in their lives the students had something to bargain with. They had a building. That's the way it is. The only way the Labor Movement got established in the thirties was through such tactics as occupying buildings and generally showing the possible strength of the workers. At school if everybody grew his hair long and dressed the way he wanted to that would be that. There would no longer be any dress code, because the headmaster couldn't kick all the students out. I think that power comes from such concerted efforts of people, united people. The voting we have in America is better than what they have in Russia, China, Cuba, Spain, and Greece, but I still don't think it brings about the necessary changes. The only effective force for social change will come from the people who need it the most. I don't happen to be one of them, but I'll help all I can.

My radicalism has to some extent been inherited. My parents were both semi-radicals or at least militant for their time. I came from the radical tradition of the New Deal era, in the middle of the Korean War. Many of my friends who grew up with politically moderate parents were radicalized by exposure to their friends. I would say that a good deal of my radicalism came from my parents. My parents share many of my views, and I think it's fair to say that they nourished my radicalism.

I also think that my own first-hand experience with America's political system helped to foster my radicalism. I saw the incidents of police brutality at Chicago on my television screen, and I was appalled to see what was going on. It's no exaggeration to say that I was left gasping and breathless. While I certainly did learn something about America from the Chicago scenes, I don't think they had a radicalizing effect on me, and that's because I wasn't there. Later on in the fall of 1968 I did take part in various demonstrations against the candidates, and it was here that I saw with my own eyes what I had earlier seen on television. The police beat up defenseless demonstrators just because they were out there protesting. I had at that point become somewhat radical, but was still more or less uncommitted to any form of revolution. I didn't totally believe what I was doing at that time, and I was more or less along for the ride. However, from that point on I think my radicalism grew. I found it in an identification with the history of American radicalism, from the Revolutionary War up through the beginning of the Labor Movement to the present. I saw one big historical progression, and that we who were on the streets in 1969 were the true descendants of Big Bill Haywood and the Molly Maguires. They along with the other early champions of radical causes, were our real forefathers. I found in this tradition something to be committed to, something that I truly respected. I hadn't truly respected what I had been doing before—such things as shouting at the candidates, and yelling "pig" at the cops. I had participated in the demonstrations, but only half-heartedly. After seeing, however, what a respectable heritage we young radicals had, I began to involve myself more sincerely in the Movement. I respected what my parents had done, I admired the earlier unionists, and I began to see that what we were struggling for, or should I say against, was as respectable an aim.

This Movement of ours is different, however, in that most of us are not from working-class backgrounds. In fact, I think the Student Movement in this country, both in the colleges and in the high schools, is the first leftist movement in the world that is made up of affluent middle-class students. Most of us have never suffered from financial want —in fact we have been the chief beneficiaries of the society we'd like to change. I personally grew up in comfortable surroundings. My parents live in Manhattan, we have a summer cottage in Amagansett, I've been to Europe several times, and I attend the private school which I've described. My life has never been lavish, but I have always enjoyed financial security, a condition which many people in this country and in the world only dream about. If this society remained the way it is, then I and all the other middle-class radicals would probably continue to prosper and enjoy material comforts. But these rewards for success, these bribes for compliance, no longer interest us. We were born near the top of this society, we are accustomed to tasting the best that it has to offer, but we cannot enjoy these things if there is so much poverty and want around us. Even if it means forsaking all the personal benefits of our middle- and upper-class position, we want to change this society into something better. We want America to begin living up to its ideals, and to become a truly democratic country, a country where blacks and whites can live in harmony, and a country where one man's profits do not come from the sweat of another.

Nuns Against The Wall

by Paula Smith

Paula Smith is seventeen years old. She comes from a middle-class home. Her father owns trailer courts in Indiana and her mother is a housewife. Paula is very active in the high school radical movement in Chicago, and last year she gave a major antiwar speech before a rally of over 35,000 people.

My name is Paula Smith. I am seventeen years old, and a Junior in a Chicago Catholic girls' school. I come from a middle-class background, with typical conservative parents —the type that say "we think black people should have all the rights," but wouldn't let one in the door. That type. I live in a typical, all-white, middle-class neighborhood. My parents aren't radical in any sense. No early friends of mine were radical in any sense. Till first year high school I never participated in any political activities, and I hadn't read anything to make me radical. However through experiences, some common, and some unusual experiences that most students don't go through, I have come to certain conclusions, conclusions that probably classify me as a radical.

When I was a little kid, my parents used to take me on travels inside the United States and out. You read various things and you hear various things, but as they say, there's nothing like seeing it for yourself. Then you know it's real. I was down in Mexico when I was in about fifth grade, down

South, in the Midwest, the Southwest, and Canada when I was in the sixth and seventh. When you don't have much exposure to the country you're not hostile toward the government and you're not all for it, but you're in between. You just start to form ideas. What you see and what you hear has a certain influence on you. Now I remember things, just certain incidents, like I remember the Southwest. Mexican-American kids used to come up to you with no clothes on trying to sell you beans for ten cents. That is how they live. Down South only about four years ago they still had three washrooms: Men, Women, and Colored. These are things that are impressed upon you, and you realize whether you are middle class, working class, or what, that there is something wrong. You can't pinpoint it. You're not sure what's the cause of it. But you begin to realize that there are certain inadequacies in this country. They must stem from somewhere. You come to the conclusion that you want to do something. You don't know how, but you want to help change things for the better, to change conditions in the country and the world. I decided that I wanted to become active as an individual. I didn't know what to do until I got my hands on some antiwar literature. It was from a high school city-wide antiwar organization, and I decided to join it. That was my first year in high school, and I wanted to see what the organization was like. Maybe it could help me get involved.

I wasn't very political at that point. I knew that there were certain things that were wrong in the country. I was, in a sense, against the war. I felt that the struggle of the Vietnamese people was correct, and I didn't think that American intervention should take place in Southeast Asia. I was for equal rights for black people, free speech, this and that. But why and to what extent, I hadn't really come to any conclusions. My education was not complete at this point and I was still looking for answers and the best ways to involve myself in various situations to find these answers. So I went to a couple of meetings of this antiwar group, participated in a couple of demonstrations, and read about how these organizations functioned and what their grievances were. I decided to become as politically active as possible against the Vietnam War. That was my main activity at this time. I was mostly antiwar.

Another thing that played an important part in my development as a radical, and in a lot of other people's, was the events of the Democratic convention. I went to look on as a neutral observer, with the nice attitude that everything's going to be fine: I'm just going to have a good time like everybody else. I went down as a photographer, and like a lot of other kids, I was arrested. I had my head beat in. I saw a friend of mine shot by the police and killed for nothing. Two policemen were beating up on a demonstrator who was carrying a Viet Cong flag. We chased the policemen in return—some other people, I'd say about fifty people, and I. The policemen got scared and ran. We chased them into an alley where they were cornered and one of them got hysterical. He started shooting, just shooting all over the place at random. He hit a friend of mine who was about five feet away from me; I saw the kid grab his side and just fall down. At that point I was scared as was everybody else, and we just cut out. Needless to say, the whole thing horrified me. From that point on I became very anti-police, and I was determined that the apparatus of the city was as inadequate as the apparatus in the country. Certain things had to be changed. The government as it stood did not function in the interests of the majority of the people. That was when I started to become a socialist. I saw something wrong. There had to be something changed. Yet there has to be an answer at the same time, as you don't change something without replacing it. So I started looking for the correct solution, or what should replace the system that we now live under.

The people I had talked to at this point, and the experiences I had gone through, led me to believe that I as a citizen had not really been given my full rights in certain situations, but had experienced injustices. I had also seen other people in the same situation. By viewing the government's foreign policy in Vietnam and in South America, I came to the conclusion that the American government all over the world is not really so peaceful. It's out for its own interests. That is perfectly good to a certain extent. Any country or any individual has a right to his own interests, "as long as they don't infringe on anybody else's rights." Now that is just the point, they do. And I feel that that is one of the reasons things must be changed. From that point on, September of 1968, I started to look for some organization or group with politics for changing the government of the United States as it now stands, and replacing it with a suitable government. That is how I found the organization that I now belong to—the Young Socialist Alliance. The YSA is a revolutionary socialist youth organization which is struggling for the construction of a socialist world. Abroad, the YSA supports the struggle for socialist democracy in Eastern Europe, the Soviet Union, and China, and the revolutions in Vietnam and Cuba. At home it supports the antiwar movement and the black liberation struggle. Advocating a working-class socialist revolution, the YSA had the concrete goals I was looking for.

As a high school student I felt that my main work, if I wanted to talk to people, discuss ideas, discuss various issues, the war, the government, foreign policy, and the black struggle, would be in the high schools. Just as a black person living in the ghetto would work among the people he lives around: his neighbors, the people he goes to school with, the people he works with.

As I said before, I attend a Catholic girl's school on the South Side of Chicago in a neighborhood which is mostly all-white, conservative, middle-class, quiet, very stable, and content in its situation. Especially in a Catholic school, high school students in general are content with their lot. They are even more apathetic than in most other schools, and apathy was the big problem I ran up against. Although there were some who thought like me, most of the students' discussions in school would revolve around such subjects as—is there life after death?, is God's real name Jesus

Christ?, and so on. We did have one course in the school called World Culture in which we learned world history, current events, and things like that. The topic of Vietnam came up. Of course I felt we should have opinions from both sides, especially since I was amazed to see how little most of the students in the class knew about the situation in Vietnam. In fact I was really appalled.

Our teacher was a typical, right-wing, excuse me, old, senile nun. In a Catholic school you usually have a certain Order of teaching nuns or brothers. They don't have to have the same qualifications as a teacher in a public school. In short, the quality of teaching in a Catholic school is usually much worse because there are no qualifications imposed— like you don't have to have a degree in this or that. And they can get anybody who joins the Order to teach, whether he is qualified to do it or not. As a result, in a lot of courses, you receive a terrible inadequate education. Also there is no age limit. In a private or Catholic school, a teacher can be eighty and going up, and still be allowed to teach. The only one hurt is the student, who has to sit in the classroom and take in this kind of education which is so inadequate.

The education which we supposedly received on the Vietnam War was a one-day discussion on the history up to about 1960. Of course, early American military activity was sort of glossed over, but the Viet Cong were described as bloodthirsty terrorists. One of the speakers who was brought in to educate us was a right-wing writer for the *Tribune,* one of the most conservative, right-wing papers in Chicago. It's known by everyone who lives here and reads it. He was evidently brought in for the sole purpose of attacking me and a group I had formed. I had gotten together a small group of students who were opposed to the war, or had serious doubts about it and wanted to discuss it openly. We were planning on asking the principal for permission to discuss it openly, have meetings in the auditorium, and form an official school group against the war. This was known by the principal and this writer from the *Tribune,* who came in and immediately attacked our group as communist. We were "communist" just because we did not wholeheartedly support the war.

The group was called Concerned Students Against the War Within The Catholic High School. We had no demonstrations, and no disruption of the educational process as they call it; we limited ourselves to debate among the students. In classrooms, we would present our views on the war if the subject came up. We were generally an antiwar group, and we stated our position as such. We talked to people, had meetings outside of school to discuss our politics, and generally discussed what sort of actions we could have against the war, both outside the school and maybe in the future within the school, if we were permitted. As I said before, this writer who was brought in attacked us as "communists" and other nice labels. At this time the Chicago Peace Council was publicizing an action in Chicago for April 5: a massive antiwar demonstration which subsequently did turn out to be a success, drawing thirty-five to forty thousand people out in the streets to protest the Vietnam War. Our group supported the Chicago Peace Council, and we were talking to the kids and building for the demonstration. The writer from the *Tribune* accused the Peace Council of being "communist" and "subversive." He said he had attended one of their meetings, and that they were planning violence. He implied that, because we supported them, we were as bad as they, and as a result, that same day, some of our people were attacked by other students. You'd be surprised how vicious some girls can be, especially if they are provoked by certain teachers and authorities in the school to do this. Later, certain individuals in the group were called down to the office and interrogated. We had had a meeting at my house on a Saturday evening, which obviously did not interfere with school activity. We had tried to make our activities as independent of the school as we could so as not to be accused of anything. After this meeting, the principal was supplied—I don't know who did it and I don't really care—with a list of the people who attended the meeting or people they thought were sympathetic. These people were brought down to the office and questioned.

I was brought in along with the others. We were accused of wild charges. They said it wasn't really an antiwar meeting. They said it was rather a meeting where everybody sat down and smoked marijuana. And all sorts of really weird things; I mean it was unbelievable what they accused us of. They said that our real purpose was to disrupt the educational process. They brought me in and said that I was "militant, defiant, and revolutionary," and that they didn't feel I belonged in the school. Another time they brought me down and said that they heard rumors that I was inciting to riot, "trying to set the blacks against the whites, and the whites against the blacks."

This was the exact opposite of what I was trying to do at this point. I had become more active in the antiwar movement in general and I supported other movements in this country such as the black struggle. Now on the borderline to our school there's a street. On one side it's white and on one side it's black. The attendance at our school has been growing increasingly black, year by year, much to the alarm of the white mothers who were thinking, "Oh, the school's going to ruin, the neighborhood's going to ruin"; they were pulling their daughters out and not sending them there. Their fear has made things really wild. After the death of Martin Luther King we had police and dogs in the school. Of course there were no incidents, except a dog bit somebody. But things like that had been happening. I'd say the school is about 65 percent black now, with each Freshman class becoming increasingly black. The teachers were still all-white, the principal was all-white. There were no black counsellors, black aides, or black anythings in the school; just black students. The black students decided to call for a meeting. They wanted to form an organization, since they wanted to demand certain improvements in the school—things such as black literature in the library. About the only black literature we had was like *Uncle Tom's Cabin*. Now if we can study in school the works of Shakespeare and early English writers, there's no reason why the black students can't study Richard Wright and other black writers and poets from this country and Africa. The education you receive in the Catholic school is all-white, and it's not acceptable for the black students. That's why the group wanted to bring about some changes in the school curriculum.

They held a meeting of about 250 black students one night after school. All of them crammed into one room. Everybody in the meeting was black except for me and three other girls I brought along. In the middle of the meeting, we got up and we endorsed the demands of the black students present. We endorsed the formation of a black student organization. We said we would aid them, in whatever means we could, in actions they were planning, and we formed an alliance with them. That is, our antiwar group, Concerned Students Against the War, formed an alliance with the black student group, the Black Young Ladies of Longwood. Oh yes, it's a very conservative name, but their actions are much different. A white teacher happened to come into the room. She saw me and some other girls speaking. We were very concerned at this point with getting the ideas, and what the black students had done, out to the white students. There was no racial tension at the school, but there was a gap, due to the administration's insensitivity toward black students, and its favoritism of whites. Also, the administration's lack of response to the black demands, and the relative apathy of most white students toward these demands, created a racial gap which we were trying to bridge. After this meeting, I worked with the heads of their organization as much as I could, trying to draw our groups closer together and draw more white students into the black organization. I at least hoped to draw support from the white student body for the black students and their right to form an organization. It was at this point that I was accused of inciting a riot—trying to set the blacks against the whites and the whites against the blacks. This was obviously the direct opposite of what we were trying to do. I was expelled. Not on the ground that my grades were bad or anything, because I am an almost straight-A student. They couldn't do that, so they had to say, "was militant, defiant, revolutionary," and this and that.

Among other ridiculous accusations they made was that I admired hippies, revolutionaries, and all these other weird things. Now in a Catholic school or in a private school, unfortunately, they have the right to look at you and not like you. The principal can get into a consultation with you in a back room, and maybe you say something, he says something, and you get in a heated argument. No matter what your grades are, your behavior, and your deportment in the school, they can expel you. It can be on whatever grounds they want, whether it's throwing a piece of paper down on the ground or being "militant, defiant, revolutionary." They did just that. We students objected by calling a press conference, and having a publicity campaign to counteract all the accusations they made—like that our meetings were really drug sessions, and that we were doing vandalism and all these other wild things in the school. I was eventually successfully expelled by the principal, but the antiwar group and the black student group are, I am happy to say, still in operation. They both have a growing number of members and sympathizers.

The situation in my school and in most of the Catholic and private schools in my area is pretty bad. First of all, you have to wear a uniform. They are pretty ugly, but that doesn't make any difference: it's the fact that you have to wear one. They go below the knee. You can't show the knee because that's a sin. You buy books from the school; they don't supply them. And they just recently installed police in the halls, which causes a bit of friction here and there. The students resent it very much. In our school I've even seen some right-wing students walk behind a cop in the halls whispering derogatory remarks. He gets very mad and he'll turn around and whack a couple of them. The police are not wanted and they are not liked. They serve no purpose in our school. We've never had any racial tensions, we've never had any big disturbances like fights or walk-outs, and I don't feel there is any justification for their being there. I think they are just brought in, like in other schools, to harass the students, to intimidate them, to keep them from expressing their ideas, and to just keep them in a state of inaction. The principal will use any means possible to keep the kids "quiet."

In my school specifically, with the growing number of black students, the level of education has dropped considerably. And it's not the fault of the black students, but the failure of the school to maintain its standards. A lot of academic courses have been dropped, such as cultural courses and writing courses, and they have now installed such things as Business Math and Typing. It has now become sort of a vocational school. Most of the students who graduate from the school do not go on to college, but go straight into business; and the education they receive in my former high school limits them to secretarial jobs, office jobs, and things like that. If they want to go further on, they have to continue their education in a better school. Instead of trying to bring up the level of education by getting in black teachers for the black students, and setting up black courses, what the school is doing now and will probably do within the next five years is closing down. They don't want to make the changes necessary and spend the money, and they say it's because Catholic schools are not financed by the state or federal government. They get their money from tuitions, or in contributions from the parents who send their children there. They tell the growing number of black students enrolled in the school that the money's not coming in and that they just can't operate the school anymore. I think it's a lie. They get more than enough money from the Catholic Church to make up for the smaller contributions they may be getting from the poorer black families. It would take very little concession on their part to install programs and to have teachers and books brought in that would do the school and the students some justice. The black and the white students. But instead, they're closing down the school on the ground that it's inadequate, "we don't have the money, we can't afford to, the neighborhood's going black." This kind of prejudice is affecting Catholic schools all over Chicago. In the past year in Chicago, five Catholic schools were closed down, mainly all-boys' or all-girls' schools, on the pretext that there were no funds to run them. I think that it's really a result of the unwillingness on the part of the principals and the High Order of Nuns to meet the needs of the black students.

My first attempt to talk to students and to organize them into a group or an organization which had differences with the ideas set by the school or with certain issues in the society, got an amazingly good reception from the student body. Most of the students are never exposed to new ideas. Few of them have ever been to a demonstration or been in any organization or done any sort of work in this field. As a result, when you start talking and bringing out antiwar views or socialist views, they are just amazed; most of them have never thought of ideas like this. And they are very interested. Most of them don't get different points of view. They get one view all the time, and they know it. But they're not really sure where to get another view, and when somebody comes in with opposing ideas—ideas contrary to what they have been brought up on—they want to learn as much as they can about them; and I'd say about half of them want to become active. Most of the work in the Catholic schools at this point has been very hush-hush. You see very few examples of open political activity. Most of it is either outside the school, in a small area of the community, or just not publicized.

I hate to say it, but very few Catholic girls will become active on their own. They just don't have the opportunity and they don't know where to turn. And I don't think religion has anything to do with it. If they are given the opportunity to become active, they will very readily. In

Catholic schools at this point most of the activity has been centered around such things as dress codes—"Should we have to wear uniforms?" In guys' schools—"Can we wear long hair and mustaches?" These are the issues that affect them directly. Rarely do you find organized opposition to the war, or involvement with groups that sponsor antiwar activities or open protest.

To gain their objectives in the schools, most of the Catholic students still use liberal methods. Most of them are brought up with the philosophy that, "You can change things through legal channels, disruptive tactics are not necessary. That's only for hippies and violent people." They will present demands—I know this has been done in certain schools. They will get a petition for the abolition of the dress code and they will present it to the administration, only to find out to their surprise that it won't be acted on. It will be shelved away, and they will never hear about it again, unless they bring up the issue. The reaction then is to keep trying. I personally know that measures like this usually will not produce a favorable response on the part of the administration, which is indifferent to students who present their demands in these ways. As a result, the students must use different means. They organize themselves, and they have rallies outside the school office to present demands. Or they go down in a body and present demands. Or they talk to students on a large scale and hold a meeting or a rally to discuss what can be done. Usually Catholic students or students from conservative backgrounds and private schools will not initiate any sort of large-scale protest or disruptive tactics, because that is not the way they have been brought up and that is not the way they think to change things. They try peaceful, legal procedures first. But as I said before, these very often will not work; they see this, and then they progress to new stages which lead to more militant and more radical methods.

More and more Catholic students are beginning to see that to change schools takes action, more than just opening one's mouth and voicing discontent. What is good is that they are beginning to see that it takes unity of action. Not just a group of individuals but a lot of students. As they say, "In unity, there is strength." More and more students are getting together: about such things as dress codes, organizing political groups, improving school conditions. Just about everybody is getting drawn in.

There's a difference between the tactics used, unfortunately, by students in a public school and those in a private school, because in a Catholic school or private school there's always an overhanging fear. In a public school, students have (under a ruling by the Supreme Court this year) the right to wear armbands and buttons to school. It is now more difficult for the administration in a public school to repress them, victimize them, suspend them, or expel them for political expression. They have, in short, some freedom within the law to work together. The atmosphere in public schools is more favorable to political activity than in private schools. The administration of a Catholic or a private school has the right to expel, suspend, or impose any kind of punishments on students who use tactics that are legal in the public schools. The students know it. As a result, there is sort of an overhanging fear from above. God has the almighty power, and God seems to side with unresponsive principals over active students. The students are thus reluctant to engage in activities for which they know they will be struck down.

Despite all this repression, however, I think that most students, when they see that their demands cannot be met by the means they are using, that is, legal means, will become more active. A successful tactic used in a lot of Catholic and private schools is a free speech movement. "We want the right to voice our ideas, we want the right to demonstrate in the school, we want the right to organize." Once students win these rights, they can have more militant actions. They can move on from there. Many fights for things like free speech have been successful, because it's very easy to draw a large number of students around such demands as "freedom to organize." Even in a Catholic school, the administration will be willing to capitulate and grant these concessions. You can draw large numbers of students around demands such as these, and it's easy to get a majority. And in almost any school situation, whether it be private or public, when you have a majority of the students on your side, the administration is forced to give in.

This fall and in the coming months and years, there are going to be more and more students in the Catholic schools voicing their opinions. You are going to see large-scale free speech fights in almost every Catholic and private high school. There will be fights for the rights to organize, have a paper, have political organizations in the school, leaflet, wear armbands, and carry on activities such as protests and rallies. These are going to become more evident in the Catholic schools. I think in most Catholic schools you are going to have open political organizations, such as antiwar organizations, or human relations clubs as they're often called. In some schools, these may be socialist clubs or something to that effect. We are moving toward a period of increased activity in the Catholic schools, mainly around the fight for free speech. I feel that in a few years, or maybe even this coming year, these fights are going to be successful. Where they've already been waged, there've been favorable responses from the students and concessions made by the administration. I think, in short, that Catholic students are going to win the right to become more active, and as a result, will be more active.

VII

THE POLITICS OF THE HIGH SCHOOL MOVEMENT

High school student unions and underground papers have arisen throughout the country. Why are they being established? What power and strength do students gain from organizing themselves? Do these structures provide an outlet for the intelligence and imagination that is squelched in schools? Are students learning more by creating their own organizations and choosing their own life styles? Why have underground papers evolved?

Steve Wasserman from Berkeley and Tom Lindsay from New York describe their experiences in organizing high school unions. Toby Mamis of New York describes why underground papers have to do the work of official school papers.

VII

THE POLITICS OF THE HIGH SCHOOL MOVEMENT

We Will
Exercise Our Rights

by Steve Wasserman

Steve Wasserman lives in Berkeley, California and is the president of Berkeley High School. He is a founder of the Berkeley Student Union and is on the staff of Pack Rat, *the Berkeley Student Union newspaper. He has been active in radical politics since the sixth grade.*

My name is Steve Wasserman. I am president of Berkeley High School in Berkeley, California. I have been in Berkeley since the sixth grade and have been involved in radical activity for the last five years. Since Berkeley has been the center of some of the most radical activity in the country, I naturally have been caught up in it. I have been through all the struggles: the Free Speech Movement, the Vietnam Day Committee, the Troop Train Demonstrations, the Eldridge Cleaver sit-ins, and the Peoples' Park demonstrations.

My first involvement was in the eighth grade when some friends and I organized an antiwar rally. We attempted to set up a Vietnam analysis committee which would be for political education, where kids could come and discuss the war and investigate its origins. The committee turned out to be very effective. We got a lot of student interest. We didn't know all that much about Vietnam, so it was helpful in that it motivated us to do a lot of reading and investigating.

Shortly after this, the hippie phenomenon emerged in the Bay Area. I was somewhat involved in that but not to a great extent. By the time I was in the tenth grade, the hippies were being suppressed and distorted by the media. In addition there was a political crackdown, which radicalized the hippies and led to a synthesis—at least in the Bay Area—between the hard politicos and people like the hippies who wanted a radical life-style. To create a life style that is radical in a society which represses that life style is to become political. This synthesis of life style and politics turned out to be very beneficial to the Movement in the Bay Area, and consequently to the High School Movement.

High school students from all over the area began to question the way the schools were being run. They could see the similarities between the way the hippies were being repressed and the way the schools were forcing students to wear their hair a certain length, to comply with rigid dress codes, and not to question the school's authority. Students began to question; they began to question the school's authority to regulate their life styles and censor their political beliefs.

Students began to organize, and the first thing we did was create a Student Union. This is a union of students—black and white—designed to move for necessary changes in the school. It is an organization that students can relate to, one they can participate in. The Union is decentralized, each Union local formulates its own program independently of any central authority. Yet all schools support and aid each other. We feel that the kind of programs and projects that we will be embarking upon can specifically relate to and involve more students than ever before.

Previously, radicals have made the mistake of talking to students in abstract terms they can't understand or relate to. Like talking to kids about imperialism! Most kids don't even know what imperialism is; however, it is a concept which can be understood through specific examples, like the conditions in the schools that repress them. We can show how that relates to the general society, and what that society does. That's how we radicalize students. Not by telling them, "Here's what's happening man, don't you want to join in on it, don't you dig it," but by relating to them on the basis of their own oppressions.

What students want is action. Students were apathetic in the past because what happened was connected with bullshit student organizations. These organizations said there was a lot to do but never did anything. Students will participate if they have a chance.

For example, last year, during the Peoples' Park episode, we organized a sleep-in at the high school to protest the occupation of Berkeley by the military forces. We refused to leave the campus until peace was returned to the streets. Forty-three Berkeley High kids had been arrested the previous day, some kids had been shot, and it was dangerous just going to and from school. So we organized this sleep-in. We got a few hundred kids to participate: it was an action which they could identify with and believe in. It was a specific thing which related to them; it wasn't some abstract kind of thing which said: sign your name to this petition and that will do it. It was something they could do —something with their bodies. They could participate in an action which had meaning. The sleep-in was very crucial for the development of our kind of politics and how we think the Movement should relate to people. For example, we found that as a result of this repression we developed a great sense of community by just working together. It was really a beautiful thing. We woke up about 6:30 in the morning. The sun was up and we all sat around in a circle to have a communal breakfast and then go to school. It was really a beautiful thing, and the kind of togetherness that grew out of the sleep-in was really wonderful to behold. The alienation that students experience from the school system and from each other was overcome with their willingness to participate in a move that they could identify with.

As a result of this action and other events that occurred

during the year, we developed over the summer a program which we feel speaks for the real needs of Berkeley High students. One of the basic points of the program concerns the exercise of our rights: the right of free speech, the right to leaflet, the right to have independent newspapers, the right to assemble and organize ourselves for our own needs, the right to take political action in our own interests without penalty, the right to do all of these things without administrative restrictions, interference, or approval.

Another point in our program concerns our commitment to struggle against racism. We will struggle against the racism that is institutionalized in the school system, in others, and in ourselves. Racism is used by big business, government, and school administrators to keep us divided and controlled. The competitive tracking and grading system, the daily classroom brainwash (American History, Civics, etc.), and disciplinary procedures are all examples of this racism. In addition there is the racism that is exercised against women.

High schools perpetuate the idea that women are inferior. They discourage girls from preparing for well-paying jobs, and channel them into Home Economics and Business classes. This does a great service to the business interests by supplying cheap office labor and unpaid household laborers. Schools prepare women to produce the next generation of workers and to buy expensive (status) products. Girls are taught to be docile, to be obedient to men, to be cute and stupid, in short, to "know their place." The oppression of women gives the guys a false sense of power. They don't mind being so powerless in the system as long as they have a woman to feel superior to. This is another form of divide-and-conquer by the system. We must all fight male supremacy and struggle for the equality of women.

Our program also calls for an end to the tracking system. The tracking system must be destroyed and replaced by education that has real meaning to us. The tracking system channels students into certain types of jobs. Blacks, Chicanos, and lower-income whites are put into classes that train them for factory jobs and the army. Women are trained for secretarial jobs and household work. Wealthy white kids are prepared for college, leading to professional and managerial positions. We must fight this system that keeps us competing against each other. Our education should not be based on the needs of employers or corporations, but on the needs of people.

We also plan to develop programs and activities that will appeal to students who are turned off the kind of hardline politics that don't integrate a life style with what they are doing. We want to have a joyous Movement. We have to create organizations which reflect the liberated society that we wish to achieve. These organizations can't be disguised in revolutionary rhetoric and merely reflect the class and authority that we oppose. In order to reflect that society which we want to achieve, we have this idea about having a joyous Movement. We want to create fairs, festivals, and centers of communication where students can meet for fun, for expression, and for communication. We will resist all puritanical restraints on what we can or cannot do, what we can say or cannot say, what we can think and what we cannot think. We will be open to a whole realm of things—like cultural fairs, like expressing our feelings about our art work and school work; in sum, we will do what we want, and resist all puritanical restraints.

And in relation to developing activities that are joyous, we intend to end oppressive Physical Education as it now exists. We really resent the military regimentation of Physical Education, the drill sergeant mentality of gym teachers who train us to be submissive, unquestioning, and who try to instill in us an attitude that prepares us for the army. We will not tolerate it any longer. Physical Education has been one of the most overt physically repressive institutions in the modern school; it is indicative, to a large extent, of the medieval conditions in our schools. We believe that Physical Education is a good thing, but we believe that Physical Education doesn't have to subordinate the individual. We recognize the right of any student to refuse to participate in

PE without academic penalty. At the present time you can complete all of your academic courses and get an F in gym for four years and not pass high school. They keep you in high school until you pass gym. We believe in Physical Education but feel it should be an open class where students can be free. I've seen kids who have flunked out of gym go all out and expend a hell of a lot of energy in an after-school game of soccer or something like that. After-school games are voluntarily entered into, not imposed from above. For example, as it is now, everyone has to wear the same kind of uniform with a gray sweatshirt. Well, we plan to organize a spontaneous demonstration where everyone will wear multi-colored sweatshirts. We envision mass refusals to run one more lap around the track, or a mass sit-down strike.

Our program also calls for an end to administrative control of student elections and organizations. We have to have student government that belongs to the students—that isn't manipulated by the administration and isn't a puppet or a rubber stamp for administration policies. We have to turn control of student elections and student activities over to students.

Similarly, we want to end suspensions and expulsions. The majority of suspensions and explusions are for things like cutting. It seems ridiculous to suspend a student if he doesn't want to come to school in the first place. In addition, suspensions and expulsions serve to repress high school kids for political activities. They slap you with a suspension based on being disobedient to a teacher or inter-fering with a teacher in the performance of her duties. The definition of interference is left up to the administration. As they define it, it can cover anything. Talking back could be interference. We want to end suspensions and expulsions, and to develop human and humane means of dealing with disciplinary problems. And that means use of counselling and extensive sensitivity sessions with kids, parents, and teachers, where the whole problem can be talked out.

Basically, our program is one that students can relate to. Students can relate to getting screwed up by gym teachers, they can relate to having a good time in school, they can relate to an end to suspensions and expulsions, and they can relate to uniting with other people. They can relate to ending racism, and girls can relate to liberating themselves. Students can relate to having control over their own lives and control over their own activities, and they can relate to exercising their rights.

Part of the program that we have developed can't be put into practice within the existing system, since we would have to work on its terms: those terms are inherently repressive and bog us down in a lot of red tape. That is why we have formed a Student Union. The Student Union is inherently a more responsive and representative kind of government (if you wish to call it that) than is the student government.

Our means of communicating our program will be through the underground press and the various programs and activities that I have outlined. There is no way of utilizing the official school newspaper, since it is under the control of the Journalism department and is subject to faculty review. All the articles that are submitted to school newspapers are subject to faculty approval, and if an article says something that doesn't deal with the school—like the war in Vietnam—it won't be printed.

Another point about our program is that we are not demanding it. We find that demands, in most instances, obfuscate the real nature of the struggle. And in most instances tend to co-opt it. We are not demanding any of our points because we don't recognize that the administration has the authority to give them to us. In a fundamental way the administration has no power to grant them. A lot of the things we want are against state law. The local school board and administration have no power to change state law. All they can say is, "Well, we are just carrying out state law, we are for you; as a matter of fact, we want to change those laws but can't do it." And that is why we have to carry out our program. We are not going to go to Reagan. We are not going to the state, we're not going to the federal government. We are going to begin implementing the program—and begin breaking the law. Our actions will gain respect and support among students. Students know they have rights. If the authorities don't recognize that, well, fuck them. That will be our attitude. We are going to put this into practice and get students to come and support us by exercising our rights.

For example, after we print our program we're going to start leafletting it on campus. Exercising our rights. We are going to leaflet and we are not going to ask for permission. If the administration suspends us, we enter into another phase. We will call a rally for the next day. Students will clearly see that the administration had come down on us for merely exercising our rights, and we will gain their respect. This program cuts to the core of the system, and the administration, even if sympathetic to our goals, will be put in the unfortunate position of defending the status quo. By beginning to implement this program we will put the administration up against the wall. And even if they are sympathetic, the only thing that they will be able to do—because of pressure from above—is begin to repress our movement.

Obviously there will be a conflict between what we would like to see happen and what school officials themselves would like to see; what may finally emerge may be a compromise, or one side may win out. Ideally, if we are to preserve any kind of meaningful education, all courses should be made to relate to each other. Subjects should not be learned in a vacuum. Lots of kids say mathematics is irrelevant. Well, when you look closely, mathematics is not at all irrelevant. Society needs mathematics in the technology that runs our kind of society—it is a kind of circular relationship. What has to be demonstrated, though, is the relationship between biology, history, and mathematics. All of these things have to be related.

I think a lot of the student revolt is a cry against specialization. Although specialization was once necessary for industrialization and technology, I think that there will be a return to the Renaissance Man: a man who not only knows a lot, but knows a lot about many things in depth, and can see the relationships between them. Like the relationships between people, government, society, nature, and wildlife. There has to be more emphasis on the sociological aspects of relationships. And that is what I think schools will have to involve themselves with. The fundamental questions concerning human and societal relations have to be explored and explained, and out of them has to grow a curriculum with course content which will involve and relate to people and their needs.

High School Students Unite

by Tom Lindsay

> *Tom Lindsay is a member of the New York High
> School Student Union and is on the staff of the New
> York* High School Free Press. *In 1968 Tom was a
> founder of the High School Independent Press Ser-
> vice (HIPS). He writes and draws excellent political
> cartoons for underground papers.*

Hello Boys and Girls.
I am a "High School Revolutionary."
This is a book about "High School Revolutionaries."
There are lots of books like this about lots of people.
Most of them stink.
This one will probably stink too.
But I need the money.

This country sucks. Its television, its ulcer pills, its
senators, its cities, its cars, its Miss America pageants, its
churches, its money, its objectivity in the media, its Miami
Beaches, its army, and its schools. Schools and parents are
the foundation of America's schizophrenia. Kids rebel in
lots of ways against what they feel and see going on around
them. And so I rebel against this insane society.

I'm the son of a preacher. I went to church, I was a nice
kid. But it's a drag being a nice kid. Because being a nice
kid means you get good grades, don't get drunk or stoned,
go to college, meet a nice girl, get married, kiss for the first

time, get a job, bring up nice kids, die a nice death—and nobody, least of all you, ever knew you lived.

I didn't want to be a nice kid after a while. So I started rebelling in lots of ways, I started smoking (cigarettes), got drunk, stopped going to church, started going to dances, started making it with girls, stopped getting good grades, skipped school on nice days and went riding in convertibles to MacDonald stands, and just started fucking around.

I began to feel more. The "in" crowd was hard as shit to make it in and I didn't make it, so I hung around with a lot of other guys in the same position. Wanting kicks but not making the top. All those guys and girls I hung around with were lonely and you could feel it. We were cool but somehow that didn't fill up everything. So I began to look around even more. I began to move with this one group of people at school. The "beautiful people." I became a goddam hippie.

I got stoned. I made new friends. We talked a lot, bullshit mostly, but we began to explore new things and thoughts. It was just a start but fuck it you have to start somewhere.

That was the time (half-way through eleventh grade) I started getting political. I turned against the Vietnam War. I went to the March on Washington, October 21, 1967. I saw people get teargassed.

Then there was a drug bust at my high school. I didn't get busted, but after most of it was over the Sergeant of Police of the town of Wellesley, Massachusetts, told my parents I had turned on. The school told me get my hair cut, and I decided that school sucks. Teachers suck, the country sucks, the war sucks, racism sucks. The school newspaper sucks.

I decided to start an underground paper. My friends dug the idea and we did it. In February 1968, the first edition of *The Searcher* came out.

Then the administration cracked down with THE IMMORTAL DRESS CODE. No cocksucker is going to tell me to get my hair cut unless I also have the power to tell him to grow his hair long.

We fought the dress code. We circulated petitions, a
majority of kids wanted to change it, and so we went to the
School Committee. They finally agreed but in their own
bullshit way. They formed a Dress Code Committee (Mah
fella Americans, after this brutal and senseless assasination
tonight, I am forming a commission to study violence). So
in the tradition of fine, upstanding, bullshit liberals we finally took a vote between four different dress codes (democracy of course). The first choice was no dress code, the
second was almost no dress code—just prohibiting shorts,
curlers, and slacks for girls, the third was the same dress
code, and the fourth was a stricter dress code. When the
votes came in a thousand kids out of fourteen hundred voted
for the first two with the second getting the most of all.
Eight people voted for a strict dress code. We had won. It
was a good feeling. We had beaten the administration.

From there, *The Searcher* continued to come out, getting better all the time. We held a three-day hunger strike
against the war and started a lot of programs around the
draft. On April 26, 1968, when 200,000 kids stayed out of
school in New York against the war, we in Wellesley succeeded in getting forty kids to stay out of school and march
up to a teach-in at Wellesley College. The once quiet,
efficient system in Wellesley was fucking up, then the big
bomb came.

In late May, the first three periods one day were cancelled in order to have a special program on poverty and
racism. There were speakers, films, and a selection of pieces
by black authors put on by the Boston Theatre Co. One of
those pieces was a part of LeRoi Jones' play, *The Slave*.
Jones doesn't talk to nice white liberals. There were a lot of
"fucks," "shits," etc. in the play. After the play there were
discussion groups—I didn't hear one kid complain about
the swear words. But it wasn't the same for the racist adults
of town. They had shit fits. Thirteen hundred people came
out for a School Committee meeting. The school auditorium was packed. Every goddam right winger of the town
was there, and they were out for blood. People got up to

speak; back and forth it went, those for the program and those against it. The whole place was polarized. Good guys —bad guys: clap for good guys, boo for bad guys. The place was tense as shit. Then the editor of the official school paper, a Student Council member and Varsity letter winner, got up and said, "The first time I heard the word fuck was when I was five years old and right here in Wellesley. And I know a lot of people who can't say a sentence without saying fuck in it." That blew it . . . If you think a thousand Russian Stalinists on the rampage is bad, this was really fucked up. The whole audience rose screaming "Shut him up." "Get him out. Arrest him." I think I heard "Lynch him" in there too. The crowd was crazy, stark raving mad. Two cops came in and arrested him and took him out. We were sitting there stunned with this raging audience behind us and a kid getting busted in front of us. To top it off, the vice principal got up and ripped the student dissenters up. For the next month the town was crazy, but the incident finally died away. I learned a lot out of it. For the first time I saw America revealed, and what I saw was frightening. Up until then it had been one principal or something, but now it was all these people. This was America—against me.

Shortly after that I moved to New York. I went to Brandeis High for my last year of high school (as well as school in general). Brandeis is an amazing school. Like, in New York they can't build schools right. Schools are either shitholes that are like used condoms that have been sitting around for a year, or so sterile they're like condoms straight out of the package, sterile like hospitals. Brandeis is 85 percent black and Puerto Rican. Quite a change from sterile people in Wellesley. Even though black schools have a reputation for being worse than suburban schools, Brandeis is very similar to Wellesley—with the same type of fucks running it, calling themselves administrators, teachers, guidance counsellors, etc. It is different in the sense that the school system cannot allow a majority of black and brown students to graduate and go on to college, while in white schools the majority of kids do go to college.

While in New York I also started working on the High School Independent Press Service (HIPS). HIPS is a press service for high school underground (news)papers. In the packets we sent out we had national high school news, articles, analysis, poems, cartoons, photos etc. I worked on that till January.

For the first three months of that year there was no school because of the teachers' strike. Kids and a few teachers opened their schools against the racist UFT strike. Kids started their own schools, and ran things in many schools. When the strike was finally over, the UFT and the Board of Education decided that classes would be forty-five minutes longer and some holidays cut in order for the teachers to make up their pay. (Teachers ended up making more money for striking than if they had not gone on strike.) A lot of people all over the city, including high school students, denounced the settlement. The bit about the pay was bad enough, but no kid is going to sit through an extra forty-five minutes of bullshit and miss any holidays. All over the city, black, Puerto Rican, and white students spontaneously walked out, went on strike, and shut down their schools. Thousands of kids ran through the streets, held rallies, fought the cops, took over subways, and said "Hell no we won't go. Fuck UFT."

At Brandeis a leaflet went out: "Are you going to take forty-five minutes more of this shit? No!" Thirty kids ran through the halls. Students poured out. The bell rang; students milled in the lobby. "Hell no we won't go." Finally over six hundred kids walked out. Classes were called off. Four hundred students took over the nearby subways and went to a rally downtown where they were joined by thousands more. For a week the strike went on, but the next week kids were back in school taking the same shit. In a lot of schools, holidays were given back and the forty-five minute period cancelled.

I just fucked around at Brandeis, I didn't do much work. I found out that I could graduate in January. I cut a lot of classes and ended up going to about two weeks of

classes. Near the end of the semester a few kids got together
and we put out a paper that looked exactly like the school's
official paper but had a totally different content. The administration and teachers flipped out. We were almost able
to get the teachers to hand it out unknowingly but some of
them read it. Teachers were running around screaming,
"This isn't *our Brandeis Brief!*"

No one was caught handing out the first issue because
we handed it out without teachers seeing us in school. The
second issue was even better. We had a short thing on how
people were handing out a phony *Brandeis Brief* and not to
listen to them because they were just troublemakers. This
time another kid and I were caught. The other guy they
transferred to another school, and they almost kicked me
out of school ten days before I graduated. They decided to
let me stay as long as I didn't cause any more trouble. I
didn't, or at least I didn't get caught. I graduated from one
of America's most amazing institutions—a high school.

In early March, kids from HIPS, the *High School Free
Press,* and the High School Student Union, got together and
started talking about a spring offensive in the high schools.
We wanted to really try and do something that would last
when the demonstrations were over. One thing about New
York schools is that it is easy to get kids to walk out or
demonstrate or take any type of action. On a nice spring
day it doesn't take much at all. As we saw with the forty-
five-minute strike, kids went out of school and rioted, but a
week later the same old fucked-up system was running and
doing the same old shit. We wanted to organize. There are
two ways you can hand out a leaflet. One is to let the leaflet
speak for you, the second is to let the leaflet assist you in
speaking yourself. You use the medium to get your message
across, you talk to people. Talking to people is more likely
to get your message across.

Too easily you can set yourself apart. To sit behind
four walls and publish your opinions allows no contact
with what is happening with people. SDS has a rhetoric
about what's happening in this country but most of it

doesn't mean anything because they have never talked to
the people they theorize about. The whole thing is this—
people who talk don't do shit (intellectuals, liberals, college
revolutionaries, etc.). You have to find out what is happening, where people's heads are at. YOU DON'T FOLLOW A
THEORY—YOU LIVE ONE. YOU DON'T FOLLOW CHRIST—
YOU ARE CHRIST. YOU DON'T FOLLOW MARX—YOU ARE
MARX. YOU DON'T FOLLOW THE PEOPLE—YOU ARE THE
PEOPLE.

This we felt and believed. We got ourselves together.
What we basically tried to do—and did in many cases—was
to get kids to feel themselves as organizers. Just small
groups of kids, maybe five to ten in each school and in
thirty to forty of the city's eighty-nine public high schools.
Building organizers and becoming one yourself is hard.
You're brought up in this country not to relate to people or
maybe just a small group of people. People lead alienated
and lonely lives in America. Take a look at your parents,
those little old secretaries, etc. To build a life where you do
more than comment on the weather, is hard. But it can be
done.

To help us that spring we developed a ten-point program which we elaborated in the *High School Free Press*
and in leaflets and demonstrations. The program was one of
the best in the country. The *Free Press* was dynamite. (It
was also one of the few working-class papers in the country;
but not only working-class, it was middle-class, black,
Puerto Rican, hippie, yippie, and in general everybody's
paper.) And the leaflets were fantastic. But we weren't all
that good. We had a lot of fuck-ups, we had a lot of
bullshit. We were too centralized, often too elitist, and we
didn't get stoned.

I moved out of my parents' house and into the High
School Student Union office/apartment with a couple of
other guys. Later more people (boys and girls) moved in.
We formed a commune. The commune story is another trip
in itself. I will say this about it: to be a revolutionary means
more than developing revolutionary politics. It means also

developing your emotions and the way you relate to people. The revolution means building yourself as a person, as a human being. If you have never gone through a communal experience, do it. But don't make the mistake of isolating your emotions from your politics, or your politics from your emotions. To be just political sucks. To be just emotional sucks. Everything must be together. You are one.

The commune was the service group for the Union and *Free Press*. We raised money for the *Free Press*, we distributed it to the local student unions, we got bail and lawyers for busted kids, we printed and distributed city-wide leaflets, we printed the local unions' leaflets and papers, and we helped set up film showings. We helped local leaders and organizers do their thing.

Our relations with the three black student groups in the city were very good. We related to them on a political and personal level. This didn't mean they became Toms or we became soul brothers. In many locals, leaders got together to talk about tactics, actions, what was happening, etc. In a couple of cases the High School Student Union started Black Student Union locals, and the Black Student Union started High School Student Union locals. On April 21, all four high school groups went out on strike. Black, Puerto Rican, and white kids were out on the streets or taking over schools together. One day fifty kids were busted, black and white, and the Union bailed them all out.

Right now I'm out of high school and I'm out of high school organizing. Already high school seems like a long time ago. I don't have that feeling, that way of being, now that I'm out. I don't belong in the high school scene. Too many people don't belong in the high school scene that are there now. When you're faced with the frustrations of organizing and this high school kid comes up to you and says, "We're trying to do something at our school, do you know anything that can help us?"—it's all too easy to start organizing high school kids. It's all too easy to organize kids who will listen to whatever you say because it's radical. (High school students who have offices with older Movement groups often end up with that group's type of politics.) The problem that's facing me and lots of other people is, what do you do after high school? I chose not to go on to college because it's bullshit—for my life. It's really scary at seventeen to try and live your life like you want to, with as little bullshit as possible. You're living your life *now*. Most people never do, they keep saying, "Well, after college I'm going to fuck around," but then they get jobs and, "Well, after I retire I'm going to see the world, etc. Well, after I die I'm going to . . ."

I feel a need for a major change in this country (commonly called revolution). But how the hell do you make a revolution in America? Everybody's got his, "After the revolution, we'll have . . ." But how do you get to after? I'm not really sure, but I have learned stuff through my high school experiences that will help me. I know that one of the greatest hang-ups people and organizers have is talking to people. They can talk rhetoric to you until your ears fall off, but they can't talk stuff that means something to people. You shouldn't be all that different talking to somebody you are organizing or talking to your girl friend or boy friend. That doesn't mean you tell workers you love them, but it means that you speak with the same honesty. (And vice versa. Don't tell a girl a big cool rap about yourself when you only want to sleep with her. Just ask her, "Do you want to sleep with me?") You have to know who you are. You have to have an identity, a feeling about yourself. You have to be proud of yourself as a man or woman. Not only do black people have problems knowing where they're at, but white people grow up in this same fucked-up country and get fucked over too (in different ways). We have to cut the bullshit in our lives. We have to define our own reality. We are not part of Nixon's and the other top idiots' reality. Their reality is in Vietnam with 40,000 dead, their reality is in the black ghettoes with twenty million hardly alive, their reality is in this country's high schools with passes to piss. Our reality is alive and we have to fight for it!

LONG LIVE
Elvis Presley
Jimmy Dean
The Twist
Drinking in the back seat
Saddle shoes
Smoking in the lavs
The Beatles
The Rolling Stones
Lyndon Johnson (and family)
The Mothers of Invention
Samuel Graves (Principal of Wellesley High
School)
Leo Hession
Ray dope Mungo
Eldridge Cleaver
Abbie Hoffman
The High School Commune
The High School Free Press
Tommy Agee

LET'S GO METS!

This story was written by a high school radical leader. Among his many aliases are George Meteskey, Tom Lindsay, and Abbie Hoffman.

The High School Underground Press: A Brief History of the New York Underground High School Press and Why Underground Papers Are Necessary

by Toby Mamis

Toby Mamis is sixteen and an editor of the New York Herald-Tribune, *an underground paper in New York City. A former student at Stuyvesant High School, he has quit to help establish a new experimental high school for discontented students. It is called the New World School.*

Four years ago, Paul Steiner and some friends started on a venture that has changed a lot of people's lives and a lot of people's heads. They started *Sansculottes,* a high school independent publication, at the Bronx High School of Science. Mimeographed at first, it soon grew in popularity, and gained wider distribution. It also grew in terms of format. It became a photo-offset tabloid, growing to a size of twenty pages at one point. *Sans* was a monthly for three years, until Fall 1968. At that point, the paper was city-wide. Then came a teachers union strike, which the radical High School Movement physically and loudly opposed.

Somewhere along the way, a paper was also started at John Bowne High School. Also started in mimeograph form, it soon became a tabloid, and although never as big, as well known, or as widespread as *Sans,* it served its purpose at Bowne High School. But its founders thought that something new was needed—a city-wide high school paper. In the spring of 1968, *the New York High School Free Press* was established.

That very same spring of 1968 saw the birth of the *Other Other* at Brooklyn Technical High School, and the *Flea* at Stuyvesant High School. Along the way, *Common Sense II* (the official journal of the Bronx Science antiwar group), Seward Park's *Neo-Dwarf,* the Student Mobilization's *Student Mobilizer, Neuk,* and many other papers and magazines were formed. To coordinate all the papers, Paul Steiner set up the High School Independent Press Service, so that all the papers could share advice and experiences, as well as articles. But HIPS never really got off the ground.

During the summer of 1968, some papers were folding, because of graduating staffs, while others were going through changes. The *Other Other* and the *Flea* merged into the *New York Herald-Tribune.*

With the appearance of the NYHSFP, Paul, Merry Maran, Jon Grell, and the rest of the *Sans* staff decided that their paper was no longer effective. The reason it wasn't effective was that they had changed their criterion for effectiveness. A monthly tabloid was no longer needed at any one school. City-wide tabloids would be fine, but something local would be much more effective—especially at a school like Bronx Science which had witnessed the growth of the High School Movement. So they put out *Mama* for a few months (during the UFT strike). It was almost the first radical daily. It was a one-page broadside printed as often as possible, and given out free at Bronx Science.

To replace *Sans,* some former staffers got together and formed *The Rebirth of Wonder* at Bronx Science, another photo-offset tabloid. So that made three tabloids in the city: the *Rebirth,* the *Herald-Tribune,* and the *Free Press.*

The UFT strike delayed the first issue of the *High School Free Press* for several weeks. But the *Herald-Tribune* was on sale the first day of the strike, with its first issue, and even came out with a second issue two months later—still during the strike. The *Herald-Tribune* at that point was mainly based at Stuyvesant, Brooklyn Tech, and Hunter. Its staff was instrumental in opening up Stuyvesant and keeping it open during the strike. Washington Irving, a neighboring, all-girls' school (Stuyvesant was then all-boys), was closed, even though there was more sentiment among its students and teachers for its being open than there was among the students and faculty at Stuyvesant. So, while "liberation of Washington Irving" battle plans were being prepared, the girls and their teachers attended Stuyvesant. This gave birth to what at first was only a "temporary paper." *The Weakly Reader* was formed as the official paper of the two "Liberated Schools." Rexographed at first, it later grew into mimeographed form. The paper stayed alive for the entire school year, even after the strike, until it underwent changes in the fall of 1969.

In the middle of the ten-week strike, the first issue of the *High School Free Press* came out. It covered the Chicago police riot at the convention, the founding of the High School Student Union, and other topics of interest to high school students. Much of its material was taken from the pages of a new journal coming out of the offices of Liberation News Service—the High School Independent Press Service. This was essentially the same service mentioned earlier, except that this one worked for a while. The staff of *Mama* was mostly responsible for getting HIPS out regularly. It contained news of the high school struggle all over the country, and reprinted graphics from all the different high school papers.

At the end of the strike, *Mama* disappeared, never to be seen again. But the *Rebirth of Wonder* was still there. It started out as more of a literary journal than an organizing tool, but soon grew in much the same way as *Sans*.

The next school year, 1969–1970, saw even more of a turnover. *Rebirth* had died, although there was an attempt to salvage it with an entirely new staff. The *Weakly Reader* and the *Herald-Tribune* merged, growing bigger and getting better. HIPS had died in the middle of the previous year, and frantic efforts were being made to revive it.

This has been a sort of outline of how the radical press grew in New York City. Elsewhere in the country, there was *Tradition*, the *Open Door*, *Links*, the *Freethinker*, the *Frox*, the *South Dakota Seditionist Monthly*, the *Finger*, *Smuff*, the *Sad-Eyed Lady*, the *Roach*, *Ann Arbor Gazette*, *Student Liberation Front*, *New American Mercury*, and hundreds of others.

Some were (are) more professional than others. Some appeared more regularly than others. Some were more effective than others. Some were better than others. But they were all united by common goals. The first goal was a revolution within the educational system; the second (second only because some papers were a bit wary of this position) was a revolution here in America, a REAL revolution.

To understand why we feel that revolution is the answer, how we came to that conclusion, and how we, as the high school revolutionary press, handle it, you must first understand the differences between the official school papers and the "revolutionary" press (the troublemakers).

The official high school papers vary as much in quality and format as the underground papers do. Some of them are elaborately produced journals, trying to look as much like *The New York Times* as possible on a limited budget.

Others are simple tabloids, some are magazines, and still others are merely mimeographed or rexographed.

Some are politically liberal, some are moderate, most are conservative or even reactionary; the chances are one in a million that you'll find a radical journal that is the official publication of an accredited high school. But these titles mean very little without substance. For instance, if a big city school paper in the Northeast devoted a great deal of space to the grape pickers' strike while not covering a student strike in the same school, there would be something wrong; but one can understand why a newspaper in Southern California would devote most of its space to the grape pickers' struggle.

The "official" paper is generally sponsored by the school's General (or Student) Organization. It receives funds from the school, and is required to have all material pass inspection before going to the printer. There is usually a faculty advisor (chosen from the English faculty) who looks the material over; if he finds anything objectionable, he goes to the principal with it. *Then* it is censored. When the editor of a high school paper writes an editorial opposing the administration (if he has the awareness and the courage to do so), he is usually faced with the prospect of spending several hours with the principal, defending his editorial position. The author of an article about any radical action or political topic, if he dares to write anything left of center, must learn to fight for his right to free speech and a free press. That is how the student learns at first hand that the Bill of Rights applies only to certain people, and that he usually isn't among those "certain" people.

Usually, to write for the school paper, you have to have taken the Journalism course offered in the school. Conversely, to get into the Journalism class, you must have experience on the newspaper. Another roadblock to many students (especially poorer ones) is that you must be a member of the G.O. to write for the paper, and that costs money.

During the Presidential primaries, a lot of moderate and

liberal kids woke up. They realized that even though a large majority of people in their communities wanted either McCarthy or Kennedy, it seemed that there was to be no news of their campaigns in any of the school papers; nor was there any mention of "other party" candidates, *except Wallace.* This is not to infer that either Kennedy or McCarthy offered any viable alternative to Nixon or Humphrey. My personal feelings are that there was no difference between any candidates running for the nominations, and that they were (and still are) undeserving of recognition for anything other than their wholehearted support for the American way of life (killing, stealing, lying, cheating, exploiting, and covering up badly). But a lot of kids thought Kennedy and McCarthy *did* represent some hope for the future. And when they saw what "patriotic Americans" did to the campaigns, campaigners, and demonstrators, they either realized that the radicals had been right all along, or they showed their true selves as part of the American machine of Death by supporting Humpty Dumpty.

Those that were repulsed by what they saw that summer tended to become active in the Movement. Many of them started underground papers, especially those who had worked on regular papers. So the Chicago police riot was a shot in the arm for all aspects of the Movement, especially in the high schools.

Many papers got started when the school year (1968–1969) started. That year showed a large increase in radical activity. More and more kids had been turning on to all kinds of things which were considered illegal or improper, and they got hassled or thrown out of school for it. One paper in the Midwest was started by a young man who was thrown out of school for some silly reason; he soon found a staff, and prospered in the Movement. Other papers got started during the joint High School Student Union-SDS-Black Panther Spring Offensive in the schools and communities. There have even been junior high school, intermediate school, and elementary school activists and newspapers.

As the 1969–1970 school year enters its fourth month, the drop in the number of high school radical papers is noticeable. This is probably due to the fact that people are getting frustrated to the breaking point by the Nixon Administration, and have given up trying.

The high school underground press has been the subject of a lot of coverage by the media (TV, radio, newspapers, books, magazines, etc.). As the radical papers became known to the community, TV stations would call the staffs and ask for interviews, newspaper reporters would call, etc. What this means is NOT that the papers are a hot story that *deserves* exposure so that people can see what we are doing, and understand what we're all about; it means that the journals or stations will have a story that they can advertise, and sell themselves with. There are a lot of people who want to know more about this "phenomenon," and they are attracted to the mass media when there is a story on radical media. Then they are lured into the pages of the publication, and are told, via advertising, which kind of underwear is better, why one soda is better than the other, and which movie is more "honest."

In addition to the use of anti-capitalist media to sell more copies of capitalist media, there is a dispute about responsible journalism. When members of the staffs of underground papers are interviewed and written up, what they have said inevitably comes out wrong. Does it come out wrong on purpose? Is it unconscious yet deliberate? Is it merely an accident? When *The New York Times* puts us down as "Revolutionaries Who Have To Be Home By 7:30," we know that they are making light of our Movement on the basis of age. People who refer to us as revolutionaries who have to be home by 7:30, or other such condescending names, are merely "Reactionaries Who Can't Get It Up." One-sided journalism is their tool, and they have the gall to blame us for not being objective. We have to tell our side of the story—in self-defense. It has come to that. *The New York Times* has an ad campaign:

"If It Isn't in the *Times* Index, Maybe It Didn't Happen."
And a slogan: "All the News That's Fit To Print." That's a
laugh. Who decides what is and isn't fit to print? Who
decides what goes into the *Times* Index? Does that mean
that I wasn't born? After all, it wasn't reported in the
Times. The *Times* has the power to make news happen. If
they ran a story on the front page of the paper that was
false, they could have people believing it for years. They are
that respected. People read the *Times* as if it were God
himself.

The mass media won't cover anything unless: 1) it will
make them some money, 2) it will improve their image, 3)
it is to their political liking and/or advantage. As an example, may I tell you of a piece in the *Daily News* of last
spring (1968). During the Republican mayoral primary,
some *News* reporters worked long and hard to find something wrong with Mayor Lindsay; they came up with an
office that was allegedly handling his campaign for re-
election at cost to the city. They came armed with cameras,
reporters, etc., but they didn't notify the proper city department of the infraction of the law at all. They waited until
the story broke, and let the city handle it from there. The
News was avidly supporting Lindsay's opponent in the primary, John Marchi.

The mass media are master mind-manipulators.

Whenever a high school underground paper appears,
there is considerable discussion as to what to do with the
"troublemakers." The debate is usually about whether to
suspend or to expel him/her. However, sometimes the
"commies" are lucky. They get off with confiscation, a
black mark on the record, a letter home, and probation.
Lucky. In Russia you have that kind of freedom.

Whatever happened to the idea of a free press? Reporters are beaten up all the time . . . Underground papers
have a hard time finding printers . . . Street sellers get
arrested for selling radical papers (for which you don't need
a permit) . . . Students get thrown out on their asses for
owning copies of underground papers . . . Teachers get

fired for having anything to do with radical students, activities, and/or papers. . . .

One day I decided to test the rule that was being used to prevent me from distributing my newspaper inside the school in the lunchroom. I gave out my paper, with some friends, and we all got stopped, threatened, and yelled at by the principal. The next week, we got some straighter-looking friends to give out the official UFT (United Federation of Teachers) newspaper. The teachers gratefully accepted free copies, and didn't halt the distribution of the papers. We have photos of this to prove it.

The school is a public place. It is as public as the Port Authority or a park. It is inside this country, and there is no reason why the laws should change inside one doorway and not the next.

The Emergency Civil Liberties Committee, and to a lesser extent, the American Civil Liberties Union, have been backing us up with lawyers and publicity. They will always tell us in advance whether a suggested action will bring trouble or not, and they will always tell us whether or not they can help us. William Kunstler, one of the best civil liberties lawyers in the nation (he has defended Dr. King, H. Rap Brown, Morton Sobel, Black Panthers, Freedom Riders, draft resisters, students), has fought in the courts for student rights, and is currently representing seven of the Chicago Conspiracy 8.

The administrations of the schools know this. They know that we will bring them to court at the slightest provocation, and they act accordingly. When they know a student knows his rights and isn't scared to assert them, they are scared and react like the pigs that they are. They either run and hide, or they take him on and—in the long run—lose. But with the fascist trend in this country, the courts may very well turn against us in the near future. Then there will undoubtably be more drastic action. Already, there are reactionary courts. Huey Newton found one, as did John Sinclair, as did the Panther 21 in N.Y.C. Ed Sanders wrote that we should plan jailbreaks if we fail in the courts. Judge Hoffman in Chicago is a caricature fascist. If it's jailbreaks they want, it's jailbreaks they'll get.

Why the underground high school media?
Why a radical Movement?
To struggle against the existing social structure, the present governmental system, today's consciousness.
To struggle for power over our own.
To build a revolutionary consciousness, so that the people will realize that they are oppressed and exploited, and so that they will rise up and fight back.
To build a revolution.
High school students are oppressed. We are controlled by our school environment. The teachers and the administrators have considerable control over our lives. They write our college recommendations, without which (they tell us) we can't get a "meaningful job." They channel and track us into different classes so that we cannot get to know each other. They resist letting Third World students learn to understand their own culture, while insisting that they learn white America's culture. They impose their will on the students. But students are fighting back now. We are fighting back the best way we know how.

We are fighting back with newspapers, leaflets, demonstrations, building seizures, disruptions, riots, bombings, etc. Some of these activities are led by irresponsible students, causing damage irresponsibly. But these students are *agents provocateur*. They are planted by the administration to make the Student Movement look bad. They cause trouble where trouble isn't warranted, to give teachers and pigs the excuse needed to beat on student leaders. You will *never* find a serious revoluntionary student organization taking political action unless the action will have political results, and *never* will a student organization take an action that endangers the lives of hundreds (or thousands) of fellow students.

This is the position of my newspaper, and most others. It is the only way to win.

ALL POWER TO THE PEOPLE!
POWER TO THE PEOPLE'S PAPERS!
TOGETHER WE WILL WIN . . .

VIII

WOMEN'S LIBERATION IN THE SCHOOLS

The movement for women's liberation is an effort to raise women from their second-class status. High school women are now asking for their liberation. How do high schools oppress and subjugate women? Why are women conditioned and channeled into certain courses? Do women always have to be pretty, gentle, docile, and submissive? Is their place only in the home as a wife and mother?

Maxine Orris addresses herself to these questions. Maxine wrote her statement.

Don't Miss America

by Maxine Orris

> *Maxine Orris is a member of the New York High School Student Union and a former staff member of the* New York High School Free Press. *She presently devotes all her time to the Women's Liberation Movement.*

Walking down the halls hearing "Hey! Chickie, what's ya doing tonight," or, "Nice," or, "Looks good," I look down at my feet and keep walking to my Home Economics class. But what am I ashamed of?

Being a "girl"?

When I was little I played whatever games I wanted to, like baseball. Whenever I talked loudly or got dirty from playing outside I was called "tomboy."

Why? I was a girl and I wasn't meant to be this way.

Later in the sixth grade I learned that no one liked me anymore. Women didn't like me because I was headstrong enough to play with the boys. Boys didn't like me because society's attitudes were becoming their attitudes and they didn't think playing rough games was feminine. I stopped being a "tomboy" and submitted to a woman's role.

Later when I went to parties and had dates I saw the kind of competition women were forced to engage in. They are conditioned to believe the only thing they can have is a relationship with one man and that he in turn will relate to the world for them. Consequently if a woman rebels or

withdraws from the competition to get "one man" because
she feels whole by herself, she is called "frigid." If she
doesn't have a boy friend she is considered worthless, in-
complete, and unimportant. Such attitudes and values rein-
force the competition with other women and allow us to stab
each other in the back, with cruel incessant talk: "Is she still
a virgin?" "Who is she going with?" "Did she sleep with
him?" "Can I get him?"

Our social "maturity" manifests itself in the kind of
competition that is bred into us from the time we are born.
We try to be better than the next girl, to look prettier, be
cuter, etc.: training for a dog-eat-dog world. As children
we are put into lacy, white dresses and told to "be good, stay
clean and don't be like a boy." They drum this definition of
what we are supposed to be into us from birth. A "girl" is
pretty, clean, docile, submissive, gentle, always willing to
listen but never to talk, always willing to aid but never to
initiate.

High school gives us, as women, our first conscious realization of what it will be like when we are on our own. The
daily routine of getting up in the morning and then staying
in the same place for six hours trains us to be workers
whether in a factory, an office, or a home. The needless and
irrelevant material stuffed into us at school tries to persuade
us that we are only good for being mothers or performing
other service-oriented jobs. Nothing in a high school prepares us for what we want to be—people! We are treated as
if we are merely tools, as if we have no wills, minds, or
emotions.

Teachers, school principals, and guidance counsellors
make slave labor at home seem like the only thing a woman
is meant to or is able to do. In "girls" high schools there are
three main courses, or tracks: the secretarial track, which
prepares you to become either a clerk, a "girl friday," or to
hold a general service job that pays poorly and offers no opportunities, no union membership, and no benefits; the vocational track for lab technicians or nurses, which trains you
to be a nurse's aide, take bed pans, take blood, clean beds,

and maybe get into nursing school; and the academic track, which equips you to go to college and—after another four years of "education"—to become a secretary, a nurse, or house slave.

In addition, every woman must take a Home Economics course to prepare for the most important job of all—the unpaid job of housekeeping. They teach you to cook, clean, sew, and manage a budget without ever expecting any power or opportunity for advancement, and always feeling obligated to submit to the will and desire of one man.

Because society ordains that a woman's primary responsibility is housework and child care, a woman must continue with this main responsibility even if she holds another full-time job. She has two jobs—one full time and the other twenty-four hours a day. Wives and mothers act as individuals—each cooks, has her own washing machine, her own car. They produce no commodities which can be sold as such, as the factory worker does, but their production is still necessary and vital for the survival of the family unit. Yet society tells us our labor is not "real" work because it has no commercial exchange value. In this way women are virtually slaves of the family structure, a huge, essential, surplus army of cheap labor.

The kind of oppression we feel when we reach high school increases rapidly, and Women's Liberation is trying to end that oppression.

IX

THE HIGH SCHOOL DROPOUT AS INTELLECTUAL

The fact that a student has dropped out of high school does not mean that he stops learning. Does the freedom for self-education offer unlimited possibilities? Should an intellectual have the liberty to let his mind develop freely? Are there virtues to spontaneous free thinking?

In the following essay Pat Gunkel reveals an imaginative way of perceiving the world. His basic assumption is that human society will evolve into something higher, perhaps even a superman-and-machine complex, and that revolutionary efforts should be used to prepare for such long-range change. To the untutored mind his essay may seem abstract, difficult to follow, and even boring. But for his own generation and for anyone who allows his imagination to follow these unusual insights, his style is refreshing and stimulating.

IX

THE HIGH SCHOOL DROPOUT AS INTELLECTUAL

The Year 3000

by Pat Gunkel

> *Pat Gunkel is a hyper-intellectual high school dropout. Irked by the lack of stimulation, he left school to devote full energy to reading, writing, and cerebral conversation. Pat lives in a single-room occupancy building in St. Louis, Missouri. He usually ekes out his room and board by taking temporary, part-time jobs. He has, however, done serious research with the Institute for the Future in Connecticut. When not wasting his time earning a subsistance, he reads and writes. He has written an eight-inch thick behemoth of a manuscript called A Catalogue of Futures.*

As an eleventh-year dropout and a student of the future, I was asked to say for this book what there might be instead of today's schools.

My eleventh year was my last year. My disenchantment with school came early since I was ejected from several kindergartens, the first and second grades. I suppose I was a bit of a nuisance, but it did seem stupid the way my class was chaotically led about, and subjected to the defocused and perfunctory attention of the obviously confused, often emotionally unsure supervisor. Actually, I had very little idea why I was there or how I was to interact with the material. This would not seem to be due to a mental lack, because I was described at the time as "extraordinarily intelligent," and because I remember all kinds of situations that "turned me off" to school. Further description won't do here, but it's useful to see the earliness of my alienation. Since the third grade I always maintained a basement science lab, and pursued outside interests that often conflicted with schoolwork. But one day in school I remember a visitor pinned a ribbon representing the electromagnetic spectrum to the board, and that was exciting.

After the fifth grade my participation plummeted as my enthusiasm for my own ideas and experiments increased. Throughout high school I averaged C's and D's with occasional A's. I formed a philosophy club, wrote a satire of the mobocracy, and ran a classroom for a few days, lecturing on everything from cosomology to theoretical physics, ecology, and philosophy; classmates protested my being stopped by the teacher, since I "was more interesting." Entertainment consisted of my "contests" with teachers by vocabularial or cognitive overbearing. I was eventually stressed to the point of severe migraines by the faculty's pandemonium and manipulation. Sadism, mediocrity, irrelevance, and the failure of the teachers, counsellors, and administrators, made change through objectivity and integration impossible in an environment which was inhumane to cattle and in an extraparietal society which was itself uninteresting and pathogenic. The psychological and pedagogical situation was so complex that I am unable to review or analyze what was wrong. I know plenty of the highest performers and model students, and their subsequent careers demonstrate that even they were misguided—partly because the external environment, the real world, and the genuine character of people were misrepresented. I admit that there are not many nonphilosophical things I can say to correct the typical school, since to change it would take a social system, a class of changers, a scholastic staff, and students—none of which we have nor have promise of getting for a century, if ever. It takes people with inbred responsiveness to mystery, each other and their sensory world, people (beyond homogeneity, mediocrity, and inauthenticity) absorbed in the life of their studies and tuned to the reality of the world, people who delight one another and revel in responsive and unpredictable growth of a mind in all its intimate aspects. It takes a world that is organic, self-explanatory, deep, brilliant, sane, evolutionary, and friendly.

When I sat in a class I raised questions which were fundamental and which demanded answers, thousands of questions beyond the time, capacity, knowledge, depth, reality, or interest of the teacher. I envisioned my subjects, tried to see them as wholes, not just as books or quizzes, parents or personal successes. I pursued these questions in the library, in my head, and in personal essays. Naturally, for all my enthusiasm, I had grave self-doubts which hampered my private activity—how could I, alone amid thousands of students and adults, be right? What a threat, this isolation by massive error! The evil of this environment extended over a gigantic range of subtlety, depth, and sheer gross pathology. Unconscious elements define the fundamental nature and impact of human experience and behavior, and they do so decisively. The origin of all my scholastic pursuits was a culture tainted by its past, and—like all cultures—under monstrous psychic and conceptual stress.

People are determined to a large extent by environment. Environments in the past were able to civilize man while allowing him to preserve his animal nature, his stability, integrity, and sense of his own worth. Now, however, changes in urban and technological environments have upset this natural balance, and put in its place abstractions and caricatures of "man"—making him into an irresponsible, hopeless, brain-damaged creature who cycles through the system in morbid absurdity.

It is undoubtable that the young, by their insights, by their relearning, randomness, and formlessness, are an asset promising renewal to society. Because of youth's freedom, sincerity, and clarity, many people pin their hopes on a new humanistic world, though at the same time there is fear that technology or some other order will evolve to politically fix or pervert generational traits. Here one is relieved with youth's spite for technocracy and stratocracy.

I will delineate my balancing position below.

The conformist "protest" which has recently gripped our schools is valuable, to the extent it: 1) increases political sensibility, in that there are countless inertial fallacies and utter illusions in the politics of Left and right; 2) rejuvenates the populace into fervor for action though juvenility and fervor are already hyperactive and in some ways don't need being counterstimulated; 3) increases objectivity about the scholastic material—texts, curricula, personnel, and classrooms; 4) accelerates a reflective wisdom (any social change is good, in permitting self-recognition). Its excessive Left polarization has, of course, been nonsensical, but a conservative should push for Left experimentation. In some situations the protest has signaled otiosity, boredom, and administrative incompetence.

Society is the way it is today largely by accident, drift, and accretion. It needs total institutional overhaul and theoretical commitment in different experimental directions. It's easy to see how obsolescent are the classroom and don. Since our teachers have such low standards, professionally and humanly, we welcome the time when the teacher's role will be eliminated or modified by education automation. We are entering an entopial age when the environment will be designed like a machine, and the attitudes and attention of the student will be oriented toward—and stimulated by—equipment which flexibly alters the environment. The amount of present and imminent technology affecting the environment this way is enormous, and the operating costs of this equipment are decreasing as income rises to a senseless infinity. To anyone with a simple brain unencrusted by inertia it is evident that automation may displace man in all nonquaternary occupations and perhaps create temporarily residual quinary jobs demanding the fullest capacity of man's mind.

Maybe the exercise of birth controls will dominate the population rise, but it's probable that nations will competitively pursue the occupational advantage of maximum future growth, while anachronistic, dogmatic religions will persist. Therefore the fifty billion ecumenopolis, reached megalopolitanly, may be delayed in arriving. But short of "apocalyptic" philosophic developments, I think: 1) population quality is compatible with population denseness; 2) whatever its consequence, limitation of population is equivalent to genocide; 3) this planet can easily harbor over a trillion people; 4) the globe will be occupied by a trans-terrestrial architecture, the surface and the interior of Earth will be manhandled and mechanized, and the artificial environment will become supreme and fabulously advanced— like a fairy-tale museum, an ubiquitous, iridescent, and intelligent cartoon, an extraordinary universe of architectural, esthetic, psychologic, and social engineering.

It's absolutely essential that goals and attitudes be propagated because success and meaning in the future—and thus the present—are possible. The great political challenge we face is reconciliation with world planning for transition to world futures. Democratic opposition to this activity is stereotypically ill-advised. The left-right spectrum omits essential tertiary possibilities, and we must, in the most subtle sense, stop being simplistic. It is possible, desirable, and necessary to plan on time-scales exceeding our present lifetimes by decades, centuries, and millennia. As an instance of the last, I think it can be proven requisite that commitment should be made to industrial and scientific development even at the sacrifice of present values and concerns. Indicators and machines will evolve which will make such ideological gaps as East-West seem meaningless. The impact of future technologies is going to destabilize that split, whether for war or peace, erosion or enforcement. We are evolving technologies and intellectual disciplines such that it will be possible to predict and illustrate in detail and overall concept alternative futures—of ideologies, cities, nations, scientific development, war, or history—and quantitatively relate present acts and actions thereto. People are going to know a lot and as much as each other, regardless of national or local boundaries. Those boundaries are going to be very seriously questioned. There has never been a society in which the populace possessed a "four-dimensional" view of itself and an ability to understand everything political. One way or another, men are going to become conscious of the hellishness of their state. Like it or not, this world is going to become an organism of motives with philosophic conscience conquered.

I anticipate an increasing number of men who will be autocatalytically self-developing, -disciplining, and -controlled. These men will recognize themselves as learning and ethical machines creating objectively designable consequences, and will work to reconstruct the environment, and to explore and extend human potential. They will prove to one another that successive heights are possible. Their job will be to measure and assess the present universe and design its futures. They will involve both constriction and amplification in their personalities, and will learn to measure, cause, control, direct, and transform their emotions and thought. Society, presumably, will stop generating passive, reckless, feckless, moronic, and superficial human beings; proliferation of this new type will be autocatalytic, and whole new macrosocial possibilities will evolve from group *resonance*. Such genii will feel an identity with their material and environment, and will emphasize such theories or principles of behavior as probability, experimentalism, typology, synechism, compossibilism, synaesthesia, holism, generalism, futurism, ecstasy, Zen Buddhism, "insane" imagination, complex and quasi-paradoxical behavior, planning, humility, agapasticism, criticism, self-sacrifice, extreme empathy, social therapy.

The possibility of the existence of the proliferation of these genii is created by larger populations and/or contagion and stimulus. It is absolutely essential that we overcome our present population mediocrity. I assert that it should be possible to make every soul on the globe unique through transformations in the form and apparati of knowledge, greater psychological and social knowledge, and some political organization of the sphere. To advance this goal I think it only necessary to eradicate the burden of defective psychology upon us all. Surprising as it seems, sociology and psychology show promise of continued and perfective theoretical progress: computers and other techniques will multiply findings and experimental bases. Drug training will amplify aspects of intelligence in inspective individuals, affording them insight into the structure and pattern of others.

Pretentious and fundamental, student liberation will extend down to some earliest age and across and through all ages, revising the relation of the student to the teacher, the school, his classroom, and his fellows, creating new channels and emotions.

There are a number of trends revolutionizing education: enhancement of the common school by improvement of textbooks, absorbing and suggestive audio-visual aids, flexible and variable extraordinarily pleasant architecture of schools, and new styles and patterns in the teaching process and student rules. We are beginning an era of learning aids that can come, and stay, home. This complements the redesign of the house and implies new mores for the home. Into the home will come videophonic consoles relaying information and communication. Devices with ranges of diverse personality and intelligence will substitute for social contact, which is deficient for lack of intimacy and constancy.

Beyond this, imagine a *pedoculture* that will attend to the detail and total growth of the mind and potential of human beings from birth to maturity and perhaps old age. Responsive, theoretically organized or noetic machines will have this ability. True human potentiality and form is not at all understood so far. New and iconoclastic indication from such schools as cybernetics, Skinnerianism, Montessori, and Piaget promise to continue; these schools will confront or penetrate multiple levels behind the appearance of the mind, and will liberate new percepts, concepts, and general modes of behavior. Other findings indicate that various chemicals and physical practices can alter and manipulate human character, expanding intelligence, awareness, and all psychologic dimensions, divulging superior and greater human possibilities than hitherto described or suspected. These changes, when brought into being, will revolutionize values and the form of society and our world.

Another trend is implied by evidence of our capability for, and the powers of, bioengineering, which may produce a new transcendent species. Yet another which I would judge of overwhelming import is the emergence or imminence of artificial intelligence, then superintelligence, and ultraintelligence; such "engines" will develop increasingly larger concepts of the world, and will act to permute it to maximal efficiencies. They will also, apropos, succeed man.

Given these outré and bizarre expectancies, what do I suggest as the goal of youth? A new political force is starting to appear: futurism, the study and active planning of the future, usurping all previous irrelevant ideologies, parochial values, and social types, what I've called "the science of possibility." Thousands of alternative worlds are now possible. A moral response and orientation to the next million years and the seemingly ultimate future is now possible and deserved. Men have an obligation to change themselves. The world and the universe are classrooms. We must develop an orientation to a new science of man and an extirpation of our dreaded past vestiges, subtlest and simplest; a concentration on the mysterious and decisive origins of ourselves, in womb, school, and home.

Youngster simplism is good. Adult gruffness, superciliousness, and despair—malarky. Much of the language of the latter is complex without being understood. The student has a plastic, fluid, and energetic view of the world that is often realistic, psychically unscarred, happy, and intuitive. It's very difficult for adults to talk to kids because adults are so dense; we should challenge all our "great men" to explain to their ideas, behavior, and advocacies to the small people. The old people don't own this world, the oncoming generations do. The really important things are objective, not solipsistic; they are poietic, not fixed. People need much nonchalance and comity. It's unnecessary to wince at a supposedly "ugly" person or maintain all of the meaningless distinctions of prejudice that we do; the lovely eye sees the world as lovely, or a challenge to compassion. Most people talk too much: they should look, feel, have sex, and cry over the absurdity of their ways. One day promiscuity and homosexuality will be seen and used as virtues.

There is no reason why we shouldn't extend some types of puerility, mystery, affection, autism, conation, disorder, bliss, and eupsychia unto death. Sometime go and kiss your face in the mirror, dance about to music, try to see the world as a big joke, eat soap, scream "Fuck God!," and buy and use a bike. Play baby with your wife in a tub, bounce on the bed or stimulate an animal, or give away free dollars on the street. It is this kind of purposeful freedom that'll liberate this moronic movie, "World." It's hopeless if adults rush around in the rotes of their jobs and conformist habits, laced with fears and tensions: they'll perpetuate and intensify insidious forms in the world, witness pejoration of slums, ecology, and wars. It's amusing or pathetic the way many retiring oldsters cripple up or suddenly realize the waste of the rest of their lives and the mess of the state of the world. Don't reconcile yourself to normalcy and neutrality, have the nerve to be a source, build yourself and participate. The occupying army of tomorrow will be the kids, so we ought to invest our sums in them.

THE POEM

His skin was black
His eyes were wide
As he lay in the sunbaked mud
Faraway his wife and children prayed
As his jacket was drenched in blood
The sun of scorn warmed the golden fields
As the young were buried in the dirt
In Washington a few old men laughed
And sat with swastikas on the side of their shirts

SIMON SHATTNER, eleven years old

MARC LIBARLE, 24, was born in California. He studied history, philosophy, and political science at the University of Florence in Italy, and graduated from Columbia University with Honors in Government. He has taught in the New York City school system. Mr. Libarle, who intends to study law, is the Science and Technology editor of *Scanlan's Monthly,* a new investigative and reporting magazine.

TOM SELIGSON, 24, grew up in Westport, Connecticut. He graduated from Phillips Academy in Andover, Massachusetts, and Columbia College, where he studied government and history. He has taught for two years in the New York City school system, and is presently teaching in West Harlem. He is also a free-lance writer.